ACTFL 2(
Realizing Our Vision
of Languages for All

Edited by
Audrey L. Heining-Boynton

PEARSON
Prentice
Hall

worLd
Languages

Upper Saddle River, NJ 07458

Executive Editor: Bob Hemmer
Editorial Assistant: Debbie King
Executive Director of Market Development: Kristine Suárez
Director of Editorial Development: Julia Caballero
Project Manager: Heidi Allgair
Production Liaison: Claudia Dukeshire
Asst. Director of Production: Mary Rottino
Supplements Editor: Meriel Martínez Moctezuma
Media Editor: Samantha Alducin
Media Production Manager: Roberto Fernández
Prepress and Manufacturing Buyer: Brian Mackey
Prepress and Manufacturing Manager: Nick Sklitsis
Interior Design: GGS Book Services
Cover Art Director: Jayne Conte
Cover Design: Bruce Kenselaar
Cover Image: Bob Rankin
Sr. Marketing Manager, Jacquelyn Zautner
Marketing Assistant: William J. Bliss
Publisher: Phil Miller

This book was set in 10/13 Times Roman by GGS Book Services, and was printed and bound
by Courier/Stoughton. The cover was printed by Courier Stoughton.

© 2006 by Pearson Education, Inc.
Upper Saddle River, NJ 07458

Printed in the United States of America
10 9 8 7 6 5 4 3 2 1

ISBN: 0-13-196347-3

Pearson Education LTD., London
Pearson Education Australia PTY, Limited, Sydney
Pearson·Education Singapore, Pte. Ltd.
Pearson Education North Asia Ltd., Hong Kong
Pearson Education Canada, Ltd., Toronto
Pearson Educación de México, S.A. de C.V.
Pearson Educación—Japan, Tokyo
Pearson Education Malaysia, Pte. Ltd.
Pearson Education Upper Saddle River, New Jersey

Table of Contents

Introduction   iv

1 Going Beyond *2005: The Year of Languages*® to Realize
Our Vision   1
Martha G. Abbott, Christine Brown

2 Does the US Need a Language Policy, or Is English Enough?
Language Policies in the US and Beyond   15
Bernard Spolsky

3 A Blueprint for Action on Language Education   39
Kurt E. Müller

4 Realizing Our Vision: Teachers at the Core   55
Myriam Met

5 Assessment Now and into the Future   75
June K. Phillips

6 Teacher Leadership in a Learning Community   105
Anne Conzemius

7 Foreign Language and Special Education   117
Sandra Brunner Evarrs, Steven E. Knotek

8 Toward an Ecological Vision of *Languages for All*:
The Place of Heritage Languages   135
Guadalupe Valdés

9 Technology and Foreign Language Instruction: Where We Have Been,
Where We Are Now, Where We Are Headed   153
Jean W. LeLoup, Robert Ponterio

10 Globalization and Its Implications for the Profession   175
John M. Grandin

11 Advancing Less Commonly Taught Language Instruction in America:
The Time Is Now   199
Antonia Y. Schleicher, Michael E. Everson

About the Authors   217

Introduction

For this American Council on the Teaching of Foreign Languages (ACTFL) volume entitled *2005–2015: Realizing Our Vision of Languages for All*, the chapter authors have answered a variety of questions while raising others. The eleven chapters approach language education from a variety of perspectives including the history and current status of language policies; language needs of our government and our international businesses; teachers, teaching, and learning; assessment; instructional technology; heritage learners; less commonly-taught languages; and special learners.

The impetus behind this compilation and self-reflection for our profession was *2005: The Year of Languages®*, a campaign for the benefit of the entire profession that was crafted and implemented by ACTFL to celebrate, educate, and communicate the power of language learning. The introductory chapter of this volume describes what led to the initiative, what occurred during the year, and what were the ultimate goals and next steps of *2005: The Year of Languages.*

This volume's authors accepted the challenge of answering the following basic questions related to their topic, as well as that of expanding upon their themes.

- Where are we now?
- Where should we be? or Where could we be?
- How do we realize our vision of languages for all?

Appreciation and thanks to go ACTFL and to ACTFL's Executive Director Bret Lovejoy for supporting the vision and realization of this volume, as well as to Prentice Hall Publishers. Additionally, I am extremely grateful for the careful and thoughtful copyediting by W. Joyce Bettini.

Audrey L. Heining-Boynton
Editor

Going Beyond *2005: The Year of Languages*® to Realize Our Vision

Martha G. Abbott
Christine Brown

The year 2005 marked a notable event for the language community: *2005: The Year of Languages*®. It is important for the language teaching profession in the United States to reflect on the accomplishments during the first ever Year of Languages celebration. We must create the road map for the continuing journey to celebrate, educate, and communicate the power of language learning. In some ways, we must build the car while we are driving it, and we might wonder, even with a working vehicle, "Do we really know the way to San José?" Our efforts at language promotion during 2005 have given us some clear insights into our present strengths and weaknesses in this national effort.

While not all language professionals may agree on the most direct route to creating a more language-competent citizenry, we do agree, for the most part, on what the end of the road should be. The goals outlined for the *2005: The Year of Languages* initiative identified areas of common concern to the entire language profession:

- Raising awareness of the benefits of knowing another language;
- Motivating people to learn languages;
- Promoting multilingualism and cultural understanding in the United States;
- Launching a media campaign to yield sustained attention and public awareness for years to come;
- Providing information about the teaching and learning of languages; and
- Supporting lifelong learning of languages.

In the 2005 campaign the overall goal was to begin to fundamentally change the public attitude in the United States about the importance of language learning. This most important goal is a long-term goal for all language educators and language organizations. At the outset, we knew this goal could not be accomplished in only one

The authors would like to thank Bret Lovejoy, Executive Director of ACTFL, for his review of and input into this article.

year; it would take many years of professional collaboration, sustained public aware-ness efforts, ever-increasing funding, and much patience in order to be accomplished. The 2005 launch of the Year of Languages was designed to be the kickoff of a sus-tained public awareness campaign that will indeed move the language profession to-ward the goals listed above. It is important at this point to provide a summary of what was accomplished during this year-long effort and to outline a plan to keep the mo-mentum from the Year of Languages building for the long-term campaign.

Building the Momentum and Setting the Stage Within the Profession

Although the American Council on the Teaching of Foreign Languages (ACTFL) was the lead organization in the 2005 effort, the Year of Languages campaign was enthusi-astically embraced by the entire profession. Throughout years of discussion about the need for a public awareness campaign at the Joint National Committee on Languages/National Council on Languages and International Studies (JNCL/NCLIS)[1] Delegate Assembly, at the ACTFL Assembly of Delegates, and throughout the New Visions project,[2] leaders in the profession often pined for a coordinated public awareness cam-paign that would bring the same limelight to language learning as had been given to the fine and performing arts through their public relations efforts.

In 2003, officers of ACTFL and the ACTFL Executive Council, working to promote language learning at all educational levels, decided to launch a language promotional effort based on the successful 2001 European Year of Languages cam-paign. The ***2005: The Year of Languages*** in the United States endeavor was devel-oped through the leadership and diligent efforts of a working committee comprised of language leaders from the state, regional, national, and language-specific organi-zations. Informational materials and promotional products were developed to assist with local events and celebrations, and the campaign was launched at the 2004 ACTFL Annual Convention in Chicago with the release of a series of public service announcements asking people to "speak up for language education" in their local communities. Delegates to the ACTFL Annual Convention, made up of representa-tives of all the organizational members of ACTFL, were solicited to become Year of Languages Ambassadors and to contact their local media to air and print the public service announcements. In addition, a Year of Languages Web site[3] was developed

---

[1] JNCL/NCLIS is the Joint National Committee on Languages/National Council on Languages and International Studies, a coalition of language organizations which advocates for language education and international studies on Capitol Hill. For more information see <www.languagepolicy.org>
[2] New Visions in Action: A Project of the Iowa State K-12 National Language Resource Center and ACTFL. For more information, see <www.educ.iastate.edu/newvisions/>
[3] 2005: The Year of Languages Web site: <www.yearoflanguages.org.>

specifically to support individuals and organizations that wanted to participate in the effort as well as to provide information to the public at large about how they could get involved in this promotional effort. The Web site also served as a location for all language educators to post their local, state, and regional *2005: The Year of Languages* ideas, activities, and events.

Year of Languages Accomplishments

During the two years of development and implementation of the initiative, many tangible and long-lasting accomplishments came from the *2005: The Year of Languages* effort:

- ACTFL and the Working Committee[4] of the Year of Languages forged stronger ties with the international language teaching community, including three meetings in Johannesburg, Brussels, and Beijing.

- The Year of Languages Honorary Council was established to draw support for the initiative from notable figures from the political, academic, humanitarian, and business worlds. The membership of the Council evolved throughout its first year and will continue to evolve with Senators Christopher Dodd (D-CT) and Thad Cochran (R-MS) as co-chairs and with members such as Dr. Maya Angelou, Governor Mark Warner, heads of academic institutions, representatives of major corporations, school board presidents, city mayors, and ambassadors representing the countries of Canada, China, France, Germany, Great Britain, Italy, Japan, Mexico, Russia, and Spain. For a complete list, see <www.yearoflanguages.org>. This Web site will continue to be enhanced and updated as the initiative continues to the next phase of the language promotion campaign.

- The U.S. Senate passed Resolution 28 declaring 2005 as the "Year of Language Study" and the U.S. House of Representatives passed Resolution 122 declaring 2005 as the "Year of Languages" (see appendix). Both resolutions encouraged the President to support the effort.

- A working committee, comprised of language leaders from the state, regional, and language-specific organizations, helped to create professionally broad-based ideas and organizational support for the effort.

- From around the country, resolutions, proclamations, and endorsements were received from 16 governors and an additional 45 local, regional, state, and national associations. These documents can be viewed at <www.yearoflanguages.org>

---

[4] Year of Languages Working Committee members: Marty Abbott, Christine Brown, Keith Cothrun, Dan Davidson, Carrie Harrington, Audrey Heining-Boynton, Elizabeth Hoffman, Janis Jensen, Catharine Keatley, Yu-Lan Lin, Barbara Lindsey, Lynne McClendon, Lynn Sandstedt, and Helene Zimmer-Loew.

- ACTFL-sponsored public service announcements (PSA) were aired on television and radio stations around the country and printed in media that included newspapers, journals, newsletters, and other print materials. Some television stations even aired the PSA during primetime. More than one hundred language professionals volunteered to serve as Year of Languages Ambassadors and continue to contact the media to request that the PSAs be given airtime and print space. The three print ads are included in an appendix to this chapter and, as with all the public service announcements, can be accessed from the Year of Languages Web site.

- The Year of Languages theme was embraced at all the regional conferences as well as at many state conferences during the year. In addition, over 50 Year of Languages presentations were made by ACTFL staff and Council members.

- ACTFL and the Year of Languages Working Committee raised more than $250,000 from organizations and individuals to offset the cost of the development and implementation of the campaign. The fundraising efforts continue with all monies raised being used to directly support the initiative.

- National events that reflected the monthly themes of the year were held all over the country with support from state and regional organizations as well as from the members of the Year of Languages Working Committee. These events ranged from a panel of representatives from various careers discussing their use of languages in their jobs held at the University of Missouri in St. Louis to student performances demonstrating early language learning held at the Texas State Fair in Fort Worth. This effort to promote language learning all across the country provided local forums where language educators could have an impact on local and state policy makers.

- A national language policy summit was held at The University of North Carolina at Chapel Hill in January 2005 to reflect that month's theme of Language Policy. Over 3,500 individuals from around the nation and from several other countries tuned in via videoconferencing and a streamed Internet broadcast to listen to and participate in a summit on language policies in academe, government, and business. *A Blueprint for Action* (Müller, 2005) was written following the summit detailing concrete steps that each area can take to move the language policy agenda forward.

- "Language ambushes" or "pop quizzes" proved to be very effective in getting the attention of local media. Used at the 2004 ACTFL Annual Convention in Chicago as a kickoff for the Year of Languages, these ambushes were staged in cities around the country by alerting the media and then giving the "man on the street" a pop quiz by asking a question in a language other than English and keeping a tally of correct and incorrect responses. When interviewed by the media, the "ambush" members would then use it as an opportunity to highlight the need for knowledge of other languages as an important need for national security and economic competitiveness.

While this list provides tangible evidence of the results of waging this campaign, the impact of this effort transcends the data. Thousands of language professionals across the country—members and nonmembers of ACTFL—rallied around the fact that 2005 had been declared the Year of Languages. This was evidenced by the stream of e-mail messages, celebratory materials, and pictures that were sent to ACTFL headquarters as well as by the national media coverage and visits to the Web site. Schools, both public and private, institutions of higher education and community colleges, and organizations related to languages were able to leverage the Year of Languages to promote their programs and departments. Many colleges and universities received institutional accolades, media attention, and higher visibility because of their efforts to celebrate the year. Language and cultural organizations were able to do the same by staging rallies at state capitols, testifying before school boards, and adding the Year of Languages imprimatur to their annual events and celebrations. The Year of Languages logo was widely printed on materials from parade banners to course syllabi to billboards. Students were actively involved from fundraising efforts to service-learning projects that resulted in a Year of Languages calendar and an interactive crossword puzzle. Through the language promotion activities conducted throughout the year, hundreds of first-timers learned how to advocate for their own programs and students. They learned to "celebrate, educate, and communicate the power of language learning." Some language educators reported that they have seen increased budgets for language education and increased support from the public at large. New coalitions have been formed in local communities and in states. This campaign was a national training effort in advocacy that will provide the infrastructure of the sustained public awareness campaign.

Hearing the Message Beyond the Language Profession and Taking Action

The context surrounding the development of the Year of Languages initiative was ripe for finding support among government and business. The cornerstone of the effort was to *Celebrate . . . Educate . . . and Communicate . . . The Power of Language Learning* and was designed to build on language needs and concerns from the three arenas of academe, government, and business. These three sectors have varying needs and motivations regarding languages. The collaboration of all was, and is, deemed important in the attempt to coalesce the language promotion effort.

The Role of Government

The government role was clear after September 11, 2001. The United States was, once again, caught short-handed in terms of linguists, not only to decipher texts in foreign languages, but to actually conduct negotiations in languages such as Pashto, virtually unheard of in the United States. Negotiation and other such language skills call for a very high level of language competence. To address this shortfall, the Department of Defense in conjunction with the Center for Advanced Study of Language (CASL) organized the first National Language Conference[5] to identify the needs in the areas of government, business, and academe. A resulting white paper, published in September 2004, laid the groundwork for the ACTFL/Year of Languages National Language Policy Summit: A Plan of Action at The University of North Carolina at Chapel Hill which produced *A Blueprint for Action* (Müller, 2005). Only weeks after the Policy Summit, one tangible result of the *Blueprint* was the development of the K-16 Flagship Program for Chinese, which was funded through the National Security Education Program (NSEP) in response to the call for well-articulated K-16 language programs that would develop students' proficiency levels to the Advanced Level on the ACTFL Oral Proficiency Interview (OPI).[6] In addition, the Interagency Language Roundtable (ILR), made up of representatives of government agencies that have language needs, declared 2005 as the *Year of Languages in the Government* and embarked on support and outreach efforts that complemented the ACTFL effort. Evidence of that is the Web site developed by the National Virtual Translation Center (NVTC) which is directly linked to the ACTFL Year of Languages site and provides a wealth of opportunities for students and teachers to learn more about languages. Furthermore, ACTFL staff were invited to make Year of Languages presentations at the Pentagon to the Senior Language Authorities for each branch of the armed services and to linguists at the National Security Agency (NSA).

The Role of Business and Commerce

The corporate world is beginning to realize how important linguistic capabilities are to conducting business negotiations in our global economy. Business leaders are perhaps more difficult to convince than the government realm because English is so widely used outside the United States. Nonetheless, in order to sell our goods abroad, many understand that a knowledge of the language and an understanding of the culture of the client are critical. In his remarks to the participants at the National Language Conference, the Honorable Sam Mok, Chief Financial Officer in the U.S. Department of Labor said, "... with international trade extending the reach of many

---

[5] National Language Conference, sponsored by the Department of Defense and the Center for the Advanced Study of Language (CASL) was held in June 2004. For information on the conference proceedings, visit <www.nlconference.org>

[6] OPI is the Oral Proficiency Interview, an oral proficiency test that can be taken to measure one's level of language proficiency. For more information, see <www.languagetesting.com>

companies overseas, companies benefit greatly by having bi- or multi-lingual employees who can communicate with foreign clientele. In order for us to be internationally competitive, we must know the language of our trading partners." He added, "95% of the potential customers for American products live outside the U.S. and the majority of them speak languages other than English." Even for Americans employed by foreign companies but working in the U.S., knowledge of languages plays an important role.

At the ACTFL/YOL Policy Summit in January, John Grandin, Director of the International Engineering Program at the University of Rhode Island, noted, "The official language of DaimlerChrysler is English, but that policy is misleading. Even though senior management may have strong English language skills, day-to-day business in Stuttgart is done in German. Their employees at many levels throughout the world, whether in Detroit, Japan, Alabama, or Brazil, are well served by being able to interact with their headquarters in their native tongue!" The Committee for Economic Development (CED) released a treatise on the importance of linguistic ability in international business during 2005 which will serve to further build the awareness of this critical need in the business world. Much work in language promotion remains to be done in the sectors of business and commerce. Although they have supported local *2005: Year of Languages* activities, CEOs and other corporate executives need to be educated and convinced about the power of language learning to their bottom line. Efforts to work with business, industry, and commerce form a large part of the road map for the sustained language promotion efforts in 2005 and beyond.

The Role of Academia

The interest on the part of government and business is critical to the effort to build public awareness and support for language education. Both fields then are obligated to turn to academe to create the much needed pipeline leading to a multilingual citizenry—the acquisition of languages other than English for monolingual English students and the maintenance and development of heritage languages for those who already speak another language. While some educators outside the field of language education see the need for more language education for all Americans at all ages and stages of life, many administrators would not make learning languages a priority in schools and universities today. Many areas of the curriculum compete for increasingly limited dollars. Language and cultural knowledge are not a part of the tested curriculum and therefore not "on the educational radar screen" of the vast majority of educational policy makers and administrators. The road map for continuation of a language public awareness campaign needs to include a "mapquest" to local, state, and national educational decision makers, who then must be held accountable for putting languages on the radar screen.

Building on What We Learned: Taking the Message to the General Public

The development of the public service announcements was the most visible outreach to the general public. Changing public attitudes and beliefs takes time—a long time—but we have many indications that the vast majority of Americans today think language education is vital to American interests at home and abroad. Polls conducted after 9/11 by the American Council on Education (ACE) indicate strong support for language education among parents and students. Older Americans are showing increased interest in enrolling in language courses for personal benefit, a further indication of a growing awareness of the value of support for language education.

ACTFL conducted a Roper Poll just prior to a December 2004 press conference in order to have some timely data regarding foreign language literacy. The random sampling poll was conducted by telephone between November 19–21, 2004, among American adults in the contiguous United States. The key findings included the following:

- Nearly half (45%) of Americans believe there is "too little" foreign language instruction in America's public schools

- A plurality (50%) of Americans also believe there is "too little" funding of foreign language instruction in America's public schools. Younger Americans are especially likely to hold this view, that is, 75% of those polled who were between 18 and 24 years old versus 31% of those 65 and older.

- One in four (26%) live in a household with someone fluent in more than one language. Younger Americans are most likely to live in such a household (42%).

- Nearly half (48%) of Americans have at least weekly dealings with someone whose first language is not English. The majority of those between 18 and 34 years old make this claim, which is perhaps why they are the most likely to believe foreign language instruction and funding should be a bigger priority.

If we consider this baseline data prior to the launch of the public awareness campaign, we can possibly gauge the direction of public sentiment about languages in similar polls in the future.

Discover Languages®: A Sustained Language Promotion Effort

The logical next step is to build upon the enthusiasm and base of support that has been created during *2005: The Year of Languages* with the implementation of a sustained public awareness campaign. Many of the same types of activities that took place during the Year of Languages can and will continue to build support for this effort. However, in addition to the exciting activities that took place during the Year of Languages, it is important to engage academe, business, and governmental agencies, as well as foundations, to support this effort financially. Paid advertising and multiple series of public service announcements are necessary to reach all facets of the American public. Language educators need to continue to build on the relationships that have been forged through the Year of Languages and continue to make inroads through new venues in the business world. If the language community is to financially sustain a language promotion effort over time, the profession needs the financial resources to do so. Support from the business community will be key to finding those resources. As we continue to work with our international counterparts, it will be necessary to seek their advice and counsel in how to harness the support of the global corporate world.

Another aspect of a sustained promotional effort is the need to work very closely with the broader education community. Presently educational policy makers are focused on adequate yearly progress in content other than languages. Our sustained language promotion campaign must focus on town halls and school board rooms across the nation. Whether through new legislation or through state mandates, language education must be placed on the radar screen for all educational policy makers. We need to help educators outside our field "Discover Languages" and realize the academic power of a K-16-and-beyond language education.

The overall goal of changing the hearts and minds of Americans about the critical need for language learning is the linchpin for the ***Discover Languages***® campaign.[7] In addition, we need to reach out internationally and connect to language professionals around the world. Just as we consulted with the European Union organizers of their effort in 2001, ACTFL was consulted by language educators in Thailand during their planning for a World Congress and Year of Languages in 2006. The Web site for ***Discover Languages***® includes these international connections as well as information about teacher certification and recruitment, language learning for people of all ages, and outreach to teachers with information about languages and careers for students. The intent is to connect language initiatives happening in the government and business worlds with the educators who are being charged with the task of equipping their students for a multilingual world. This effort will serve to ensure a place for languages in the curriculum of America's schools K-16 and will promote the language teaching profession. It needs to be well-coordinated to involve all the major stakeholders and sustained so that the impact can eventually be felt and evidenced by wide public acceptance of languages in America's schools as well as by an expectation that all children will have access to learning a second or

---

[7] **Discover Languages!** is a registered trademark of the American Council on the Teaching of Foreign Languages.

even a third language. The interest, enthusiasm, and drive are there to truly change the way Americans interact with the world!

References

Hayward, F. M. & Siaya, L. M. (2001). Public experience, attitudes, and knowledge: A report on two national surveys on international education. American Council on Education. Washington, DC.

Mok, S. (2004, June). Address given at the National Language Conference, Adelphi, Maryland.

Müller, K. E. (2005). *A blueprint for action on language education: Summary of the proceedings at the National Language Policy Summit, January 10–11, 2005.* [white paper]. Alexandria, VA: American Council on the Teaching of Foreign Languages. Retrieved from the ACTFL Web site: <www.yearoflanguages.org>

Roper Poll. (2004, November). Americans talk about foreign language literacy. Alexandria, VA: American Council on the Teaching of Foreign Languages. Retrieved from the ACTFL Web site: <www.yearoflanguages.org.>

Appendix

Whereas the people of the United States have growing social, cultural, and economic ties to the international community that present new challenges as the United States seeks to communicate . . . (Engrossed as Agreed to or Passed by House)

HRES 122 EH

H. Res. 122
In the House of Representatives, U.S.,
March 8, 2005.

Whereas the people of the United States have growing social, cultural, and economic ties to the international community that present new challenges as the United States seeks to communicate with and understand international partners from different language and cultural backgrounds;

Whereas communities across the United States are welcoming many new neighbors, friends, employees, and citizens from many countries throughout the world;

Whereas increased language learning is a critical national interest and is necessary to maintain the economic edge the United States has in the worldwide marketplace;

Whereas developing a workforce that is skilled in languages and cultural understanding is vital for conducting international commerce;

Whereas both the 2000 Cox Commission and the National Intelligence Council have reported that a shortfall of experts in foreign languages, particularly the languages of Asia and the Middle East, has seriously hampered information gathering and analysis within the intelligence community of the United States;

Whereas studying other languages has been shown to contribute to increased cognitive skills, better academic performance, and a greater understanding of others, while also providing life-long learning opportunities;

Whereas language education in the 21st century includes a commitment to the study of long sequences of world languages, beginning in early grades and continuing throughout the academic career of an individual, in order to develop the levels of proficiency needed to effectively communicate with people from other cultures at home and abroad; and

Whereas the American Council on the Teaching of Foreign Languages, along with its affiliate organizations, is urging the public to support increased language education for students, which will expand the cultural and literary horizons of adult learners and strengthen the position and security of the United States throughout the world: Now, therefore, be it

Resolved, That it is the sense of the House of Representatives that—

1. the study of languages contributes to the intellectual and social development of a student and the economy and security of the United States;

2. there should be a Year of Languages in the United States, during which language study is promoted and expanded in elementary schools, secondary schools, institutions of higher education, businesses, and government programs; and

3. the President should issue a proclamation calling upon the people of the United States to—
   A. encourage and support initiatives to promote and expand the study of languages; and
   B. observe a Year of Languages with appropriate ceremonies, programs, and other activities.

Attest:
Clerk.

109th CONGRESS
1st Session
S. RES. 28

IN THE SENATE OF THE UNITED STATES

February 1, 2005

Mr. DODD (for himself, Mr. COCHRAN, Mr. AKAKA, Mr. BAUCUS,
Mr. BINGAMAN, Mr. DURBIN, Mr. FEINGOLD, Mr. HAGEL, Mr. KENNEDY,
Mr. LAUTENBERG, Mr. LIEBERMAN, and Mr. LUGAR) submitted the following
resolution; which was referred to the Committee on the Judiciary

---

RESOLUTION

Designating the year 2005 as the 'Year of Foreign Language Study'.

Whereas according to the 2000 decennial census of the population, 9.3 percent of Americans speak both their native language and another language fluently;

Whereas according to the European Commission Directorate General for Education and Culture, 52.7 percent of Europeans speak both their native language and another language fluently;

Whereas the Elementary and Secondary Education Act of 1965 names foreign language study as part of a core curriculum that includes English, mathematics, science, civics, economics, arts, history, and geography;

Whereas according to the Joint Center for International Language, foreign language study increases a student's cognitive and critical thinking abilities;

Whereas according to the American Council on the Teaching of Foreign Languages, foreign language study increases a student's ability to compare and contrast cultural concepts;

Whereas according to a 1992 report by the College Entrance Examination Board, students with 4 or more years in foreign language study scored higher on the verbal section of the Scholastic Aptitude Test (SAT) than students who did not;

Whereas the Higher Education Act of 1965 labels foreign language study as vital to secure the future economic welfare of the United States in a growing international economy;

Whereas the Higher Education Act of 1965 recommends encouraging businesses and foreign language study programs to work in a mutually productive relationship which benefits the Nation's future economic interest;

Whereas according to the Centers for International Business Education and Research program, foreign language study provides the ability both to gain a comprehensive understanding of and to interact with the cultures of United States trading partners, and thus establishes a solid foundation for successful economic relationships;

Whereas Report 107-592 of the Permanent Select Committee on Intelligence of the House of Representatives concludes that American multinational corporations and non-governmental organizations do not have the people with the foreign language abilities and cultural exposure that are needed;

Whereas the 2001 Hart-Rudman Report on National Security in the 21st Century names foreign language study and requisite knowledge in languages as vital for the Federal Government to meet 21st century security challenges properly and effectively;

Whereas the American intelligence community stresses that individuals with proper foreign language expertise are greatly needed to work on important national security and foreign policy issues, especially in light of the terrorist attacks on September 11, 2001;

Whereas a 1998 study conducted by the National Foreign Language Center concludes that inadequate resources existed for the development, publication, distribution, and teaching of critical foreign languages (such as Arabic, Vietnamese, and Thai) because of low student enrollment in the United States; and

Whereas a shortfall of experts in foreign languages has seriously hampered information gathering and analysis within the American intelligence community as demonstrated by the 2000 Cox Commission noting shortfalls in Chinese proficiency, and the National Intelligence Council citing deficiencies in Central Eurasian, East Asian, and Middle Eastern languages: Now, therefore, be it

Resolved, That—

1. it is the sense of the Senate that foreign language study makes important contributions to a student's cognitive development, our national economy, and our national security;

2. the Senate—

    A. designates the year 2005 as the 'Year of Foreign Language Study', during which foreign language study is promoted and expanded in elementary schools, secondary schools, institutions of higher learning, businesses, and government programs; and

    B. requests that the President issue a proclamation calling upon the people of the United States to—

        i. encourage and support initiatives to promote and expand the study of foreign languages; and

        ii. observe the 'Year of Foreign Language Study' with appropriate ceremonies, programs, and other activities.

2

Does the US Need a Language Policy, or Is English Enough? Language Policies in the US and Beyond

Bernard Spolsky

What Is Language Policy?

Hardly a day goes by that we do not come across a newspaper headline dealing with a language issue.[1] In October 2004, a commission chaired by Claude Thélot that had been charged with organizing a national debate on the future of French schooling recommended that English no longer be treated as just one of a number of foreign languages taught in the system; rather, in recognition of its role as the international language of communication, it should be considered together with French and mathematics as the core of the curriculum. A month later, the Russian Constitutional Court ruled that Tatarstan cannot switch the Tatar language's alphabet from Cyrillic to Latin, saying that regional authorities have no jurisdiction over the alphabets of ethnic groups and peoples. In Canada, some 40 years after the Official Languages Act, fewer than 10% of non-francophones claim to be bilingual, and the newspapers are starting to ask why the federal government is spending so much money on attempts to change the situation. At the same time, in Boston, a health clinic gave in to pressure from the U.S. Equal Employment Opportunity Commission and the National Labor Relations Board and cancelled a policy that forbade its employees speaking Spanish with each other.

These are all examples of language policy. Language policy has three distinct but closely interrelated components (Spolsky, 2004). The first is language practice; the second, language belief; and the third, language management. Members of a speech community know when to speak, when to keep silent, which language to choose, which variety of a language to use, what words to avoid when other people are present. When I am in Jerusalem, I speak Hebrew with the bus driver although I realize he probably speaks Russian at home; I speak English with my grandchildren although I know that they use Hebrew with their classmates. The merchants whose shops line the *shuk* along which I walk to the Jaffa Gate are particularly adept at

---

[1] This paper is developed from the keynote address I gave at the American Council on the Teaching of Foreign Languages (ACTFL) Year of Languages Policy Summit which took place at The University of North Carolina at Chapel Hill on January 10–11, 2005.

guessing which language to use with residents and tourists passing by. These language practices are rule governed and generally acquired in everyday life rather than taught in any formal way, so that we are usually unaware of them. But also because they are learned through experience and because they are not salient, they are particularly difficult to modify.

In this sense, the language policy of a particular community[2] constitutes its sociolinguistic ecology, the languages and varieties that people choose in various circumstances. We all realize that there are many speakers of Spanish and other languages in the United States, but most people who look at the MLA Language Map on the Web[3] are likely to be astonished both at the number of languages represented and at the way that they are spread across the whole country. It is the complexity and fixedness of language practices that sets a major challenge for anyone who wants to modify them. This I refer to as the King Cnut phenomenon: royal authority does not extend to the waves nor to the way people speak.[4]

A second aspect of language policy is the beliefs about language held by members of the speech community. One belief that seems to be common to most societies, especially those with an organized educational system, is that there is a correct form of language. Another very common belief is that some languages are inherently better than others—richer, purer, and more beautiful. In much of the world now, the belief expressed by the French commission on the national debate that English comes at the top of any list for its usefulness is commonly accepted. Similarly, in the United States and in many other countries, there is constant tension between the belief in the need for unity expressed in a monolingual policy and the values of multilingualism, plurilingualism, and diversity. Language beliefs constitute a critical and seldom studied component of language policy; to change them is a major challenge (see Kroon & Vallen, in press).

The third component is language management,[5] the effort of anyone or any institution within a speech community that claims authority to attempt to modify the language practices or beliefs of other members of the community. It is language management when parents or caretakers try to make sure that their children speak clearly and speak the kind of language that will ease their relations with other members of the community, or when school teachers endeavour to control the language of their pupils, attempting to eradicate what they consider stigmatized forms and to

---

[2] A speech community is not defined by size, but rather by the existence of a recognized set of sociolinguistic practices and beliefs.

[3] URL: <http://www.mla.org/census_main>.

[4] Cnut, I was reminded, was not himself attempting to stop the waves, but rather trying to show his people the limits of royal power.

[5] I prefer the term management to the commonly used planning, or to language engineering. Cf. Jernudd (2000; 2001).

help them acquire the language of school whether or not it is a language of their home. And it is language management when a government determines what languages should be used and for what purposes.

Managing Language Status

The first language management task for the government of a nation-state is determining what variety of language should be used by citizens for what purpose (Kloss, 1969, called this *status planning*). When a constitution declares a language to be official, it is usually saying that all formal bureaucratic, legislative, and judicial activities should be conducted in that language. It also expresses a hope, which it has less possibility of enforcing, that its citizens will use that language in their interactions with each other. The status of the various languages spoken in a community is commonly determined by a constitutional clause or by a language law.[6] When countries achieve independence after a period of foreign or colonial rule, one of their first concerns is often to foster and declare this independence by proclaiming a new national language. After independence from Denmark, Norway set out to invent a new national language, Norwegian (Haugen, 1966). After independence from British rule, India adopted a constitution recognizing 11 languages and planned to drop English from the list (Annamalai, 2001). After the end of British rule, Israel amended the trilingual policy adopted for the League of Nations Mandate by dropping English and leaving Hebrew and Arabic as official languages.[7] With the end of apartheid, the new South Africa revised its constitution to add seven named African languages to Afrikaans and English which were already there (Heugh, 2003). With the establishment of the Soviet Union, a constitution was drawn up under Lenin that promised equality to all languages. After the breakup of the Soviet Union, which under Stalin had effectively ignored the constitution by enforcing Russian language hegemony, the newly independent states attempted to reestablish the dominance of their national territorial languages (Grenoble, 2003). In Russia itself, a new wave of nationalist feeling is working again to bolster the status of Russian over regional and minority languages. In Afghanistan and Iraq, one of the most disputed clauses in the new constitutions deals with recognition of minority languages.

Sometimes the new policy is laid down not in a constitution but in a law. Taking advantage of the new British policy of devolution, the Scottish parliament has just passed a law to recognize Scots Gaelic as a national language alongside English. In the Good Friday agreement which, it was hoped, would resolve the tension in Northern Ireland, two languages, Irish Gaelic and Ulster-Scots were given special

---

[6] For the latest version of national constitutions, see <http://confinder.richmond.edu/>.
[7] But see Deutch (2005), Saban & Amara (2002).

recognition (Nic Craith, 2001). In Wales, autonomy made it possible to continue reversing the historical policy of discouraging Welsh (Williams, 1987). In Catalonia (Strubell, 2001; Woolard & Gahng, 1990) and Quebec (Larrivée, 2002), language laws were passed to strengthen the positions of Catalan and French respectively. In New Zealand, responding to legal and political pressure, the government passed a law declaring Maori an official language (Benton & Benton, 2001). In France, a long tradition of enforcing French hegemony was capped by the passing in 1994 of the Toubon law and about the same time by the addition to the constitution of a new clause declaring French the national language (Ager, 1999).

Managing Language Form

A second major branch of language management is concerned not with the status of languages but with the prescription of their form. Called somewhat confusingly *corpus planning* (Kloss, 1969), a better term is perhaps *cultivation* (Garvin, 1973). It involves all the activities undertaken to standardize and modernize a language. While agreeing at one time with the general conception that status planning was "the engine which pulls the language planning train" (Fishman, 1988), Fishman (2000) reported that in extensive reading of arguments by written proponents of language reform he had found that corpus-related statements calling for purification tended to appear earlier.

An early cultivation issue is the selection of a writing system (Fishman, 1977). Writing has been invented *de novo* only three or four times, with the result that most writing systems are adaptations of systems that were being used for other languages. The basic choices are fairly limited: a system like Chinese that uses different characters to represent different words or meaning units or a system that uses a limited number of letter forms to represent individual sounds (an alphabet) or combinations of sounds (a syllabary). There is however a wide choice of scripts that might be used, and when setting up new alphabets, it is common to invent new letters (Coulmas, 2003). The choice of a writing system is partly pragmatic and partly symbolic: the argument in Russia between insistence on the use of Cyrillic and the desire of the speakers of many languages to use the Latin alphabet or Perso-Arabic is really a political rather than a linguistic argument. When Pakistan and India wanted to divide the Hindustani language that they both used into Urdu and Hindi, they distinguished the two by writing the Urdu in Perso-Arabic and Hindi in Devanagari (King, 2001).[8] North and South Korea maintain different forms of their writing system, and Taiwan has refused to accept the script reforms made on the mainland.

Once a writing system has been adopted, the need for language management is far from exhausted, for spelling remains a critical issue as long as it is being used to

---

[8] They modified lexicon too, for Hindi choosing Sanskrit and for Urdu, Arabic words.

represent a sound system for a language that varies in time and space. The problems we have with English derive from the fact that many of its conventions remained fixed long after pronunciation had changed. Difficulties like these encourage many people to propose spelling reform. It has never worked for English (Webster's effort to develop a more logical American system affected only a tiny group of words, and Bernard Shaw's efforts [Shaw, 1962] faded rapidly without notice), but it was undertaken successfully by the Netherlands (Geerts, Van den Broeck, & Verdoodt, 1977) and, most recently, with considerable compromises, by the Germans (Johnson, 2002). Proposals for far-reaching changes, such as suggestions that Chinese and Hebrew should be romanized, have so far been firmly resisted (Cheng, 1986; Rabin, 1977), but in China proper the script has been simplified (Zhou, 2004). The possibility of a radical change was demonstrated in the case of Turkish, when Kemal Atatürk carried out major reforms changing not just the script but also a large portion of vocabulary (Lewis, 1999); a recent study by Bingol (2002) suggests however that Persian and Arabic words persist in spoken and literary Turkish and that some of the earlier reforms have been reversed under Islamic influence.

Because of the widespread belief that there is a correct form of language, it is not uncommon to grant authority to some organization or institution to decide what it is or should be. The classic example of such institutions is the language academy (Cooper, 1989), common in countries with Romance languages and successfully resisted in Britain and the United States. The language academy is expected to resolve controversies over the form of language by laying down rules for correct spelling and grammar. It is usually given a second task which takes up most of its time, the coining or approval of new terminology to cover all the rapid developments of modern culture and technology (Antia, 2000; Wright & Budin, 2001). Making up lists of new words is not difficult: the second part of the task, disseminating these words and making sure that they are used, turns out to be the kind of problem that King Cnut faced with the waves (Rubin, Jernudd, Das Gupta, Fishman, & Ferguson, 1977). In spite of the general belief that there is a correct form of language, few people are willing to make the effort to use it regularly or to find out what words the academy will ultimately[9] propose for their new gadgets and concepts.

Managing Language Learning— Language of Instruction

The first two tasks of language management are making decisions about the *status* of languages, namely what they should be used for, and making decisions about the *form* of languages, namely attempting to standardize their use and elaborate their

---

[9] It took 225 years for L'Académie française to publish its first grammar.

vocabulary. The third task, called generally either *language acquisition planning* or language education policy, is concerned with modifying the ability of selected community members to use specific languages (Cooper, 1989).[10] Regularly, children come to school speaking the language of their home and of their neighborhood,[11] and, just as regularly, schools set out to modify their language practices either by developing parallel control of new varieties or languages or by attempting to replace their home language with another (Spolsky, 1974a). The gap between home and school language may be total, as when children of immigrants need to learn the language of their new country, or it may be partial, as when speakers of a nonstandard dialect are called on to start learning the standard variety.

The first challenge of language education is determining which language to use as the language of instruction in the classroom. The normal choice is the official language of the nation,[12] whether or not it is the language of home and community. A second approach, called mother-tongue[13] education, is to use the language of the home when it is practical, that is to say, when teachers know it and when materials are available and when all the children in the class have the same mother-tongue (Kecskes & Papp, 2000). A third approach, much debated and misunderstood, called *bilingual education*, is to work out some combination of home language and national language that will efficiently produce students able to work in both (Baker, 2001). These straightforward approaches are often confounded when a school system or nation has decided to switch to another language, as for example in Singapore, which chose to make English language of instruction (Xu & Wei, 2002), and most recently in Malaysia, which has just also decided to conduct education in English after 50 years of cultivating Bahasa Melayu (Gill, 2002).[14]

Conquered lands and colonies constitute special cases in which the relevant question is the status to be granted to the metropolitan language in language education. Here, there are two major approaches. One approach, adopted from the beginning of Spanish colonization of South America (Mar-Molinero, 2000) and maintained as a

---

[10] Language diffusion planning or management, the attempt to have people not under your direct control learn your language, is either a fourth task, or a sub-category of the third. Examples are the work of the Goethe Institute to spread German or the Dante Alighieri Society to promote Italian.

[11] Howard (2004), for instance, gives a detailed account of how Thai village children have to learn not only "the ideologies and linguistic practices of respect," but also the Standard Thai in which to express them, a language related to but different from the Kam Muang they and their fellow villagers speak (40% of the lexicon is not cognate, and half of the cognate words are pronounced differently).

[12] Some constitutions define what functions an official language should be used for; most leave it vague.

[13] Mother tongue (home language, first language, native language) is a complex concept (Haugen, 1991; Khubchandani, 2003).

[14] A bill to replace bilingual education by English medium is currently (May 2005) moving through the Philippine House of Representatives.

policy by Spain, Portugal (Vilela, 2002), and France (Bokamba, 1991; Chumbow & Bobda, 2000) in their overseas territories, was to require the use of the metropolitan language for all government-supported education from the first day of school. The effect in South America was to destroy indigenous languages wherever schooling was offered; the fact that some languages have survived is evidence of failure to introduce universal education (Hornberger & King, 2001). In French colonies, the result was that even after independence no question ever arose of developing indigenous languages for official status or for education (Bokamba, 1991). The second approach was developed in arguments in the 19th century in India over the strategy to be followed in education (S. Evans, 2002). While many of the British administrators accepted the Spanish or French approach, assuming that the goal of colonial education was to westernize and that this was best done in the Western language, there were others (the Orientalists) who argued that it was more efficient to conduct the first few years of schooling in the local language. This was a policy that the British followed in most of its African colonies (Armstrong, 1968; Phillipson & Skutnabb-Kangas, 1995a). Elementary schooling started in a selected indigenous language (practical conditions limited the number of languages that could be used). During this period, a start was also made on teaching English, which became the language of instruction no later than secondary school.

One advantage of using the metropolitan language is that it was already standardized and developed, with the terminology required to present the subject matter of the school curriculum. Where the choice was made, for whatever reason, to use an indigenous language in education, the immediate result was the need to cultivate that language. Thus, a decision on language education policy required action in corpus planning. The first requirement was often to choose a writing system, for the large majority of local languages had no need for or history of literacy, unless missionaries had already undertaken this task. The second was to develop the terminology needed for schooling. When in the 1970s a few schools on the Navajo Reservation started to teach in what was then the language of 90% of their entering pupils, an immediate challenge was to find ways to express in Navajo the basic concepts of school arithmetic (Holm & Holm, 1995; Spolsky, 1974b). I can recall sitting in one of the first classrooms in New Zealand that decided to teach in Maori and observing teacher, visiting inspector, and pupils discussing vocabulary problems (Spolsky, 1989).

Managing Language Learning— Additional Languages

The first and most disputed decision in language education management is what is to be the language of instruction. The next decision is what additional languages, if any, should be taught. Here again, the answers are best explained historically or politically. Western education started as a general rule in Latin; when it moved to teaching in the vernacular, it preserved the teaching of Latin and sometimes Greek as a central part of the curriculum (Clarke, 1959). The main goal of classical language instruction was to give access to what was considered a vital aspect of Western culture. Emphasis was naturally on literature, on developing the skill to read and write the classical language. In more recent times, Greek at first and Latin later were replaced by other major European literary languages, with French commonly taking pride of place in English-speaking countries.

A second common pressure on the choice of languages to teach is the language situation of the country, in other words, the sociolinguistic ecology or language practices of the community. In bilingual or multilingual countries, it seems logical to teach at least one other major language: in Belgium, French is taught in the Dutch regions and Dutch in the French regions (Aunger, 1993; Deprez, 2000; Murphy, 1993); in Switzerland, German has priority in French- and Italian-speaking cantons, and French in German-speaking cantons (Harlow, 2004; Hürdegen, 2001);[15] this principle accounts for the current importance of Spanish in the United States. An extension of this policy was the three-language policy adopted in independent India: pupils started their education in the mother-tongue, next learned the regional language, and then added the national language and English (Khubchandani, 1997). In the United States, both demographic and regional factors argue for the importance of Spanish as the first additional language. In Europe, the first language of choice to be added is English, which is why there is strong pressure for European countries to have two compulsory foreign languages. In Israel, Arabic-speaking pupils whose schooling is in their mother-tongue have first to start learning standard Arabic,[16] then to add Hebrew, which is the dominant language of public life, and finally to learn the English needed in the modern global society (Amara & Mar'i, 2002). There are additional reasons for adding languages to the school curriculum: religion is an important one, for many religions have a traditional sacred language associated with them (Spolsky, 2003).

A third pressure is provided by the existing status quo. French was so well established as the major foreign language to be taught in Britain and United States that any modification has been difficult (Lambert, 1994). Major changes can occur, as witnessed by the way that many East European teachers of Russian were retrained as teachers of English after the collapse of the Soviet Union.

Does the United States Have a Language Policy?

While most countries state their language policy in a constitutional clause or in a language law, the United States has no such explicit policy. United States language practices are essentially the result of an initial colonization period, leaving a small

---

[15] There has recently been controversy over the proposal to make English the first foreign language in Zurich and other cantons.

[16] It has major differences in grammar and lexicon from the language they speak at home.

residue of autochthonous languages and larger remnants of the languages of two former colonial powers (French and Spanish), an English-speaking dominance at the time of independence, and large influxes of immigrants speaking other languages generally allowed, encouraged, or forced to adopt English for public life at least. The result is a complex blend of changing individual pluringual proficiency (mainly in the direction of adding English for more and more purposes) and an uneven mosaic of societal multilingualism as presented clearly by Fishman (1966) and represented spatially by the MLA language map. There are thus many individuals who continue to use languages other than English at home and many neighborhoods where other languages are salient and even dominant.

American beliefs about languages, societal multilingualism and individual pluringual proficiency are equally complex. The General Social Survey[17] reveals that about two-thirds believe that English should be (or is) the official national language, although the campaign to make this the case has had quite limited success (Baron, 1990). The majority (64%) also seem to believe that there is value in plurilingualism (at least to the extent that teaching foreign languages is about as important as teaching mathematics); only 10% actually oppose teaching foreign languages. A third think all teaching in schools should be in English, nearly a half think that the first year or two should be in the child's native language, and a small group (16%) believe that native language education should continue through the school. The majority (75%) think that English unites Americans, but nearly the same number agree that ballots should include other languages. A third see the existence of a threat to English, but two thirds favor bilingual education. These are overall scores from a national sample, and presumably vary by region and sector of the population, but they suggest a general acceptance of multilingualism (Robinson, Brecht, & Rivers, in press).

In the early years after independence, multilingualism and bilingual education were in fact widely supported. During the period of intense immigration in the second half of the 19th century, growing ethnocentrism encouraged an ideology of English hegemony (Ricento, 2001), only modified more recently by developing acceptance of cultural pluralism. Essentially then, the public position is not negative towards the notions being developed during the Year of Languages.

Language management activities reflect this ambivalence. There have been, I believe, two major forces driving U.S. language management: civil rights and national security. The first of these is the application to language of the civil rights laid down in the Constitution and the Bill of Rights. The important statement of civil rights is in the 14th Amendment to the U.S. Constitution, passed in 1868 and

---

[17] A regular survey of a national population sample collected by the National Opinion Research Center (NORC) at the University of Chicago.

establishing the principle of equal protection. A number of laws starting with the 1957 Civil Rights Act prohibited discrimination on the basis of race, color, and national origin. Subsequently, in the 1970s, court decisions used Title VII of the Act and the 14th Amendment to tackle language discrimination.

This approach was strengthened by the passage in 1968 of the Bilingual Education Act, intended, according to all the testimony given to Congress before the passage of the Act (*Bilingual Education,* 1967; *Bilingual Education Programs,* 1967), to provide a more efficient method of teaching English to minority pupils. While it was in place, the program had many educational successes (Brisk, 1998; Crawford, 1999; Hornberger, 1987) but came under increasing political pressure and finally (Crawford, 2002) was dropped, swallowed by the No Child Left Behind Act (see following).

However, the impact of the Civil Rights Act was extended when in August 2000 President Clinton signed Executive Order 13166, entitled "Improving Access to Services for Persons with Limited English Proficiency." Federal agencies and other organizations receiving federal funding were required by the Order to develop plans on how to provide necessary services to people who did not know English well enough (Brecht & Rivers, 2005). Implementation of the program has been uneven, but it remains a major force protecting the civil rights of speakers of other languages. Like similar programs in Europe and elsewhere, these are policies to protect the rights of individuals, and not policies to enforce the desire of language groups to maintain their own languages. They accept the right of speakers of minority languages to attempt to maintain their language, provided this does not interfere with the learning of the national civic language by members of the group. They insist on the right of individuals living within a state to have access to government in spite of the fact that they speak another language.[18]

A second force which has led to U.S. government language management activity is national security. One early program was the Armed Services Training Program in the Second World War, a brief but celebrated effort to make up for the failures of U.S. education to teach languages over the previous two decades (Keefer, 1988; Spolsky, 1995).[19] The various government agencies, especially defense and intelligence, have been forced by the inadequacies of U.S. foreign

---

[18] Stronger claims for the rights of languages rather than individuals are advocated by some; for example, see Phillipson & Skutnabb-Kangas (1995b), Skutnabb-Kangas & Phillipson (1995) and Varennes (2001).

[19] While the announced aim of the program was to produce soldiers with language skills that would be useful to the army, in fact the main motivation appears to have been keeping the colleges open when their male students were being conscripted.

language teaching (Henmon, 1934) to set up their own language schools.[20] With the threat of Soviet scientific superiority after Sputnik, the National Defense Education Act also included a language program. The inadequacy of these programs, even bolstered later by the National Security Education Program, was one of the major issues brought up in the investigations of the intelligence failures before 9/11. Since then, defense and security agencies of government have come to recognize the need for higher priority for language management.[21]

There has been a major recent development: the new Defense Language Transformation Roadmap, approved by the Deputy Secretary of Defense Paul Wolfowitz on February 14, 2005. The preparation of the roadmap began in November 2002, starting with a review by all military departments, commands, and defense agencies of their requirements for language professionals and a detailed study of their current capacity to meet these needs. It was based on four assumptions: the continuation of conflict against enemies speaking other languages and the consequent need for "robust foreign language and foreign area expertise" in maintaining coalitions and conducting missions, including post-conflict operations; the widening range of potential conflict zones and likely coalition partners; the development of forces with improved foreign language capabilities; and the likelihood that adversaries will attempt to divide international coalitions. The first goal is to recognize "language skill and regional expertise" as "warfighting skills" to be incorporated in operational planning. To carry out this goal, a Defense Language Office is to be established, language requirements are to be developed within service doctrine, an annual "strategic language list" and a language readiness index are to be developed, language skills of all military and civilian personnel are to be measured and reported, guidelines are to be developed for recruiting heritage and language-qualified personnel, the National Flagship Language Initiative is to be supported, the language testing program is to be improved and implemented, study abroad opportunities for military personnel are to be developed, and foreign language ability is to become a criterion for promotion to the rank of general. The second goal is to develop a method to meet the requirements of operational units for language and regional

---

[20] In November 1941, the US Army began a secret school with 60 students to teach Japanese at the Presidio of Monterey and produced in the course of the war some 6000 graduates. After the war, the renamed Army Language School added other languages—Russian, Chinese, Korean, and German among the largest programs. In the 1950s, the US Air Force conducted training through universities, but all these programs were consolidated in 1963 when the Defense Language Institute was established. The Department of State, CIA, NSA, and FBI also operate language schools.

[21] Among the various steps taken was the establishment of a university-affiliated research center at the University of Maryland, the Center for Advanced Research in Language, where some of the ideas in this paper were nurtured. For detailed discussion of these issues, see Brecht & Rivers (2000; 2005) and Brecht & Walton (1994).

area expertise. This will include hiring linguists, maintaining a database of retired personnel with language qualifications, building civilian career paths for soldiers with language proficiency, recruiting personnel from heritage communities to provide translators and interpreters, supporting the establishment of a Civilian Linguist Reserve Corps, developing courses for language and regional training, and building a reserve of people with expertise in less commonly taught languages. The third goal is to establish a cadre of language professionals with functional skill in reading, listening, and speaking.[22] Currently, training programs do not reach this level. A first step will be to identify tasks and missions that require this level of proficiency and to estimate the number of people required for these positions. A system is then to be developed to meet and fill these positions. The fourth goal is to study the hiring, maintenance, and promotion of military personnel with language and area competence. Associated with these four goals will be a major transformation of the Defense Language Institute Foreign Language Center. The roadmap assigns primary responsibility for each of the tasks it identifies and sets a date for full operational capability. Transformation is an appropriate term for this new policy, which continues and deepens the concern of the federal government and especially of Defense to develop the national language capacity.

The fact that national security has come to play such a significant role in U.S. language policy raises some concerns, not unlike the realization of physicists that their scientific work was being boosted and exploited by the development of the atomic bomb during the Second World War. This paper is not the place to discuss this issue in any detail, but it is perhaps worth mentioning some points. First, as has been argued, it results from a failure of the educational enterprise as a whole to produce a citizenry with plurilingual proficiency able to support not just defense concerns but also the demands of global business, international diplomacy, and the needs of social justice and civil rights. Second, while the Defense initiatives focus on security demands, the effects can be beneficial to a much wider range of social needs, such as (for the first time) a serious government commitment to multilingualism and a recognition of the importance of heritage language communities, seen as a resource rather than as a problem. Third, a scholar who recalls a lifetime of fruitless arguments in favor of multilingualism cannot scoff at hearing the chief of staff of the U.S. Air Force publicly stating that his highest priority was an air force with foreign language proficiency and cultural sensitivity.[23]

U.S. language management then currently focuses on two ends of the continuum, providing for access to civic services for those who do not know English and

---

[22] Level 3 in the government scale.

[23] General John Jumper, Chief of Staff, US Air Force spoke on "Operational perspective of military language needs" at the National Language Conference at the University of Maryland on June 23, 2004.

attending to the advanced professional foreign language education of government employees in defense and security. The obvious gap that this leaves is a national language education policy that can produce a citizenry with adequate skills in languages other than English. The absence of such a program means that government and industry generally suffer from serious shortages in potential employees with the level of proficiency in foreign languages required for their efficient operation (Brecht & Rivers, 2000; 2005; Lambert, 1994). But as Lambert pointed out, the constitutional assignment of authority over education to the states rather than the federal government makes it harder to determine blame. However, when the federal government wishes to take charge of an educational matter, as in the National Defense Education Act, or the Bilingual Education Act, or the current No Child Left Behind Act, there are ways to do this.

There have, of course, been attempts in the United States to fill the gap in producing language capacity. From time to time, the federal government has been persuaded to set up programs to improve foreign language teaching: the National Defense Education Act involved strong efforts to revise teaching methods. There are components in place that could be built upon. There are some elementary schools— two-way immersion or bilingual or content-based—that provide a small group of children with the needed basis for plurilingualism. There are high school programs, mainly in Spanish and French, which carry on the traditional policy of foreign language teaching. There are college programs teaching the same traditional subjects but also some offering lesser taught languages. There are even university programs, supported by Title VI, offering a wide range of languages at the doctoral level. Basically, however, as Lambert (1994) pointed out, the fact that U.S. educational policy is constitutionally left to the states and that there is an absence of concern for foreign language education in such federal programs as No Child Left Behind has meant that the gap remains. There is continuing evidence of the reduction of instructional time devoted to liberal arts and the teaching of foreign languages in schools (von Jastrow & Janc, 2004). In fact, the No Child Left Behind Act of 2001 (2002) is starting to show significant differences in the valuing of languages other than English.[24] Evans & Hornberger (2005) lament that the new policy considers language a problem rather than a resource or a right. It presents an ideology opposed to multiculturalism and multilingualism (Ricento & Hornberger, 1996; von Jastrow & Janc, 2004).

Recent congressional resolutions do offer some signs of hope: Senate Resolution 28, introduced by a dozen Senators, designated 2005 as the Year of Languages and called

---

[24] The "Perspectives" section of *The Modern Language Journal* 89(2), pp. 242–282, reviews the Act from the point of view of the foreign language profession. It notes that it is an exceptionally strong attempt at a Federal intervention in education and sets a major challenge to foreign language educators.

for encouragement of initiatives to promote and expand the study of foreign languages; the resolution was passed on February 17, 2005. A similar resolution, sponsored by Representatives Rush Holt and Patrick Tiberi, passed the U.S. House of Representatives on March 8, 2005.[25] However, a summary of activities of the 108th Congress show that only two out of eighteen bills dealing with languages and international studies were passed, both dealing with intelligence. Most federal programs dealing with language were either decreased or their funding kept at the same level: there were some increases in the Foreign Language Assistance Program and the International Education program; and some money was added to the National Security Education Program. The new budget request eliminates funding for more than a dozen small federal programs which in the past have provided support for language. Essentially then, apart from activities related to defense and intelligence, the progress so far for federal support for the Year of Languages is disappointing.

There has however been an effort by the Department of Defense to encourage the development of a national language policy, recognizing the fact that long range planning is needed (Brecht & Walton, 1994) and that meeting its language goals will depend in part on recruiting heritage speakers (Brecht & Ingold, 1998; Spolsky, 2001). In July 2004, the Department of Defense organized a conference to which were invited 300 people from federal, state and local government, academia, international institutions, language associations, and business to discuss national foreign language capabilities. At the end of the three-day meeting, a white paper was drafted and circulated among participants and government agencies. The document, with the title "A Call to Action for National Foreign Language Capabilities," was released finally by the Department of Defense on February 1, 2005. It is signed by David S. C. Chu, Undersecretary of Defense for Personnel and Readiness, under whose responsibility falls also the Language Transformation roadmap, and is presented as the "thoughts of the conference participants" including views which "do not necessarily represent the views of the Department of Defense." The rhetoric is strong: this may well be "a Sputnik moment" and there is an "urgent need for national leadership."[26] The paper lists seven major actions that are needed: the development of language and cultural competency, engaging federal, state, and local government in solutions, integrating language training in various career fields, developing critical language skills, strengthening teaching capabilities, integrating

---

[25] Senators Lieberman (D-CT) and Alexander (R-TN) introduced the United States-China Cultural Engagement Act in May 2005; the legislation provides for Chinese language instruction in American schools. On May 23, Senator Christopher Dodd introduced the Dodd-Cochran International and Foreign Language Studies Act, S.1105, on behalf of himself, Senator Cochran, and Senators Levin, Kennedy, and Akaka. This bill increases funding for language programs and overseas study.

[26] William Rivers reminds me that in fact it took nine years between the first arguments for the relevance of Sputnik to foreign language education and the inclusion of language in the National Defense Education Act (Parker 1961).

language into educational requirements, and developing instructional materials and tools. The weakness of the document is that it is not signed by any other agency—the absence of the Department of Education is obvious—and that a government department cannot officially advocate national policy in an area beyond its immediate concern.[27] It is a signal that Defense needs a wide support if it is to achieve its own language goals, but also evidence that this wide support has not yet developed in other branches of government or at the key levels of political leadership.

The Year of Languages organized by the American Council on the Teaching of Foreign Languages is of course part of the struggle to mobilize this support. The Year started in January 2005 with a policy summit, a video conference to which representatives of government, business, and the professions were invited.[28] The goal of the summit was to create a plan of action that would take the next steps, basing these steps on the Department of Defense's *A Call to Action for National Foreign Language Capabilities* (National Language Conference, 2005). A report entitled *A Blueprint for Action on Language Education* (Müller, 2005) details steps to be taken and by whom.

Are There Models for U.S. Language Policy?

A colleague of mine has just completed an article on foreign language education policy for an encyclopedia (Lambert, in press). He was somewhat distressed to find that for most countries in the world, foreign language education means teaching English. This clearly has an important influence on U.S. beliefs about language policy: if everyone else wants to learn English, why should we bother learning other languages?

Of those countries that do teach foreign languages other than English, the main examples are in Western Europe, where the Council of Europe and the European Union have exerted steady pressure to develop a consistent language policy which will recognize the rights of a select number of identified autochthonous minority languages and promote common standards for developing the proficiency of European citizens ideally in two languages other than the national language (Council of Europe, 2001; Scharer & North, 1992).

The policies of multilingual European countries like the Netherlands or Finland or the Scandinavian countries are not directly applicable to the U.S. situation. As

---

[27] On May 19, 2005, Senator Daniel Akaka (Democrat from Hawaii) introduced S. 1089—The National Language Coordination Act of 2005, establishing a National Language Director and a Coordination Council with representatives of major government departments. This was one of the recommendations of the White Paper.

[28] This paper is a development of remarks made in a keynote address at that meeting at The University of North Carolina at Chapel Hill. Kurt Müller's paper in this volume is also a result of the Policy Summit.

Lambert notices, most non-English speaking countries in the world do not have a foreign language education policy so much as an English teaching policy. Their first goal is to maintain and strengthen their official national language (or languages); their second is to teach English to as many pupils as possible; their third is to deal with languages of neighboring countries and minority groups. The Netherlands feels reasonably safe with Dutch, works hard to maintain the high standards that it has achieved in English, tries to provide a reasonable level of plurilingualism including German and French and other European languages, and tends to ignore minority and immigrant languages except for some token support for Friesian.[29] Countries with significant minority languages like Belgium, Switzerland, and Finland are starting to find it increasingly difficult to grant those languages priority over English. But still there are important lessons to be derived from Europe, for it is committed to national language education policies that produce a plurilingual citizenry. Indeed, we might soon be able to cite France as a prime example: after 200 years of asserting the hegemony of one national language, it might well be about to recognize the critical need of bilingualism in the modern world by including English in its core curriculum alongside mathematics and French.

That leaves English-speaking countries to search for models. Canada, South Africa, New Zealand, and the United Kingdom apart from England, while also exemplary in their growing commitment to multilingualism, have first to deal with powerful minority interests before they can talk about adding other languages. In Canada, since 1969, the key problem has been to change a situation where the meaning of bilingual was a French Canadian who had learned English;[30] in South Africa, the struggle is how to protect Afrikaans against English while paying at least lip service to a handful of selected African languages; in New Zealand, the issue is the role of the Maori language; and in the formerly conquered peripheral UK territories, the issue is the nonthreatening revival of the symbolically important territorial languages, Welsh, Scottish Gaelic, and Irish. That leaves Australia and England. At one stage, Australia offered a promising solution. A coalition of language interests— heritage and community language groups, foreign language professionals, autochthonous language groups, academic linguists—formed first in Victoria and then spread to the federal level encouraging the development of an Australian language policy that appeared to be a model for a multilingual society with plurilingual citizens (Lo Bianco, 1987). In practice, however, most of the effort went into the establishment of some university research centers which, however necessary they were and however valuable their scientific output, did not lead to any major revision in language teaching.

---

[29] They have just agreed to translate the European Constitution in Friesian.
[30] Ghosh (2004) notes the fundamental conflict between the federal multilingual policy and the Quebec ideology of French-Québécois nationalism.

The policy was later revised, first to concentrate on the teaching of "Australia's national language" (meaning English) and then to add the teaching of commercially relevant Asian languages (Lo Bianco & Wickert, 2001). Canada and Australia are potentially relevant in their attempts to find a way to develop a national policy while respecting regional autonomy.

England, leaving aside its granting of autonomy to Scotland, Wales, and soon Ireland, has in fact recently adopted a foreign language teaching strategy. In 1988, the National Curriculum made it compulsory for all secondary schoolchildren in England and Wales to study modern foreign language up to the age of 16. Only 10% carried on with their studies after this, so that many university language departments were forced to close. The Nuffield Languages Inquiry in 2000 pointed out problems and needs, and, as a result, the Department for Education and Skills issued a new plan in December 2002. The first component of the new plan was a commitment to offer every primary school pupil between the ages of seven and eleven the opportunity to study at least one modern foreign language. The second component will be a strengthened framework for teaching modern foreign languages in the first three years of secondary education, where it will be compulsory. A National Director of Languages has been appointed and the new curriculum is slowly moving towards the precise statement of goals in the Common European Framework. As promising as this plan sounds, the actual situation remains disturbing. Languages are to be made optional at the GCSE level, and the Qualifications and Curriculum Authority have reported that high school French and German are in "chronic decline." The House of Lords European Union Committee has concluded that "the United Kingdom is already falling badly behind in language-learning capability," which will seriously limit its ability to take advantage of EU training programs. UK businesses will be "severely hampered."[31]

None of these other countries offer simple and obvious models to deal with the situation in the United States. In the areas of civil rights and defense, we have been able to present obvious arguments that have more or less convinced some appropriate federal agencies and a few Senators and members of Congress to venture into the realm of language management. It is much harder to find arguments that will convince state governments and the general public that a language education policy is needed.[32]

While people all over the world are trying to learn English, why should speakers of English bother with other languages? And if so, which of the very many should be given priority?

---

[31] *BBC News*, 14/4/2005.
[32] National Association of State Boards of Education Study Group (2003) draws attention to a study for the American Council on Education which found that 77% of respondents felt that foreign languages should be required in high school.

In this volume, you will read many excellent arguments on topics such as efforts to develop a national language policy aiming to produce plurilingual citizens, the cognitive value of being plurilingual, the access to many cultures and literatures, the trading advantage when you understand the language of your customer, the added security that comes from understanding the language of your potential allies and enemies. If we are to turn this dream into reality, we need a major change in attitude and belief, an abandonment of our false assumption that monolingualism is normal and efficient. A society that accepts multilingualism and that encourages plurilingualism in its citizens is safer, stronger, and richer. The United States is a multilingual country; many of its residents and even more of their parents and grandparents are and were plurilingual. In recognition of this, we will need to find ways to modify our educational system so that it develops a goal that all its graduates can be proficient not just in English but also in a second language.

My tone has been more pessimistic than usual in what should be a celebratory volume. I am not saying that language management is impossible: there have been many cases, at all levels, of degrees of success—families which have maintained traditional languages while acquiring new ones, religions which have kept sacred languages alive, local and global businesses which are learning how to succeed in a multilingual world, legal and health institutions that can cope with multilingual clientele. And there have been national language policies which have achieved major changes—the revitalization and revernacularization of Hebrew,[33] the protection of French and Catalan in Quebec and Catalonia,[34] the establishment of Malaysian and Indonesian, the re-establishment of languages suppressed during the Soviet period, the symbolic valuing of Maori and Irish and Basque. None of these approach the difficulty and nature of the challenge facing the US, the successful development of a functionally plurilingually proficient population. In the civil rights area, a program is struggling to protect individual rights; in the defense and security domain, a roadmap is being implemented; and an ambitious action plan has been proposed to fill the gap. However, absent two vital forces—a strong popular belief and a political and educational leadership committed to multilingualism—it is hard to be optimistic.

References

Ager, D. E. (1999). *Identity, insecurity and image: France and language.* Clevedon, UK: Multilingual Matters.

Amara, M. H., & Mar'i, A. A.-R. (2002). *Language education policy: The Arab minority in Israel.* Dordrecht, Netherlands: Kluwer Academic.

---

[33] Albeit at the cost of loss of many traditional languages (Spolsky & Shohamy, 2001) and traditional Jewish plurilingualism (Ben-Rafael, 1994).

[34] Admittedly producing problems for English and Spanish speakers.

Annamalai, E. (2001). *Managing multilingualism in India: Political and linguistic manifestations*. New Delhi, India: Sage.

Antia, B. E. (2000). *Terminology and language planning: An alternative framework of practice and discourse*. Amsterdam: John Benjamins.

Armstrong, R. G. (1968). Language policies and language practices in West Africa. In J. A. Fishman, C. A. Ferguson, & J. Das Gupta (Eds.), *Language problems of developing nations* (pp. 227–236). New York: John Wiley and Sons.

Aunger, E. A. (1993). Regional, national and official languages in Belgium. *International Journal of the Sociology of Language, 104*, 31–48.

Baker, C. (2001). *Foundations of bilingual education and bilingualism* (3rd ed.). Clevedon, UK: Multilingual Matters.

Baron, D. E. (1990). *The English Only question*. New Haven: Yale University Press.

Ben-Rafael, E. (1994). *Language, identity and social division: The case of Israel*. Oxford: Clarendon Press.

Benton, R. A., & Benton, N. (2001). RLS in Aotearoa/New Zealand 1989–1999. In J. A. Fishman (Ed.), *Can threatened languages be saved?* (pp. 422–449). Clevedon, UK: Multilingual Matters.

Bilingual Education, United States Senate, 90th Congress, First Sess. 681 (1967).

Bilingual Education Programs, House of Representatives, 90th Congress, First Sess. 584 (1967).

Bingol, Y. (2002). *Revisiting Turkish language policy in light of the actors' norms and identity model*. Unpublished PhD, Indiana University, Bloomington.

Bokamba, E G. (1991). French colonial language policies in Africa and their legacies. In D. F. Marshall (Ed.), *Language planning* (Vol. III of Focusschrift in honor of Joshua A. Fishman on the occasion of his 65th birthday, pp. 175–214). Amsterdam: John Benjamins.

Brecht, R. D., & Ingold, C. W. (1998). *Tapping a national resource: Heritage languages in the United States* [Position paper]. Washington, DC: National Foreign Language Center.

Brecht, R. D., & Rivers, W. P. (2000). *Language and national security in the 21st century: The role of the Title VI/Fulbright-Hays in supporting national language capacity*. Dubuque, IA: Kendall-Hunt.

Brecht, R. D., & Rivers, W. P. (2005). Language needs analysis at the societal level. In M. Long (Ed.), *Second language needs analysis*. Cambridge, UK: Cambridge University Press.

Brecht, R. D., & Walton, A. R. (1994). National strategic planning and less commonly taught languages. *The Annals of the American Academy of Political and Social Science, 532*, 190–212.

Brisk, M. E. (1998). *Bilingual education: From compensatory to quality schooling*. Mahwah, NJ: L. Erlbaum Associates.

Cheng, C.-C. (1986). Contradictions in Chinese language reform. *International Journal of the Sociology of Language, 59*, 87–96.

Chumbow, B. S., & Bobda, A S. (2000). French in West Africa: A sociolinguistic perspective. *International Journal of the Sociology of Language, 141*, 39–60.

Clarke, M. L. (1959). *Classical education in Britain, 1500–1900*. Cambridge, UK: Cambridge University Press.

Cooper, R. L. (1989). *Language planning and social change.* Cambridge, UK: Cambridge University Press.

Coulmas, F. (2003). *Writing system: An introduction to their linguistic analysis.* Cambridge, UK: Cambridge University Press.

Council of Europe. (2001). *Common European framework of reference for languages: Learning, teaching, assessment.* Cambridge, UK: Cambridge University Press.

Crawford, J. (1999). *Bilingual education: History, politics, theory and practice* (4th ed.). Los Angeles: Bilingual Education Services.

Crawford, J. (2002). Obituary: The Bilingual Education Act: 1968–2002.

Deprez, K. (2000). Belgium: From a unitary to a federalist state. In K. Deprez & T. Du Plessis (Eds.), *Multilingualism and government: Belgium, Luxembourg, Switzerland, Former Yugoslavia, and South Africa* (pp. 17–29). Pretoria, South Africa: Van Schaik.

Deutch, Y. (2005). Language policy in Israel: The legal perspective. *Language Policy, 4*(3).

Evans, B. A., & Hornberger, N. H. (2005). No Child Left Behind: Repealing and unpeeling federal language education in the United States. *Language Policy, 4*(1), 87–106.

Evans, S. (2002). Macaulay's Minute revisited: Colonial language policy in nineteenth-century India. *Journal of Multilingual and Multicultural Development, 23*(4), 260–281.

Fishman, J. A. (Ed.). (1966). *Language loyalty in the United States: The maintenance and perpetuation of non-English mother tongues by American ethnic and religious groups.* The Hague: Mouton.

Fishman, J. A. (Ed.). (1977). *Advances in the creation and revision of writing systems.* The Hague: Mouton.

Fishman, J. A. (1988). Reflections on the current state of language planning. In L. LaForge (Ed.), *Proceedings of the International Conference on Language Planning* (pp. 406–428). Quebec: University of Laval Press.

Fishman, J. A. (2000). The status agenda in corpus planning. In R. D. Lambert & E. Shohamy (Eds.), *Language policy and pedagogy: Essays in honor of A. Ronald Walton* (pp. 43–52). Philadelphia: John Benjamins.

Garvin, P. (1973). Some comments on language planning. In J. Rubin & R. Shuy (Eds.), *Language planning: Current issues and research* (pp. 24–73). Washington, DC: Georgetown University Press.

Geerts, G., Van den Broeck, J., & Verdoodt, A. F. (1977). Successes and failures in Dutch spelling reform. In J. A. Fishman (Ed.), *Advances in the creation and revision of writing systems* (pp. 179–245). The Hague: Mouton.

Ghosh, R. (2004). Public education and multicultural policy in Canada: The special case of Quebec. *International Review of Education, 50*(5–6), 543–566.

Gill, S. K. (2002). *International communication: English language challenges for Malaysia.* Serdang, Malaysia: University Putra Malaysia Press.

Grenoble, L. A. (2003). *Soviet language policy.* Dordrecht, Netherlands: Kluwer Academic.

Harlow, R. (2004). Switzerland. In P. Strazny (Ed.), *Encyclopedia of Linguistics.* London: Taylor and Francis.

Haugen, E. (1966). *Language conflict and language planning: The case of Modern Norwegian.* Cambridge, MA: Harvard University Press.

Haugen, E. (1991). The "mother tongue." In R. L. Cooper & B. Spolsky (Eds.), *The influence of language on culture and thought: Essays in honour of the 65th birthday of Joshua A. Fishman* (pp. 75–84). Berlin: Mouton de Gruyter.

Henmon, V. A. C. (1934). Recent developments in the study of foreign language problems. *Modern Language Journal, 19*(4), 187–201.

Heugh, K. (2003). Can authoritarian separatism give way to linguistic rights? A South African case study. *Current Issues in Language Planning, 4*(2), 126–145.

Holm, A., & Holm, W. (1995). Navajo language education: Retrospect and prospects. *Bilingual Research Journal, 19,* 141–167.

Hornberger, N. H. (1987). Bilingual education success, but policy failure. *Language in Society, 16*(2), 205–226.

Hornberger, N. H., & King, K. A. (2001). Reversing language shift in South America. In J. A. Fishman (Ed.), *Can threatened languages be saved?* (pp. 166–194). Clevedon, UK: Multilingual Matters.

Howard, K. (2004). Socializing respect at school in Northern Thailand. *Working Papers in Applied Linguistics, 20*(1), 1–30.

Hürdegen, S. (2001). The Fribourg linguistic case—Controversy about the language of instruction in schools in the light of freedom of language and equal educational opportunities in Switzerland. *European Journal for Educational Law and Policy, 5,* 73–82.

Jernudd, B. (Ed.). (2000). *Language Management and Language Problems: Special Issue of Journal of Asian Pacific Communications 10.2* (Vol. 1). Amsterdam: John Benjamins.

Jernudd, B. (Ed.). (2001). *Language Management and Language Problems: Special Issue of Journal of Asian Pacific Communications 11:1* (Vol. 2). Amsterdam: John Benjamins.

Johnson, S. (2002). On the origin of linguistic norms: Orthography, ideology and the first constitutional challenge to the 1996 reform of German. *Language in Society, 31*(4), 549–576.

Kecskes, I., & Papp, T. (2000). *Foreign language and mother tongue.* Hillsdale, NJ: Lawrence Erlbaum.

Keefer, L. E. (1988). *Scholars in foxholes: The story of the Army Specialized Training Program in World War II.* Jefferson, NC: McFarland.

Khubchandani, L. M. (1997). Language policy and education in the Indian subcontinent. In R. Wodak & D. Corson (Eds.), *Encyclopedia of language and education* (Vol. 1: Language policy and political issues in education, pp. 179–187). Dordrecht, Netherlands: Kluwer Academic.

Khubchandani, L. M. (2003). Defining mother tongue education in plurilingual contexts. *Language Policy, 2*(3), 239–254.

King, R. D. (2001). The poisonous potency of script: Hindi and Urdu. *International Journal of the Sociology of Language, 150,* 43–59.

Kloss, H. (1969). *Research possibilities on group bilingualism: A report.* Quebec: International Center for Research on Bilingualism.

Kroon, S., & Vallen, T. (in press). Immigrant language education. In K. Brown (Ed.), *Encyclopedia of languages and linguistics.* Oxford: Elsevier.

Lambert, R. D. (1994). Problems and processes in U.S. foreign language planning. *The Annals of the American Academy of Political and Social Sciences, 532*, 47–58.

Lambert, R. D. (in press). Foreign language education. In K. Brown (Ed.), *Encyclopedia of languages and linguistics*. Oxford: Elsevier.

Larrivée, P., (Ed.). (2002). *Linguistic conflict and language laws: Understanding the Quebec question*. Basingstoke, UK: Palgrave.

Lewis, G. (1999). *The Turkish language reform: A catastrophic success*. Oxford: Oxford University Press.

Lo Bianco, J. (1987). *National policy on languages*. Canberra: Australian Government Publishing Service.

Lo Bianco, J,, & Wickert, R, (Eds.). (2001). *Australian policy activism in language and literacy*. Canberra: Language Australia.

Mar-Molinero, C. (2000). *The politics of language in the Spanish-speaking world: From colonisation to globalisation*. London: Routledge.

Müller, K. E. (2005). *A blueprint for action on language education: Summary of the proceedings at the National Language Policy Summit, January 10–11, 2005*. [white paper]. Alexandria, VA: American Council on the Teaching of Foreign Languages.

Murphy, A. B. (1993). Linguistic regionalism and the social construction of space in Belgium. *International Journal of the Sociology of Language, 104*, 49–64.

National Association of State Boards of Education Study Group. (2003). *The complete curriculum: Ensuring a place for the arts and foreign languages in America's schools*. Alexandria, VA: NASBE.

Nic Craith, M. (2001). Politicised linguistic consciousness: The case of Ulster-Scots. *Nations and Nationalism, 7*(1), 21–37.

National Language Conference. (2005). *A call to action for national foreign language capabilities* [white paper]. Washington, DC: Office of the Undersecretary of Defense (Personnel and Readiness).

No Child Left Behind Act of 2001, United States Congress (2002).

Parker, W. R. (1961). *The national interest and foreign languages* (3rd ed.). Washington, DC: US Government Printing Office.

Phillipson, R., & Skutnabb-Kangas, T. (1995a). Language rights in postcolonial Africa. In R. Phillipson, M. Rannut, & T. Skutnabb-Kangas (Eds.), *Linguistic human rights: Overcoming linguistic discrimination* (pp. 335–346). Berlin: Mouton de Gruyter.

Phillipson, R., & Skutnabb-Kangas, T. (1995b). Linguistic rights and wrong. *Applied Linguistics, 16*, 483–504.

Rabin, C. (1977). Spelling reform—Israel 1968. In J. A. Fishman (Ed.), *Advances in the creation and revision of writing systems* (Reprinted from *Can language be planned?* ed., pp. 149–176). The Hague: Mouton.

Ricento, T. (Ed.). (2001). *Ideology, politics and language policies: Focus on English*. Amsterdam: John Benjamins.

Ricento, T., & Hornberger, N. H. (1996). Unpeeling the onion: Language planning and policy and the ELT professional. *TESOL Quarterly, 30*(3), 401–428.

Robinson, J. P., Brecht, R. D., & Rivers, W. P. (in press). *Foreign language speakers in America: Correlates, trends, and possible consequences.*

Rubin, J., Jernudd, B., Das Gupta, J., Fishman, J. A., & Ferguson, C. A. (1977). *Language planning processes.* The Hague: Mouton.

Saban, I., & Amara, M. (2002). The status of Arabic in Israel: Reflections on the power of law to produce social change. *Israel Law Review, 36*(2), 5–39.

Scharer, R., & North, B. (1992). *Toward a common European framework for reporting language competency* [Position paper]. Washington, DC: National Foreign Language Center.

Shaw, G. B. (1962). *Androcles and the lion, an old fable renovated; by Bernard Shaw: with a parallel text in Shaw's alphabet to be read in conjunction, showing its economies in writing and reading.* London: Penguin.

Skutnabb-Kangas, T., & Phillipson, R. (1995). Linguistic human rights, past and present. In T. Skutnabb-Kangas, R. Phillipson, & M. Rannut (Eds.), *Linguistic human rights: Overcoming linguistic discrimination* (pp. 71–110). Berlin: Mouton de Gruyter.

Spolsky, B. (1974a). Linguistics and the language barrier to education. In T. A. Sebeok, A. S. Abramson, D. Hymes, H. Rubenstein, E. Stankiewicz, & B. Spolsky (Eds.), *Current trends in linguistics: Linguistics and adjacent arts and sciences* (Vol. 12, pp. 2027–2038). The Hague: Mouton.

Spolsky, B. (1974b). The Navajo Reading Study: An illustration of the scope and nature of educational linguistics. In J. Quistgaard, H. Schwarz, & H. Spong-Hanssen (Eds.), *Applied Linguistics: Problems and solutions: Proceedings of the Third Congress on Applied Linguistics, Copenhagen, 1972* (Vol. 3, pp. 553–565). Heidelberg: Julius Gros Verlag.

Spolsky, B. (1989). Maori bilingual education and language revitalization. *Journal of Multilingual and Multicultural Development, 9*(6), 1–18.

Spolsky, B. (1995). The impact of the Army Specialized Training Program: A reconsideration. In G. Cook & B. Seidelhofer (Eds.), *For H.G. Widdowson: Principles and practice in the study of language: A. Festschrift on the occasion of his sixtieth birthday* (pp. 323–334). Oxford: Oxford University Press.

Spolsky, B. (2001). Heritage languages and national security: An ecological view. In S. J. Baker (Ed.), *Language policy: Lessons from global models* (pp. 103–114). Monterey, CA: Monterey Institute of International Studies.

Spolsky, B. (2003). Religion as a site of language contact. *Annual Review of Applied Linguistics, 23*, 81–94.

Spolsky, B. (2004). *Language policy.* Cambridge, UK: Cambridge University Press.

Spolsky, B., & Shohamy, E. (2001). Hebrew after a century of RLS efforts. In J. A. Fishman (Ed.), *Can threatened languages be saved?* (pp. 349–362). Clevedon, UK: Multilingual Matters.

Strubell, M. (2001). Catalan a decade later. In J. A. Fishman (Ed.), *Can threatened languages be saved?* (pp. 260–283). Clevedon, UK: Multilingual Matters.

U.S. Department of Defense (2005). *Defense language transformation roadmap.* Available: http://www.defenselink.mil/news/Mar2005/d20050330roadmap.pdf

Varennes, F. de. (2001). Language rights as an integral part of human rights. *MOST Journal of Multicultural Studies, 3*(1).

Vilela, M. (2002). Reflections on language policy in African countries with Portuguese as an official language. *Current Issues in Language Planning, 3*(3), 306–316.

von Jastrow, C., & Janc, H. (2004). *Academic atrophy: The condition of the liberal arts in America's public schools.* Washington, DC: Council for Public Education.

Williams, G. (1987). Policy as containment with democracy: The Welsh Language Act. *International Journal of the Sociology of Language, 66*, 49–60.

Woolard, K. A., & Gahng, T.-J. (1990). Changing language policies and attitudes in autonomous Catalonia. *Language in Society, 19*(3), 311–330.

Wright, S. E., & Budin, G. (Eds.). (2001). *Handbook of Terminology Management* (Vol. 2: Applications Oriented Terminology Management). Amsterdam: John Benjamins.

Xu, D., & Wei, L. (2002). Managing multilingualism in Singapore. In L. Wei, J.-M. Dewaele, & A. Housen (Eds.), *Opportunities and challenges of bilingualism* (pp. 275–296). Berlin: Mouton de Gruyter.

Zhou, M. (Ed.). (2004). *Language policy in the People's Republic of China: Theory and practice since 1949.* Dordrecht, Netherlands: Kluwer Academic.

3

A Blueprint for Action on Language Education

Kurt E. Müller

ACTFL/Year of Languages National Language Policy Summit: A Plan of Action

Prelude to the Deliberations

On 10–11 January 2005 the American Council on the Teaching of Foreign Languages (ACTFL) convened a national gathering to establish an agenda for language education. The event certainly does not mark the first time an interest group sought to reform education practice across the United States with a deliberate emphasis on languages. In 2004, Robert A. Scott, president of Adelphi University, provided a convenient overview of such attempts. Some of the advocates of these attempts have been based in academe, some have been in government programs, and some have been in private philanthropic foundations. Scott's tally of legislative initiatives (p. 2) includes the Fulbright Act of 1946 and the Fulbright-Hays Act of 1961, broad-based efforts to increase citizen, student, and faculty exchanges; the original National Defense Education Act, with its support for teacher education, curriculum development, studies of language education, and materials development; the International Education Act, which, had it been funded, would have been a true watershed, expanding America's education structure to reach abroad as well as to bring "the abroad" to classrooms here; and the recent National Security Education Act. Although the President's Commission on Foreign Language and International Studies carried a title indicating White House support, it was Congressional action that created and conducted the Commission's activities and advocated expanding Americans' familiarity with the world. The academic groups Scott mentions include the American Council of Learned Societies, the American Council on Education, the Modern Language Association, and the Educational Testing Service. For the philanthropic sector Scott notes an initiative by the Ford Foundation but could as well have listed Culpepper, Dodge, Exxon, Hewlitt, Luce, Rockefeller, and others. Crucial to elementary and secondary education, the National Governors Association has weighed in on the need to emphasize language and international education. Scott goes so far as to specify that concomitant with launching both the League of Nations and the

United Nations, there were calls for attention to the world beyond our shores and the languages spoken there.

Scott's presentation helped set the background for the National Language Conference of June 2004. The ACTFL/Year of Languages National Language Policy Summit: A Plan of Action continued the call for action raised at the National Language Conference with a crucial step to create coalitions to raise language education as a national priority. Organizers of the National Language Conference circulated among federal agencies a white paper of recommendations with a vision of academe, government, and the private sector mutually supporting a polyglot citizenry familiar with various cultures (National Language Conference, 2005). Unprecedented in its call for national attention to developing citizens' language competence, the Conference emphasized language capacity in the national interest as it has never been explored before. Uniquely in America, language education has not been—and is not yet—a national priority. With a diversity of sectors represented, the Conference called for skills to meet the demands of a global economy, a post-9/11 security awareness, and an internationally collaborative approach to common challenges.

Recognizing that demands for improved language education have long-term implications for educators and that implementation strategies require consensus among stakeholders, ACTFL leadership decided its first event in 2005: Year of Languages® (YOL) should be a policy summit. Given the diversity of interests inherent in Americans' competence in international economic and diplomatic affairs and the variety of organizational structures in the education sector, ACTFL decided to convene a set of individuals who could address policy in government, business, and academic sectors and to extend this working group through off-site participation.

Recognizing Language Needs

The terrorist attacks of 2001 focused Congressional, executive, and public attention on the nation's awareness of international relations and on language competence in particular. Agencies in the intelligence community had publicly professed the scarcity of personnel with appropriate language skills to address various threats to the nation. One of several convenient summaries of the dimension of language needs for the national security sector appears in House of Representatives Report No. 107-219 (2002). In this report, the House Permanent Select Committee on Intelligence notes that language expertise

> is the single greatest limitation . . . and is a deficiency throughout the Intelligence Community. . . . CIA, NSA, FBI, DIA and the military services . . . have all admitted they do not have the language talents, in breadth or depth, to fully and effectively accomplish their missions. (pp. 18–19)

A series of Congressional actions has continued to direct federal agencies in the intelligence community to recruit personnel among the heritage community and to emphasize language skills among their personnel.[1] But the national interest is broader than countering threats to physical security. National security itself ranges far beyond matters of physical security, and it is treated accordingly at the highest levels of continuing education for employees of federal executive agencies. The national interest includes economic vigor, public health, political liberties, cultural expression, and many other factors that characterize quality of life. Agencies that contributed to the National Language Conference reflected that diversity of interests. Not only were defense and diplomacy well represented, but discussions on commerce, health and welfare, and domestic society pointed to a national need for developing a citizenry with deeper skills across more languages.

Advocates for language education have long recognized the federal interest in developing a polyglot society and usually noted a division between this need and the state-based funding of education.[2] A notable feature of the National Language Conference was the inclusion of presenters from state, county, and municipal governments, all indicating a diversity of interests in language competence, from exchanging information with communities abroad dealing with similar municipal problems to emergency medical treatment of tourists to meeting the social needs of an increasingly diverse populace.

Structuring the Policy Summit

By combination of on-site discussion, video teleconference, dial-in telephone conversation, Webcast, and e-mail, participants in the ACTFL/YOL Policy Summit were able to raise and respond to issues identified in the draft federal white paper and explore suggestions for implementation. The School of Education of The University of North Carolina at Chapel Hill welcomed over 30 on-site participants and hosted the inclusion of over 3,500 others electronically.

If indeed American society is to facilitate the acquisition of competence in other languages, individuals and groups need to take specific actions toward meeting such a goal. To determine fruitful steps to fulfill this mission, the participants of the Policy Summit formed three discussion sections, one each for business, government, and academe. Each developed a set of priorities on which the group itself could act,

---

[1] At the close of the 109th Congress, for example, P.L. 109-458 and P.L. 109-487, were passed and signed with provisions emphasizing language competence for the intelligence community.

[2] During a January 1979 hearing in New York, James A. Perkins, chairman of the President's Commission on Foreign Language and International Studies, pointed out the challenge of seeking state support in the education sector for a need that was primarily federal. For additional treatments of federal language needs, see Parker (1961), Müller (1986, 2002), Brecht and Rivers (2000).

determined the persons or organizations that will move this agenda, and set deadlines and milestones for achieving their goals. The groups reported at regular intervals in plenary session, including those participating by remote means. These priorities also informed the off-site discussions, and participants in remote sites devised priorities for their locations.

Raising the Priority of Language Education

"The focus on international education in languages can't be primarily or ultimately at the higher-education level. It's critical that we have great centers, but we must teach languages much more broadly at K–12."
—*former governor James B. Hunt, North Carolina*

Identifying the Interested Parties

Despite recent federal emphasis on education, the states remain the major source of funding for education. Looking to federal legislation and funding to raise the profile of language education will not succeed unless accompanied by state-based efforts. In his remarks at the ACTFL/YOL Policy Summit, James B. Hunt, former governor of North Carolina, set the societal context for education issues. He advised the audience that federal agencies—especially the Departments of Defense and State and some members of the U.S. Congress—understand the need for this critical skill. But the task of building support for expanded language education requires building coalitions of citizens, seeking commonalities of interest, and developing advocacy in the business sector.

America's economic security depends on international commerce. State offices dealing with economic development, exports, and regional cross-border issues and providers of emergency services to growing numbers of foreign visitors and recent immigrants all appreciate the need for effective communication in multiple languages. Numerous speakers from this sector presented evidence of their requirements during the June 2004 National Language Conference. But for education administrators to appreciate the need for language competence, these requirements need greater visibility. Unfortunately, a presentation of the rationale for attention to language competence is insufficient to achieve the emphasis the nation needs. As in most political decisions, rational argument is essential but insufficient for success. Building support is the primary requirement, and that activity requires continuous presentations before diverse audiences.

Governor Hunt suggested that the nation needs a commitment to language and international education by both the federal and state governments. Although education is primarily a state responsibility, the federal government's specific interest in international affairs requires a federal emphasis to ensure the citizenry is well prepared to meet international challenges.

Moving an Agenda of Language Competence in America

The theme of "connectedness" that Gov. Hunt proposed informs an agenda for language competence along two major dimensions: (1) language skills are connected to their use across multiple domains, all of which benefit from advanced language competence, and (2) the "agents of change" must craft coalitions of advocates in order to move a national agenda. During the ACTFL/YOL Policy Summit, Ray Clifford, former chancellor of the Defense Language Institute Foreign Language Center, noted that solving the challenge of language education demands engaging federal, state, and local government. Moreover, language education must be integrated in education across various fields rather than merely pursued in isolation. The concept of "language across the curriculum" thus takes on a significant role: when students acquire knowledge of various disciplines through multiple languages, practitioners of those disciplines can recognize the contribution that additional languages make to student competence across fields of study. Building such cross-disciplinary support for language education remains a continuing challenge: common interests offer opportunity for collaboration, and, as in international affairs, these alliances require constant tending.

Advocates need to engage local and state authorities as well. Each exercises influence on education, and none can be neglected. The danger of incomplete follow-through is not immediately evident but can be illustrated: states have mandated earlier language education, but then not followed up with adequate funding. This circumstance results in a series of "unfunded mandates;" with no accountability mechanism in place, the decision to implement early language programs is left up to individual school boards or the building principal. Among numerous competing mandates, those advocated by active constituencies are most likely to achieve priority attention.

Priorities for a Partnership Between Business and Language Education

"The official language of DaimlerChrysler is English, but that policy is misleading. English is not enough, but at senior levels you wouldn't see it. How do you get to the bowels of the company, where language skills are critical?"—Professor John Grandin, University of Rhode Island, International Engineering Program

Business groups, industrial associations, and government export planners periodically undertake studies to determine future markets, changes in clientele, and risks to development. The business discussion group pointed to surveys by the Committee for Economic Development, the Localization Industry Standards Association, the Asia Society, the American Council on Education, the Institute for International Education, and the Rand Corporation, as well as to a research series in international business and finance. As an item for immediate attention, members of the business group agreed to identify the range of extant studies enjoying current interest in the commercial sector. These findings will form the basis for a documentation survey specifically oriented toward language and cultural knowledge for international business.

The business representatives agreed to enlist the assistance of chief executive officers, strategic planners, and human resource professionals to

- Advocate support for language education in America's schools
  - Write letters to appropriate officials, such as the White House and Congress
  - Meet with senior government officials to advocate attention to language and international education
- Establish corporate climates that promote language competence
  - Recognize the contribution of heritage languages to business climate and corporate activities
  - Encourage employees to volunteer support for school programs, for example, speaking to promote international business, advocating language education before school boards and media
  - Replicate successful internship programs between universities and international business
- Expand adopt-a-school programs with a specific emphasis on foreign languages

These priorities are national, regional, and local and require the effort of language professionals across the country to enlist business support to move this agenda. For example, St. George's Independent School, Colliersville, Tennessee, took this challenge to its board members with affiliations to local industries such as Federal Express. This model needs replication across the country: public, independent, and parochial schools all have boards whose members serve because they care about the quality of education. Individual teachers, local and state language organizations, and regional leaders need to present the case for language education to such individuals, to chambers of commerce, and to boards of realtors, all of whom prosper when education meets the emerging needs of the future workforce.

Priorities for a Government Partnership for Language Education

". . . language instruction needs to begin well before high school and continue throughout the educational pipeline." —A Call to Action for National Foreign Language Capabilities (federal white paper, February 2005)

The government discussion group identified action items, leaders to implement the actions, and deadlines for each identified activity. The group decided

- To endorse the federal white paper, stressing its application to the national interest, and to circulate the endorsement to language advocates and language educators
- To promote a national strategy to develop language competence among Americans
- To implement, through the National Security Education Program, an articulated K–16 Chinese program as a model to demonstrate the feasibility of developing competence in a less commonly taught language
- To expand this model to other languages via the intelligence community's foreign language executive committee
- To move to reschedule the foreign language National Assessment of Educational Progress (NAEP) test for 2007
- To provide national leadership for language education by developing an advisory council under the auspices of the Department of Defense
- To advocate through the Joint National Committee for Languages (JNCL) new legislation to fill gaps in national support for language education
- To endorse the National Civilian Linguist Reserve Corps foreseen in federal legislation
- To develop and implement a K–12 assessment program (inherent in model programs)
- To strategize a national language outreach and support program

Congress provided authority and funding for several of these initiatives through legislation. P.L. 108-487, for example, expands the National Security Education Program (NSEP). The Chapel Hill discussion identified a K–16 program in Chinese as a near-term priority that NSEP pursued through a request for proposals.

P.L. 108-458 gives the Director of National Intelligence the task of conducting a "pilot project to assess the feasibility and advisability of establishing a Civilian

Linguist Reserve Corps. . . ." If its feasibility is affirmed, this task carries long-term implications.

Priorities for Academe in Moving a National Language Agenda

"The matter of language competence goes beyond jobs, markets, and security. It's part of who we are, and it demands public policy initiatives to raise quality and expand the cadre of teachers, to conduct research on language learning on the model of how people learn science, and to integrate language into the larger context of things that surround language experience."—Thomas James, Dean of Education, The University of North Carolina at Chapel Hill

Objectives

Common themes emerged from the three discussion groups, notably the need to work simultaneously at local, state, and national levels and the advisability of a national language advisor on the model of the national science advisor.

Academic institutions can influence American society at large by promoting language competence in their own environments and ensuring that others know that academe values such skills. Some academic actions require a commitment of resources on campus, while others require seeking resources from donors and philanthropic foundations and using an academic "bully pulpit" to bring sectors together to promote skills required in the national interest. The academic discussion group set as its priorities to

- Raise the consciousness of the American public, its leaders, and the education sector to the need and value of learning languages and cultures
- Pursue funding for language-education research and assessments
- Expand model programs of language education
- Seek support for priorities in professional development
- Expand available types of immersion language experiences

This agenda to align education resources with the national interest has numerous goals for each of these five points. Pursuit of this agenda requires building alliances and working within extant policy structures to seek financing for the necessary expansion of language education.

1. Raising the consciousness of the American public, its leaders, and the education sector.

In support of this goal, priorities are to

- Establish the position of National Language Advisor
- Support a fully funded public-awareness campaign for language skills
- Extend the agenda of education in language and culture to the US Department of Education
- Create a movement among philanthropists to support local, state, and national initiatives in language-and-culture education
- Convene a national education commission on language-and-culture education using the National Governors Association, the Education Commission of the States, the Council of Chief State School Officers, and similar groups
- Convene state and local cross-sector summits modeled on the ACTFL/YOL Policy Summit at The University of North Carolina at Chapel Hill
- Recognize, reward, and remunerate language achievements in language education
- Emphasize language requirements stated in terms of achievement and proficiency
- Replicate the language policy summit in locations across the country
- Support the States' Institutes initiative of the Asia Society

2. Pursue funding for language education research and assessments

- Collect data on all existing language programs in the U.S.
- Disseminate to policy makers and appropriate educators the relevant and reliable research on the effectiveness of long sequences of language study
- Encourage research on models for language learning across age groups and types of learners
- Fund K–16 assessments of language study at state and national levels
- Use provisions of the *No Child Left Behind Act* to conduct research on the impact of studying other languages on reading and writing in English
- Use the *No Child Left Behind Act* to support language programs in public schools
- Collaborate cross-nationally on language research and assessment

3. Expand model programs of language education and create options

- Use National Security Education Program funds for model K–16 programs

- Support new legislation to fund expansion of K–16 model programs across a broader spectrum of education

- Fund research and development of alternative models of language education, including virtual classrooms and other technologically delivered instruction as well as independent and adult learning

- Create pilot sites for assessment of longer, articulated sequences of instruction, investigating differences in starting at different stages of education and tracking progress

- Coordinate with the high school redesign movement to model new options for secondary-level language learning

4. Seek support for priorities in professional development

- Identify incentives to explore K–16 options for content and delivery of language instruction

- Seek funds for projects to offer secondary-school options, such as language maintenance, credit for language education initiatives

- Train secondary teachers to develop new course and curricular options

- Fund pilot programs of teacher education that link language and education departments in postsecondary institutions

- Use National Council for Accreditation of Teacher Education (NCATE) standards to redesign teacher education

5. Expand available types of immersion language experiences

- Support study domestic as well as study abroad, service learning, and expanded internship programs

- Promote language camps and family language experiences

- Cultivate language maintenance, weekend and technology-mediated immersion, and broad experiences requiring target language as the medium of instruction

Language Choice

"Foreign languages are to the humanities as math is to the natural sciences."—Thomas Adams, National Endowment for the Humanities

Participants in the dialogue on language capacity agree that America needs individuals with skills in a great diversity of languages. Translating this need into education policy and implementing a response in formal education require promoting, recruiting, financing, developing, and expanding various aspects of language education. Not all schools and colleges can be expected to offer a dozen languages or more, and not all should be expected to offer the same critical languages, but all should offer a choice among several high-need languages. The call for attention to less commonly taught languages does not indicate the country needs fewer individuals competent in commonly taught languages. To the contrary, the national need is for more individuals with higher levels of competence across a diversity of languages.

The need for individuals with skills in high-utility languages such as French and German has not diminished. It continues. This goal calls for a transformation of values clearly articulated in public that Americans be fully literate in English and one or more additional languages of their choice. The challenge is to harness advocacy for competing language interests to increase choice of offerings rather than frustrate potential supporters by limiting instruction to the language of the currently predominant immigration pattern.

Moving the Agenda

"Don't be cowed by those who say we don't have the money."—former governor James B. Hunt

Population and Language

The ubiquity of English in the Western world, in South Asia and parts of the Pacific, and in international conferences makes it easy for native speakers of English to rely on the advantage of speaking in one's native language and reap the benefit of the official medium of communication. But in multinational gatherings (for example, peace or development conferences), many who use English as a foreign language may refrain from full participation when their ability to articulate thoughts is limited by their proficiency. At such a point, the English speaker needs to reach out through another language to ensure full participation in multilateral dialogues. In a multilingual gathering, silence cannot be taken as signaling agreement; it is often simply a lack of voice.

The global expansion of English has facilitated the nation's indolence in language education. America is not alone in this regard: Australia and the United Kingdom, too, are challenged to educate the populace in other languages. According to the European Commission's *Eurobarometer 55* (2001, pp. 80–81), of the then 15 members of the European Union, 47% of the citizenry could converse in a language other than their mother tongue, but in the United Kingdom, only 27% could do so (and since 5% of the populace claimed another language as mother tongue, the proportion of polyglot Britons who acquired proficiency in other languages through their schooling is even lower).

> *"Language Management is any attempt by anyone with authority to change the practices and beliefs of others. Language management includes telling children, 'Don't speak that way to your mother,' not to swear, to speak a heritage language to your grandmother, or to set up a language academy to construct words for new concepts so that an English term, for example, isn't appropriated in the local language."—Professor Bernard Spolsky*

The United States is far more multilingual than education statistics portray. Depending on the manner in which the question is asked, somewhere between one in four and one in five Americans speaks a language other than English. The 2000 census asked about a language spoken at home, and 18% of the respondents indicated a language other than English. The General Social Survey 2000 asked respondents simply whether they speak another language, and 26% indicated they do (Center for Advanced Study of Language, 2004, p. 8, table 1). But neither measure elicits data on proficiency or literacy. French, German, and Russian are spoken more widely in the populace than they are represented in the schools, and these are world languages for which the education infrastructure could easily support the development of literacy. An even greater disparity between languages spoken in the populace and languages taught in schools is evident for Arabic, Chinese, Korean, Tagalog, and Urdu.

A Model for Emulation

As an anglophone, largely immigrant society with a native population whose language and culture were long disregarded by the ruling elite, Australia shares a number of similarities with the United States. Even its immigration patterns, first European, recently Asian, share characteristics with America's. Despite its own reputation as an English-speaking country, Australia is "more multilingual than it ever has been" (LoBianco, 2004a, p. 2). Australian advocates for language education fashioned coalitions of interests to advance an education model that offers promise for the United States. The country has a set of policies whereby immigrants and indigenes learn English and keep their heritage language as well; and everyone born into an English-speaking family learns another language. Such a policy facilitates trade and diplomacy and raises expectations that citizens be multilingual, the typical circumstance in most of the world.

In presenting the sometimes competing interests among language constituencies, LoBianco (2004b) notes the existence in Australia of indigenous-language interests, advocacy for European and Asian languages, concerns over English literacy, and intergenerational language-maintenance interests, all of which have found common ground. Implementation of the model is certainly not without its challenges—language advocacy requires continual tending—but the Australian experience offers a look at potential policy for school districts, colleges, and government units here in the United States.

A Revolution in Education?

Crises precipitate revolutionary changes. Even in the face of adversity, inertia exerts too strong an influence to allow for significant changes unless decision makers recognize that failure to change poses the greater threat. This principle operates as much in education as it does in a commercial firm's adaptation to competition and loss of market share, a diplomatic or military response to a foreign-policy threat, or an independence movement.

Representative Rush Holt of New Jersey (2004) suggested we are facing a *Sputnik* moment, one that offers a once-in-a-generation opportunity to increase attention to language study on an order of magnitude. The model that readily comes to mind of national legislation that improved access to language education is the National Defense Education Act. But, although Congress passed this act in response to the surprise of *Sputnik*, it did not pass language legislation overnight. Preparations had been laid for years, with a relentless advocacy program undertaken by the Modern Language Association with foundation funding. Professor William Riley Parker, who is most often associated with this legislation—and whose *National Interest and Foreign Languages* remains a landmark monograph—wrote numerous articles to raise support for national legislation among members of the academy as well as among the general public. Tirelessly admonishing audiences and readers not to forgo taking education policy as a professional responsibility, he observed that letting others determine education policy was precisely the cause of the education sector's inattention to the world, its languages, cultures, and international affairs. Addressing a commencement audience at the Middlebury College Summer Language Schools in August 1953, Parker told his audience, ". . . no change will come about until those who actually determine the course of American education are convinced that a change is overdue. You can help by making a point of persuading your friends and neighbors. Commence today to talk about America's need for foreign languages whenever and wherever you get a chance" (1966). To grasp the current "*Sputnik* moment," language advocates must write legislators, address school boards, and write supportive pieces—from op-ed pages to professional articles on language-education policy. If we fully recognize the contribution of languages to our society across numerous domains and on various points of any scale of societal needs, we must each define the pieces we can contribute to enhancing the nation's skills and improving its familiarity with other cultures. Then we must pursue this agenda to achieve not only public financial support but a societal transformation valuing competence in multiple languages.

Numerous, significant legislative measures address language competence, but they have been limited to the federal workforce. Initiatives such as the Civilian Linguist Reserve, the National Security Education Program, the Roberts Scholars program, language-proficiency requirements for promotion in the intelligence community, and the series of directives for federal agencies to recruit among America's ethnic minorities are all essential, but they are only incremental. In the absence of a revolution that emphasizes language competence throughout American society, these measures risk creating an American Janissary. The Ottoman Empire sought to incorporate—to an extent—its ethnic minorities by providing opportunities to advance in service to the empire. As with the Ottoman experience, several considerations recommend such an approach. But this cost-effective model creates separate classes of individuals who must pursue careers in specified agencies. Moreover, absent a societal transformation that values these skills, their specialty becomes more than a curiosity. It often raises suspicion.

These legislative examples all address the intelligence community. Departmental policy in the Department of Defense has recently raised the profile of language competence in the military services. This attention is not only welcome; it is long overdue. Periodically over the past 50 years, hosts of individual military officers, several senior commanders, and occasional review boards have advocated incentives or requirements to develop language competence. Time will tell if the current emphasis achieves the transformation intended and develops the depth of language skills so notable among some of our NATO allies. Review boards that determine selection for command, promotion, and professional education need to direct persistent attention to language competence if we expect of our military no less than of our diplomats that they understand the nations with which they are to interact, both as partners and as adversaries.

In its sponsorship of the National Language Conference, the Office of the Undersecretary of Defense (Personnel and Readiness) emphasized that language competence in American society should be valued not only for its importance in keeping the nation secure from military threat, but for a range of contributions to the national interest, including economic competitiveness, mutual collaboration on environmental and public-health matters, facilitation of understanding among diverse cultural groups within our society as well as between America and other societies, and a general improvement in quality of life. Applying Governor Hunt's comments at the ACTFL/YOL Policy Summit on the need for a federal–state partnership in language education to such reasoning, it becomes clear that if Congress addresses the clear and compelling need for language competence only among certain federal agencies, the country would be shortchanged. Recent legislative and policy initiatives that address language skills for government personnel constitute one component—government policy—of a broader national policy for languages. The education sector must not confuse policy that addresses government agencies with public and education policy, which address both education priorities and the climate for a polyglot citizenry in commercial and cultural affairs. As for education, the national interest requires a broader agenda to educate American society in the rich diversity of human cultures. Just as war and peace are too important to be left to diplomats and generals, language education is too significant to be left to the education sector alone. As a group, education administrators have yet to appreciate the contribution of language study to education. The rarity of an Ernest Boyer or an Earl McGrath demonstrates the dimension of the challenge to educate national education leaders. Language educators themselves tend to see the richness of cultural diversity, the aesthetics of language, and the interplay between language and thought, but to undervalue the instrumental motivation: language acquisition for practical use. As with the arts, the greater the market for artistic products, the more sophisticated the product will be. Aesthetic arguments for language, too, are far better received when more of the public has already acquired practical experience of multiple languages. Even those committed to emphasizing proficiency usually have limited experience in specific domains, thus constraining their ability to encourage using another language as the vehicle, rather than the object, of instruction. Consequently, to realize our professional goals, we must engage others in emphasizing a language-competent citizenry.

References

Brecht, R. D., & Rivers, W. R. (2000). *Language and national security in the 21st century.* Washington, DC: National Foreign Language Center.

Center for Advanced Study of Language. (2004). *An introduction to America's language needs and resources: Briefing document, 22–24 June 2004.* College Park, MD: Author.

European Commission. (2001). *Eurobarometer: Public opinion in the European Union* (Standard Eurobarometer Report 55). Brussels: Author.

Holt, R. (2004, June). *Is American security being lost in translation?* Paper presented at the National Language Conference, Adelphi, MD.

H. R. Rep. No. 107-219 (2002).

LoBianco, J. (2004a, June). *Outline of the Australian Language Policy Experience.* Paper presented at the National Language Conference, Adelphi, MD.

LoBianco, J. (2004b, June). *Dilemmas and issues in national language policies: Synopsis.* Addendum to paper for the National Language Conference, Adelphi, MD.

Müller, K. E. (1986). *Language competence: Implications for national security.* New York: Praeger.

Müller, K. E. (2002). Addressing counterterrorism: US literacy in languages and international affairs, *Language Problems and Language Planning, 26*(1), 1–21.

National Language Conference. (2005). *A call to action for national foreign language capabilities* [white paper]. Washington, DC: Office of the Undersecretary of Defense (Personnel and Readiness).

Parker, W. R. (1961). *The national interest and foreign languages* (3rd ed.). Washington, DC: US Department of State.

Parker, W. R. (1966). The language curtain. In W. R. Parker (Ed.), *The language curtain and other essays* (pp. 110–116). New York: MLA. (Originally published 1953 in *School and Society, 78*, 129–133)

Scott, R.A. (2004, June). *Many calls, little action: Global illiteracy in the United States.* Paper presented at the National Language Conference, 22–24 June 2004, Adelphi, MD.

4

Realizing Our Vision: Teachers at the Core

Myriam Met

Our vision of a nation that values foreign language learning, that dedicates sufficient resources to developing language and cultural competence, and that results in a populace that is skilled in English and at least one additional language is not a new one. In the decades during and following World War II, a number of initiatives worked to effectuate various aspects of that vision. Some of these initiatives made significant progress; others did not.

Tragic events in our own nation, coupled with a complex and rapidly changing geopolitical landscape, have made language competence, once again, a focus of policymakers. Serious discussions about options for improving our nation's capacity to meet the linguistic demands that confront us have been accompanied by significantly increased resources. How the academic language education community, defined as those who teach languages and prepare language teachers pre-K through 16, responds to this opportunity will likely shape language education for the next generation of language learners.

Many variables impact how well Americans learn foreign languages. They range from motivation to time on task to what is taught and how. It is the latter—what students learn and how we enable them to learn it—that not only impacts powerfully and directly the outcomes of language study, but also impacts the attitudes and motivations of those who currently study languages and those who will in the future. Simply put—good teaching matters.

This chapter describes the current state of language education policy, explains the role that teachers play in shaping public attitudes toward language learning, and discusses some of the challenges facing language instruction that we need to address in order to realize our vision. It then examines in more specific terms what our vision might be and how we might get there. A central premise of these future-looking actions is that teachers are at the core of effecting change.

Where We Are Now: The Government, Public Policy, and Languages

Over a decade ago, in an article on language education policy (Met, 1994), I wrote that there is no single policymaker for education in the United States. We have no national policy related to language education. As a result, (and, to my mind, even worse), a variety of stakeholders and decision makers make language education policy. This diverse group of policymakers makes decisions regarding who takes a language, when they begin and how long they study, which languages are offered, who may teach them, and so on, decisions that frequently result in an inconsistent and fragmented pattern at the local, state, and even national levels.

Since that 1994 article was published, we have made some notable policy advances. We now have National Standards for Foreign Language Learning. Consonant with these Standards are the standards developed for new, veteran, and accomplished teachers. These standards demonstrate a consistency of philosophy and approach that was heretofore absent. Unfortunately, conformity to some of these standards is voluntary. For example, the National Standards for Foreign Language Learning are not mandated. Although they have been used by a large number of state and local districts as a framework for their own curricula, a significant number of states do not require local districts to adhere to state frameworks or curricula. On the other hand, accrediting agencies such as National Council for Accreditation of Teacher Education and the National Board for Professional Teaching Standards have brought uniformly high standards to the preparation of teachers and to the recognition of accomplished teaching performance.

On the national scene, recent years have brought some semblance of a national education policy as embodied in No Child Left Behind (NCLB). NCLB seems to make clear a maxim of U.S. education: what is valued is assessed; what is not assessed is not valued. Serious sanctions for underperforming schools have caused building and district administrators to increase attention and resources on student performance in reading and mathematics, eroding resources (specifically, time and money) for foreign language instruction, particularly in grades K-8. Concurrently, recognition of the critical role language competence plays in promoting our national security has led the Department of Defense to take leadership in improving language learning in both the government and academia. For those of us in language education, these federal policies appear to be at cross-purposes with one another and yet another instance of an inconsistent policy approach to language learning (see, for example, *A Call to Action*, National Language Conference, 2005).

Where We Are Now: The Public and Languages

If public policy is made in response to public opinion, it should come as no surprise that public policy regarding language education is inconsistent. While surveys frequently show that parents and the public at large value language learning (Robinson, Brecht, & Rivers, 2005), those surveys do not always get at the critical decisions that need to be made regarding the allocation of very limited resources such as instructional time and money. Parents may express verbal support for foreign language learning, especially in the early grades, but may also be reluctant to reduce the time allocated to other subjects. They may choose to spend limited funds on desirable curricular options other than foreign language. Nonetheless, there appears to be a great deal of pent-up demand for early language learning opportunities as evidenced by waiting lists for immersion programs and PTA-sponsored programs, as well as for charter and magnet schools. These are encouraging signs of the vitality of the language education system.

Over the last decades, advocates for increasing the role of foreign languages have proposed a number of compelling arguments for early and sustained study. This rationale has included national needs (for example, homeland security, economic competitiveness), social needs (our increasingly diverse society), and the individual benefits of knowing other languages (personal enrichment, enhanced cognitive functioning, academic achievement, job opportunities). It is interesting that the effectiveness of these arguments has been as varied as the arguments themselves—and, perhaps, caused by them as well. For example, if it is expected that foreign language study will result in a skill that can be used in later life, then the emphasis on utility makes language learning more like a vocational skill than an academic one, undermining the point that language learning is beneficial in and of itself. In comparison, art and music, subjects that the public supports for inclusion in the school curriculum, do not appear to be in the curriculum in order to improve job competitiveness or performance. They are valued as academically enriching, whereas language learning earns its place in the curriculum for its market value. The disconnect between the time made available for language learning and the realities of the time required to learn language to the levels required in the workplace are rarely recognized by the public and school administrators.

Research has shown that the general public's framework for interpreting advocacy for language learning determines how much they will support language in the curriculum. Many of the arguments educators make do not find receptivity with the public. In particular, studies conducted by the Frameworks Institute that examine public views and widely held assumptions, have found that public response to particular issues depends, in part, on how the issues are framed. Analyzing public response to global and international education (which includes foreign language learning), Institute researchers found that while language competence may be proposed as a solution to improving homeland and national security, the public considers other investments more likely to protect our nation than knowing foreign languages. The *knowledge gap* frame ("Our students are behind their peers in the rest of the world"; "Our schools are failing."), evokes reminders that our schools are not producing students who are literate in their own language and simply reinforces negative beliefs about our schools that the public already holds. In contrast, the public is more receptive to international education (and language learning) as a means of updating our curricula (vs. addressing deficiencies), respecting other peoples and cultures, and preparing our country to be a cooperative partner with other world nations (Bales, 2003; Bales, 2004).

Where We Are Now: Language Educators and Language Learning

Language educators rarely make language education policy, nor do we often have much direct influence over those who do. Nonetheless, we indirectly shape policy in a fundamental way, as we create public perceptions of what it is like to learn a language in school and what can be accomplished. Our students become parents, school board members, administrators, the public at large. Yesterday's students are today's decision-makers. They have reached their leadership positions independently of foreign language competence and are not easily persuaded that such skills are necessary for success. The experiences of our students as language learners affect public beliefs about the outcomes of language study ("I took two years . . ."); they affect the perceptions of siblings and, later, their own children ("It was very hard. I never did learn to speak it." "It's all about conjugating verbs."); and they have led us to where we are today: a general populace that is either monolingual, having failed to learn another language in school, or bilingual, as a result of personal experience. Our former students, now today's leaders, determine the opportunities of today's students—who in turn will be tomorrow's leaders. Many have concluded that languages cannot be learned in school. We should always remember that what our students think has lasting effects.

Where We Are Now: Curriculum, Instruction, Articulation, and Assessment

Most students do not leave our schools competent in a foreign language. Bad teaching is not to blame. Limited time, issues of student motivation, and discontinuities in the educational system are partly at fault. Because good teaching matters so much, we should continually strive to improve our performance, no matter how good our teaching may already be. We, as language educators, can take responsibility for the results of language study—and therefore exercise some control over the future—by enhancing our performance in the areas of curriculum implementation, assessment, and articulation.

Earlier it was noted that one major policy advance has been the development of national standards that describe what students should know and be able to do. Accompanying these standards, the K-12 Performance Guidelines help to answer the question, "How well?" In tandem these documents represent significant progress in our ability to delineate expectations for our students and have been enthusiastically embraced by language teachers.

Language teachers embody the enactment of language policy. If content standards represent policy that guides decisions about what should be taught, then the degree to which teachers implement curriculum and assess students in ways consistent with those standards/policies affects policy. Curriculum, instruction, and assessment determine in large part whether students attain the standards; language teaching is therefore policy implementation. In the past, it has been challenging for language educators to be clear about what students (and parents) can reasonably expect as a result of study. We have been unclear in the promises we made and frequently failed to keep those promises.

As widespread implementation of standards progresses, we need to be much clearer with ourselves and with one another about operationalizing outcomes statements and standards. We need to specifically identify, "What would it look like if a student could . . . ?" "What would be observable and measurable evidence of *knowing* and *being able to do*?" Until we are able to do so, it will continue to be difficult to assess outcomes and to articulate across levels.

The alignment of assessments with curriculum and instruction remains a fertile ground for our efforts. Both formative and summative assessment of learning is challenging, especially when measuring performance rather than knowledge. Assessment of performance involves applying subjective, incremental, qualitative measures of performance rather than simply determining whether answers are right or wrong. Pinpointing effective mechanisms to measure whether students have attained the outcomes identified in our curricula and standards is made more difficult by the lack of standardized assessment instruments at particular grade levels, in certain modes of communication, and in some languages. These challenges are exacerbated by the constraints of our educational settings. For example, final exams at the secondary and postsecondary levels need to be graded quickly in order to turn in grades on time. In secondary schools, particularly, this time constraint often precludes many open-ended approaches to performance assessment because classroom time is unavailable and testing 150 (or more) students requires more time than is provided.

External measures such as college placement exams, Advanced Placement exams, or tests developed by other organizations can exert a subtle pressure on teachers to teach and test as others expect them to. The wash-back effect of tests on instruction has been observed in classrooms at all levels (for example, the effects of No Child Left Behind). The content tested by some (but, of course, not all) of these external measures does not align with what standards and school curricula indicate should be taught; the structure of some of these assessments does not allow measurement of performance—only of specific knowledge. Because these measures have significant consequences for test-takers and because many are associated with high-status institutions or organizations, they become the standard. Developers of the tests that foreign language learners take lead by example, and, as such, have a unique opportunity to influence the future of foreign language education.

Assessment is intricately linked to articulation. The greatest hindrance to improving level to level and institutional to institutional articulation ties back to common agreements on learner outcomes and how they are measured. Language educators across levels need to have consistent expectations, definitions, and interpretations of assessments, of what it means to *know* or *be able to do* with specific content. Because such consistency is rare, articulation problems most often stem from differing definitions of what it means to know language, how to measure what students know and can do, and how to interpret the results. If students continue language study over long stretches of their educational career, that study should not constitute frequent repetitions of the same content or, worse, repeated enrollment in level one.

Where We Might Be

I began this paper by noting that the vision of a language competent America is not new and that over the span of the last five decades numerous initiatives (many successful) have sought to bring that vision to fruition. As a longtime language educator, I have found that my colleagues in this field are very intelligent, highly committed to their work, dedicated to their students, and frequently more energetic than peers in other disciplines. Past efforts to enact changes in the U.S. language education system have met successes because of those traits; failed efforts were not because we were not smart enough or did not try hard enough. Change is neither rapid nor easily accomplished.

We can build on many productive efforts of the last decades, such as the standards projects and New Visions in Action. In 1998, a collaborative effort between the National Foreign Language Resource Center at Iowa State and American Council on the Teaching of Foreign Languages undertook an initiative to bring together the language education community, pre-K-16, to further our common agenda. New Visions began by asking a number of key questions. Some of these questions have been partially answered since 1998; others continue to be addressed. The questions continue to be a helpful way of thinking about where we might want to be and a guide for helping us determine what will get us there. Those questions are, What would it take . . .

- To ensure that all teacher educators had the necessary knowledge and skills?
- To ensure that all pre-service foreign language teachers were fully prepared in the discipline?
- To ensure that all pre-service foreign language teachers were fully prepared in the pedagogical and clinical content of foreign language teaching?
- To ensure that all experienced foreign language teachers were competent to help their students achieve the national standards?
- To have clear, measurable ways of assessing competence?
- To develop and implement varied curriculum models that reflect diverse learners/ purposes/outcomes?

- To assess whether every student had achieved the national standards?
- For the profession to gain increased control in the agenda-setting and decision-making process?
- To ensure that every child had the option to participate in a sound program of foreign language study and that every teacher had access to quality professional development?
- To define a unified professional stance regarding language policy? (*New Visions in Action*, 1998)

Making the Vision a Reality: How Do We Get There?

Complex and diverse factors set the context for language education and related policies, not all of which are within the span of control of the language education community. While efforts to influence the decisions of policymakers outside the language profession must continue, we can also work within our profession on making the vision happen.

The Context of Change

Language teachers need to recognize that they have power to make change and use that power to good effect. In recent years, American attitudes toward our schools, budget cuts in K-12, and even greater budget reductions in postsecondary institutions have made many educators feel powerless to control the contexts of their work. Undeniably, teaching is not a highly respected profession in U.S. society. The devaluation of teaching as a profession is evidenced in mandated scripted instructional materials (for example, early literacy), in "teacher-proof" materials developed in many subject areas, and in the dismantling of university departments that are not generating sufficient income for their institutions.

Institutional contexts foster or impede change. Most schools, building administrators, and state level education systems do not consider foreign language learning a priority. It is rarely in the core curriculum. In those settings where languages are valued (magnet programs, charters, themed high schools, postsecondary programs where languages are integrated into interdisciplinary programs), teachers are energized and share an *esprit de corps*. In pre-K-12 schools, far less time is available for discipline-specific professional development than for the scheduled school-wide in-service devoted to other topics that teachers are expected to address issues beyond their disciplines: recognizing the signs of substance abuse, depression, potential violence, gang membership, physical abuse, and the like.

College and university faculty are central to intervening in the cycle of language learners who, later in life, make policy decisions based on their prior experiences as students of foreign languages. This faculty produces each succeeding generation of language teachers for our schools. As such, language faculty serve as role models for language teachers. They also can impact the placement examinations that determine which high school graduates will once again repeat entry level language courses and which ones will be allowed to make continued progress.

Because their responsibility for shaping the next generation of language teachers and learners is so significant, postsecondary faculty need to acknowledge the centrality of their role and exemplify the vision of what language education should be. It is regrettable that many language faculty have little expertise (or interest) in research-based language pedagogy. On the other hand, our profession is fortunate to have a significant number of talented, well-informed faculty members in language departments as well as in education departments, faculty that do an excellent job of teaching languages and of preparing teachers for our schools.

As we recognize the value to our profession of this cadre of highly qualified postsecondary faculty, both language faculty and teacher educators, we should also be aware that, for the most part, little is known about the quality of language teacher educators in general. In fact, at many smaller institutions, pre-service language teachers receive pedagogical preparation in the same methods courses as teachers of various disciplines, taught by faculty who may be generalists or who may not be attuned to best practices in foreign language education. Pre-service teachers in such programs may learn to teach, but they may not learn to be foreign language teachers.

Effecting Change Is Hard

Turning vision into reality will require language educators and language teacher educators to be change agents—transforming the field and transforming ourselves. Current policies limit opportunities for students to begin learning languages early, thereby also limiting the number of years most students are engaged in language study. While we continue advocacy efforts to change those policies, we can also work on maximizing every single moment a student is in a language classroom. Time is one of the most scarce and most valuable resources in schooling. Therefore, making every moment count can be one avenue for improving the language proficiency of this generation of learners.

Fortunately, instructional practices, assessment, and seamless articulation patterns are within our purview—we can make these changes and we must. To do so it will be important to recognize that change is slow; change is often arduous; change requires resources we may have to work to acquire; and change will require us to call on inner resources as well as external ones.

Change is facilitated when resources are readily available and when the rewards are rapid and recognizable. For language educators, there are few incentives for improving how we teach, for revamping how we measure what students have learned, and for reconsidering how we use the results of those measurements. Student growth—the most powerful incentive for committed professionals—is gradual and incremental, making it difficult to recognize in the course of any one teacher's contact with an individual student. Because clearly observable results are not readily apparent, it is often difficult to justify to oneself the hard work that change requires. We are carrying out our work at a time when most educators at every level of instruction find themselves overwhelmed with institutional demands, when ever-increasing workloads distract from the primary focus on teaching and learning, and when language departments see themselves marginalized because languages are not a priority.

Changing Professional Practices

Language teachers must shoulder responsibility for creating language competent graduates from our schools. I use the term *teachers* broadly to include teachers in the language classroom (pre-K-16) and those related to it, such as language supervisors and language teacher educators. *Teachers* means all of us, and it means that we are all also among those whose professional practices must align with the vision we have set out to achieve.

We are not bad teachers. We do what we do well—despite many difficulties to overcome. Nonetheless, no matter how effective any teacher is, there are always possibilities for future growth. Just as Olympic athletes (already the best of the best) continually strive to improve their last performance, so, too, even the best of us can become even better. Many teachers are already teaching in ways largely consistent with the standards. We should not assume that all teachers must change or that the discrepancy between current and desired practices represents an obstacle of Herculean proportions. Most classrooms reflect some elements of the directions that the standards seek to take us, while a few classrooms are at the margins of what we might term *desired practice*. We can assume, however, that there is widespread need for all teachers, language supervisors, and language teacher educators to have opportunities to move closer to our vision of language learning (and, as a result, closer to the vision of a language-competent nation). To bring about that vision will require more than just dissemination of information. It will require that we attend to the factors that shape how we define what good teaching is, what learning looks like, and how we will know it when we see it.

Theory construction and research continue to provide information about many aspects of the science of teaching. Pre-service programs of teacher development combine theory, information, and practice to educate a skilled teacher. These models assume that continued professional growth derives from an ever-increasing knowledge base/information and continued refinement of skills and techniques that constitute improved practice. We would expect research to inform the knowledge base of teaching; however many teachers perceive second language acquisition (SLA) theory as divorced from the realities of the classroom (Markee, 1997).

The disconnect between research and practice is, in essence, a different perspective on what it means to know how to teach. Teachers base a great deal of their practice on their own experiences—first as language learners, then as language teachers—and on the collective experience of language teachers. Indeed, for many, "experience is the best teacher," and experience is often cited as more powerful than the array of mandatory pre-service or continuing education courses they are required to take. The power of personal experience in developing a repertoire of useful, satisfying, and successful instructional approaches is far greater than that of *received information* from outside sources, perhaps because the knowledge base in teaching is not perceived as meaningful or relevant by teachers. In fact ". . . teachers are expected to learn about their own profession not by studying their own experiences but by studying the findings of those who are not themselves school-based teachers" (Cochran-Smith & Lytle, 1993, p. 1).

Indeed, some research simply is not as generalizable as researchers might wish (Markee, 1997). Little of the SLA research focuses on foreign language learning, and less of that, on foreign language learning in high schools, and even less, on learning in middle schools. Extrapolating findings from studies of college-age ESL students, or even postsecondary foreign language learners, may not produce satisfying improvements in instruction in pre-K-12 settings.

Changing Professional Practices: Beliefs, Knowledge, and Behaviors

Our beliefs about instruction can be more powerful than our knowledge, and our behaviors may be more accurate reflections of our beliefs than what we say. Williams and Burden (1997), in reporting a review by Pajares of the literature conducted of teacher beliefs and practices, report that studies show that "teachers' beliefs . . . had a greater influence than teachers' knowledge on the way they planned their lessons, on the kinds of decisions they made and on their general classroom practice . . . Beliefs were also found to be far more influential than knowledge in determining how individuals organize and define tasks and problems, and were better predictors of how teachers behaved in the classroom" (p. 56). There is evidence that suggests that teacher reports of their philosophy and beliefs are sometimes contradicted by the instructional experiences they provide in their classrooms (Williams and Burden, 1997; Schön, 1988). Although espoused theories—explicit statements of teaching beliefs—may be contradicted in actual practice, the implicit belief system is always consistent with practice classrooms (Caine & Caine, 1997). Those who study teacher enhancement suggest that lasting improvements in instructional practices stem from an understanding of the relationships between what teachers believe and know about student learning and how that shapes their teaching (Freeman, 1996b; Pennington, 1995; Schön, 1983; Ulichny, 1996; Willams & Burden, 1997).

If beliefs are a potent force in shaping practices, then teacher preparation and professional development must be strongly linked to belief systems, not just to knowledge structures. Both teachers and teacher educators need to be involved in addressing beliefs and knowledge. Much of professional development for veteran teachers has focused on changing teacher behaviors: that is, on giving teachers new techniques and strategies. While changing behaviors by expanding teachers' repertoire of instructional strategies may seem relatively easy, changing our beliefs may be far more challenging. And this challenge may help us understand why, despite over two decades of emphasis on proficiency-oriented instruction, much of what takes place in classrooms consists of proficiency activities layered through and wrapped around a strong core of traditional instruction.

Changing Instructional Beliefs

Mental models, constructs, paradigms, and cultures share many features in common. They structure and determine what we know and how we use what we know. They shape our behaviors implicitly, as well as determine how we acquire new information or filter new experiences (Barker, 1993; Bolman & Deal, 1991; Kuhn, 1962). Similarly, mental models—beliefs about teaching—not only determine how we teach, they also filter and shape the ways in which received knowledge, practical experience, and personal reflection become integrated into enhanced professional competence.

Most of us experienced language learning as students first and only later as teachers. Many of us learned a language in school. We were acculturated into the society of effective language learners: we came to believe deeply in the value of language learning and deduced from our experiences some intuitively logical strategies for teaching languages. We know these strategies work because they worked for us.

Unfortunately, we language teachers are an anomalous population. Given the small numbers of American students who took a language at all in secondary school (no more than 40% in the last 30 years), language teachers are a distinct minority, a very small pool of the general student population. That pool is even smaller considering how few secondary students took more than two or three years of a foreign language. The pool shrinks substantially when limited to those students who continued to study a foreign language intensively throughout their college years. Indeed, the pool is just a few mere droplets. Thus, for teachers to judge the efficacy of instructional practices from our own successful school experiences as language learners is naive. Perhaps language teachers should assume that whatever works for us as a unique subset of the total school population does *not* work for most students. In order to reach the majority of students—most of whom are not at all like us, the successful language learners—it is important to expand instructional practices beyond what worked for us former language students/now teachers.

Veteran teachers have more than our own experiences as language learners to rely on. Our background knowledge is shaped by our experiences as teachers as well. As we gain experience, we filter evidence about the efficacy of instructional practices through our existing belief and knowledge structures. Over time, as this evidence accumulates, it is likely that teachers have developed sophisticated and strong understandings how some approaches to instruction may be more or less effective with some learners than with others. Of course most of these understandings are not wrong at all, but they are deeply held because of the reinforcing role experience plays in confirming knowledge and beliefs. Some of the beliefs we deeply hold may be inaccurate.

Professional Development: A Reflection on the Past, Directions for the Future

It may. well be that schema theory and mental models can help to assess the strengths of past approaches to professional development and inform decisions about future directions for continued teacher enhancement. Costa and Garmston (1994) have suggested that effective teaching requires that teachers have a repertoire of instructional strategies to call upon for instructional delivery and that they have the knowledge and conceptual understandings to assist them to choose wisely from their repertoire. That is, repertoire gives teachers choices about how to teach. Pedagogical knowledge and understanding gives teachers the tools to decide which instructional approaches are most likely to result in student learning, given the context of the classroom, the learners, and the learning situation. Pedagogical tools must include the kinds of knowledge and understandings that lead teachers to choose well within their repertoire.

Traditional approaches to professional development have been very effective at expanding teacher repertoire. Teachers gain new ideas for classroom activities at workshops and conferences, where they also have opportunities to gain an understanding of the theories that underlie new approaches and activities. Trends in professional development today are moving away from isolated workshops in which experts and consultants "give" and teachers "come and get" (Fine & Raack, 1994). Workshops and conferences can contribute to our growing professional knowledge and skills. Yet, even a sustained series of professional development activities such as workshops, conferences, and university courses is unlikely to have lasting impact unless linked to other forms of professional development that research is showing to be tied to improved practice. Freeman (1996a) notes that ". . . If a teacher's practice is seen solely as behavior and activity, it is possible to miss the complex basis of understanding on which that activity is based. Likewise, if change in teaching means doing things differently, it overlooks how teachers' understandings may themselves be modified or amended, possibly without external evidence in behavioral change" (p. 238).

Three current trends in professional development have been shown to improve professional practices and address belief systems: reflective practice, interaction and discourse, and job-embedded learning. These three trends are interrelated, so that incorporating all three into teacher professional development programs may be more likely to result in powerful, lasting change than the use of any in isolation.

Reflective practice. Reflective practitioners enhance their professional knowledge and skills by reflecting upon instructional situations. They analyze classroom experiences to try to solve instructional problems. In so doing, they gain increased understanding of what they teach (their subject matter) and insights into their own teaching, as well as into the nature of teaching itself. Pennington (1995) suggests that reflection is integral to the change process. ". . . The means by which teachers' awareness and practice change involves the interplay of two processes: innovation and critical reflection . . . [C]ritical reflection is the processing of information gained through innovation in relation to the teacher's existing schema for teaching." In addition, reflection on one's own practice validates professional experience as an important knowledge source. It makes teachers producers, as well as consumers, of knowledge.

To be effective, reflection must be systematic. Teachers must be careful to collect observational data that support the conclusions they derive from experience (Antonek, McCormick & Donato, 1997; Schon, 1983; Wallace, 1991). As Corcoran (1995) notes, if reflection is not based on systematic approaches to observing classroom events, conclusions may be based on anecdotal data or unreliable exemplars or incidents. Reflective practice is also more effective when tied to real-life classroom experiences as they happen. That is, reflective practice may be more effective when it is job-embedded, a concept to which we will return shortly.

Interaction and discourse. Interactions with peers and expert others can help us build common understandings of our practice. Teacher collaboratives and new teacher groups have been shown to promote change in teacher practices, giving teachers opportunities to deepen their knowledge of the subject matter as well as of effective instructional practices (Corcoran, 1995; Rogers & Babinski, 1999). Corcoran states that research shows that collegiality plays an important role in "teachers' willingness to try new approaches, share their experience, and reflect on their practice" (p. 38). Research into effective professional development programs for teachers of mathematics and science has found that professional dialogue, individual reflection, and group inquiry such as that fostered by learning communities of teachers are likely to result in changed practices aligned with research and standards (Fine &

Raack, 1994). This may be because collaboration with colleagues may promote successful reflection.

The need to verbalize one's understandings, to put ideas into words, and to make ideas understandable to others may require sharper thinking and may make explicit ideas about teaching and learning that may have otherwise remained implicit. Professional dialogue in which teachers articulate and actively examine their understandings can help teachers discern those beliefs about student language learning that are supported by research evidence and theory and those that are not. Unlike reflection on one's own teaching that is carried out in isolation, interactive professional dialogue with significant expert others can help teachers confront contradictions between evidence, their practices, and their interpretations of their observations of student learning in their own classrooms. In contrast, reflection in isolation can be derailed by the very real danger of misinterpreting or rejecting data that are inconsistent with one's belief systems, leading to confirmation of misconceptions. Donato (personal communication, 1997) suggests that one solution to the problem of selective attention to and filtering of experiential evidence that contradicts teacher beliefs is "to anchor reflective practice in evidence or concrete instantiations of experience and then to allow for the interpretative process to unfold or be constructed with others . . . If we look at the mind as discursive and development as mediated socially with tools such as language, cultural artifacts, etc., then it is quite possible that evidence can be attended to and development realized. It is only when we see the channel of learning as occurring through the individual that such problems exist."

Language, of course, is at the heart of interaction and discourse and plays a significant role in all learning. Language makes explicit understandings and beliefs; it is a vehicle for transmitting and revealing cultural beliefs.

Freeman (1996a) highlights the important role of language in changing teacher practice. He notes that novice teachers gain entry into the discourse of experienced professionals by using language consistent with that community. That is, novice teachers move from what he calls "local language" to the Discourse [sic], or jargon of the profession. In so doing, they accomplish two functions: (a) they become a member of the group/community and (b) they carry out ". . . the cognitive function of organizing one's conceptual world according to the values and meanings of that group" (p. 236). He views teacher learning as a dialectical process in which renaming practice is a vehicle for understanding how tacit assumptions about language learning can lead to new or deeper understandings, informed and molded by participation in professional discourse.

Language can also help to clarify and resolve misconceptions. Transformation theory as developed by Mezirow and discussed by Kennedy and Wyrick (1995) holds that interpretations of the meanings of experience are encoded in language. As we make meaning from our experiences, we construe it both through models and language. Thus language plays an important role in mediating our interpretations of experience and knowledge.

Talking and listening are important to teacher learning. Talk is a public process of co-constructing knowledge among teachers who have to work consciously to ensure their language is interpreted as conveying the meanings and thoughts they intend (Cochran-Smith & Lytle, 1993). Rogers and Babinski (1999) report that teachers specifically speak to the importance of listening carefully and being listened to in collegial discourse.

In addition to oral language, writing can help to support conceptual change in all learners. "Researchers have also reported that writing about thinking improves learning . . . The holistic event of writing may force integration of new ideas and relationship with prior knowledge. This forced integration may also provide feedback to the writer . . . The looking-back nature of writing seems to match the nature of changing knowledge and may encourage students to consider alternative understandings" (Fellows, 1994, p. 987). The research in the efficacy of writing in improving learning is instantiated in the growing role that interactive journals and learning logs play in classrooms. In fact, interactive journals and other uses of writing are also recommended for teacher professional development (Sparks & Hirsh, 1997). "Clearly teacher portfolios anchored in evidence, teacher journals and narrative inquiry, and some forms of action research could all be potential forms of mediation necessary to change misconception and lay the groundwork for more informed thinking about instruction" (Donato, personal communication, 1997).

Job-embedded learning. Effective staff development programs recognize that teacher learning must emanate from important instructional problems teachers need and want to solve and must help teachers explore the solutions in their own classrooms. Sparks and Hirsh (1997) suggest that job-embedded learning may take multiple forms, including classroom-based action research, teacher participation in collegial study groups, and peer observation, among others. Portfolios of teaching performance are a form of mediated reflection (Antonek, McCormick, & Donato, 1997); scoring performance assessments deepens teacher understandings of curriculum and student performance (Falk & Ort, 1998); teachers who participate in scoring portfolio assessments gain deeper understanding of instructional practices, and curriculum writing can strengthen teachers' understanding of subject matter (Corcoran, 1995). Additional job-embedded learning may include peer coaching, case discussions, and joint problem solving (Fine & Raack, 1994). Such learning-on-the-job is consistent with Schön's view (1983) that an important part of reflective practice is reflection-in-action (that is, thinking while doing) as well as reflection-on-action (that is, thinking about how classroom actions reflect implicit assumptions or beliefs about student learning). Both types of reflection are more likely to be successful when embedded in teachers' own classroom experiences. Schön has also suggested that reflection practices can be embedded in supervisory settings, resulting in a reflective practicum. To be effective, these practicums [sic] "must get at what teachers do through direct, recorded observation that permits a very detailed description of behavior and a reconstruction of intentions, strategies, and assumptions." Clearly, such reflection practicums represent a powerful form of job-embedded professional development.

Realizing the Vision: The Common Threads

A number of threads weave through this paper:

1. Teachers may not directly formulate policy, but they influence policymakers. Public attitudes toward language learning can be significantly impacted by prior experiences as language learners. As we provide positive experiences for our students that lead to observable, measurable, and usable language skills, we are also creating a more positive, receptive climate for language education.

2. Beliefs, attitudes, and values underlie current policy, public support for language learning, student and parent attitudes, and educational practices. The work of the Frameworks Institute makes clear just how powerful pre-existing assumptions are in shaping public response to policy initiatives as well as how great are the challenges language educators face in transforming educational policies in ways more favorable to language study. And, given the premise of this paper—that teachers are at the core of creating the future of language education—then an understanding of how our own belief systems have shaped (and will continue to shape) our work is essential to our success.

3. Information is not enough. Personal experience is far more powerful than information in shaping belief systems—those of policymakers, those of the public at large, and those we hold as teachers.

   Our advocacy efforts have relied on giving the public and policymakers key information. Our underlying premise—that information is a powerful weapon for advancing our cause—may be unfounded. We often assume that lack of information keeps others from valuing language proficiency as we do (the "If only they knew . . ." syndrome). We need to pay close attention to the oft-repeated refrain in the work of the Frameworks Institute, "When the facts don't fit the frame, the facts get rejected, not the frame."

   Our professional development efforts have also targeted information: knowing about research, examining the implications of research for teaching practices, expanding teaching repertoires. Perhaps we have assumed here, as well, that information is sufficient for making the transition from past practices to current, research-driven practices. As the professional development literature shows, information is a necessary but not sufficient condition for changing what we teach, how we teach, and how we determine whether students have learned.

4. Time is a precious and scarce resource. Our nation needs a linguistically competent workforce now, whether for homeland security or economic competitiveness.

Unfortunately, learning a language to high levels of competence takes much longer than most policymakers have acknowledged, leading to public policies that make early language learning difficult to implement, that leave most students beginning language learning in high school, and that only allow for relatively short sequences of language study. Because time is such a critical variable in language learning, we have to exploit every moment a student spends in a language classroom. Enhancing instructional practices requires time too. We need time to learn, to practice, and to integrate new skills into improved performance. Teachers need time to think and to plan differently in order to carry out instruction differently. The most effective forms of professional development are ongoing, extending over time.

New Visions began in 1998 with the goal of engaging the entire academic foreign language community in a collaborative drive to attain a common vision: to produce graduates of our schools who demonstrate foreign language competence. To that end, New Visions in Action sought to identify and implement the actions necessary to revamp the language education system so that it can more effectively achieve the important goal of language proficiency for all students, first by identifying "What could we do?"; then by setting priorities for those actions ("What should we do?"); and, most importantly, by gaining the active participation a broadly-based cross section of the foreign language education community ("What will we do and who will do it?"). To date, four major task forces have been formed, with numerous working groups enfolded in them. Individuals and professional organizations have committed to working on parts of the identified agenda, collaborating and pooling resources rather than competing and duplicating efforts. These have been extraordinary efforts on the part of the pre-K-16 language education community despite competing demands for their time and energy and despite a climate in which language education is not always highly valued. Much has been accomplished, yet much more remains undone.

Due to the terrible events of this century and the continuing fragility of global relationships, our role as language educators has gained greater importance than perhaps ever before in our careers. We have a unique opportunity to lead change and affect public policy. As leadership of New Visions transitions to the major language professional associations, the questions central to the New Visions efforts retain their currency and power:

- What would it take to make our vision a reality?
- What could we do?
- What should we do?
- What will we do and who will do it?

Language educators at every level, pre-K-16, must answer these questions.
    We are at the core.

References

Antonek, J., McCormick, D., & Donato, R. (1997). The student teacher portfolio as autobiography: Developing a professional identity. *Modern Language Journal, 81*(1), 15–27.

Bales, S. N. (2003). *Making the public case for international education: A FrameWorks message.* Paper presented at the States Institute for International Education, Washington, DC.

Bales, S. N. (2004). How Americans think about international education and why it matters. *Phi Delta Kappan, 86*(3), 206–209.

Barker, J. (1993). *Paradigms: The business of discovering the future.* New York: Harper Business.

Bolman, L., & Deal, T. (1991). *Reframing organizations—artistry, choice and leadership.* Jossey-Bass.

Caine, R., & Caine, G. (1997). *Education on the edge of possibility.* Alexandria, VA: Association for Supervision and Curriculum Development.

Cochran-Smith, M., & Lytle, S. (1993). *Inside/Outside: Teacher research and knowledge.* New York: Teachers College Press.

Corcoran, T. C. (1995). *Transforming professional development for teachers: A guide for state policymakers.* Washington, DC: National Governors Association.

Costa, A. L., & Garmston, R. J. (1994). *Cognitive coaching: A foundation for renaissance schools.* Norwood, MA: Christopher-Cordon Publishers.

Falk, B., & Ort, S. (1998). Sitting down to score: Teaching learning through assessment. *Phi Delta Kappa, 80*(1), 59–64.

Fellows, N. J. (1994). A window into thinking: Using student writing to understand conceptual change in science learning. *Journal of Research in Science Teaching, 31*(9), 985–1001.

Fine, C., & Raack, L. (1994). *Professional development: Changing times* (Policy Briefs, Report 4). Oak Brook, IL: North Central Regional Educational Laboratory.

Freeman, D. (1996a). Renaming experience/reconstructing practice: Developing new understandings of teaching. In D. Freeman & J.C. Richards (Eds.), *Teacher learning in language teaching* (pp. 221–241). New York: Cambridge University Press.

Freeman, D. (1996b). The "unstudied problem": Research on teacher learning in language teaching. In D. Freeman & J. C. Richards (Eds.), *Teacher learning in language teaching* (pp. 351–374). New York: Cambridge University Press.

Kennedy, R. L., & Wyrick, A. M. (1995). *Teaching as reflective practice.* Paper presented at the Annual Meeting of the Mid-South Educational Research Association, Biloxi, MS.

Kuhn, T. (1962). *The structure of scientific revolutions.* Chicago: University of Chicago Press.

Markee, N. (1997). Second language acquisition research: A resource for changing teachers' professional cultures? *Modern Language Journal, 81*(1), 80–93.

Met, M. (1994). Foreign language policy in American secondary schools: Who decides? *Annals of the American Society for Political and Social Science, 532,* 149–163.

National Language Conference. (2005). *A call to action for national foreign language capabilities* [white paper]. Washington, DC: Office of the Undersecretary of Defense

(Personnel and Readiness). Retrieved July 8, 2005, from <http://nlconference.org/docs/White_Paper.pdf>.

New Visions in Action. (1998). Retrieved June 27, 2005, from <http://educ.iastate.edu/newvisions>.

Pennington, M. C. (1996). When input becomes intake: Tracing the sources of teachers' attitude change. In D. Freeman & J. C. Richards (Eds.), *Teacher learning in language teaching* (pp. 320–348). New York: Cambridge University Press.

Pennington, M. C. (1995). The teacher change cycle. *TESOL Quarterly, 29*(4): 705–731.

Robinson, J. P., Brecht, R., & Rivers, W. (2005). *Foreign language speakers in America: Correlates, trends, and possible consequences.* Manuscript submitted for publication.

Rogers, D., & Babinski, L. (1999). Breaking through isolation with new teacher groups. *Educational Leadership, 56*(8), 38–40.

Schön, D. A. (1983). *The reflective practitioner: How professionals think in action.* New York: Basic Books.

Schön, D. A. (1988). *Teachers as reflective practitioners.* Talk given at the annual conference of the Association for Supervision and Curriculum Development, Orlando, FL.

Sparks, D., & Hirsh, S. (1997). *A new vision for staff development.* Alexandria, VA: Association for Supervision and Curriculum Development.

Ulichny, P. (1996). What's in a methodology? In D. Freeman & J. C. Richards (Eds.), *Teacher learning in language teaching* (pp. 178–196). New York: Cambridge University Press.

Wallace, M. (1991). *Training foreign language teachers: A reflective approach.* Cambridge, UK: Cambridge University Press.

Williams, M., & Burden, R. L. (1997). *Psychology for language teachers: A social constructivist approach.* New York: Cambridge University Press.

5

Assessment Now and Into the Future

June K. Phillips

Overview

There is an old *Peanuts* cartoon that depicts Peppermint Patty at her schoolroom desk; she is the only character we see and hear in this strip. She raises her hand and asks the teacher: "Ma'am? What kind of test are we having today? Multiple choice?" At the presumed affirmative answer, Patty breaks into a wide smile and proclaims: "Good! I choose not to take it" (Schulz, 1979). At the time the original cartoon was drawn, the predominant format in most disciplines for most tests, whether standardized or teacher-created, was some variety of forced choice or fill-in right answer. In foreign languages, tests focused on the language system itself where students made choices about grammatical structures or the meaning of vocabulary words or phrases; in some cases they demonstrated comprehension of listening or reading passages by choosing the correct English iteration of what had been heard or read. These tests could be developed in conformity to statistical measures of reliability and validity that pleased the psychometricians if not the Peppermint Patty test takers.

Many years later, Elana Shohamy, an international specialist in language testing, attributes her interest in research on testing to her personal experiences as a test-taker. She explains that ". . . not doing well on tests motivated me to try to understand the mystery of testing from a different perspective—that of the test taker. My training is in traditional testing. This is where I learned the psychometric truth of one correct answer. Yet my perspective of testing has always been that of the test taker, attempting to understand why so many of us could not do well on certain types of test, especially those involving multiple choice items" (2001, p. xi).

How have testing practices changed in the decades since the foreign language profession claimed that communication was the primary goal of instruction? Has testing broadened to look at the test taker, to envision that providing feedback that can improve learning might be more important than—or as important as—assigning a score, or to use multiple measures that give a more useful profile of the learner? And why do we see the term *assessment* replacing that of *testing* in much of the literature? Is the use of this term superficial, or have significant changes occurred in both the format and purposes of evaluation? In this chapter, the "now" of testing will be seen to include significant examples of the "then," for the present state of assessment consists of both innovation and tradition: we are very much in an age of transitions.

As we look toward the future, it will be essential that all the dimensions of testing and assessment be explored. This exploration must probe the purposes, contexts, and variables of specific assessments; the perspectives of the test takers; and the consequences associated with the reporting of results—consequences for learners, teachers, and educational systems. The chapter will, therefore, not impart a bank of exemplary test items but attempt to clarify and provoke thinking about assessment, its uses and abuses, and ways the foreign language profession should be pursuing assessment processes that improve student learning. The author is not a test developer and approaches this discussion as a practitioner struggling with the issue.

Definitions, Purposes, Directions

Assessment is the term used in the title of this chapter, rather than *testing* or *measurement*, which would have been the more prevailing term in similar chapters in the 1980s. Perhaps that semantic switch encapsulates the perspective influencing our practice in the late 20th, early 21st century. Overlap certainly exists between the terms testing and assessment since both encompass broad sets of procedures. A well-constructed test serves assessment purposes just as assessments may include a series of tests. In order to have a working definition for purposes of discussion, the operating classifications used by the International Baccalaureate Organization (IBO) for tests, examinations, and assessment provide meanings grounded in classroom and curriculum:

> **Test**—a collection of many short-answer questions (either selected-response/
> multiple-choice questions or questions requiring only a few words in response)
> that students must answer under controlled, isolated conditions in a set time.
> Often marked (or graded) automatically.
>
> **Examination**—a collection of one or more tasks of various types (short answer,
> extended-answer, problem-solving, or analytical questions; sometimes practical
> or oral tasks) that students must respond to under controlled, isolated conditions
> in a set time. Generally marked/graded by examiner (or rater).
>
> **Assessment**—a term used to cover all the various methods by which student
> achievement can be evaluated. Assessment instruments may include tests, examinations, extended practical work, projects, portfolios and oral work, some carried out over a prolonged period and sometimes marked by the students' teacher.
> (1994, p. 3)

The IB program serves as a good model for explicating the role of assessment in its curriculum, and it informs teachers about the purposes of assessment as being both formative and summative. Moreover, the program describes assessment in a way that acknowledges underlying theoretical premises by linking assessments to the work of Vygotsky (1978, 1986). Assessment is envisioned as a means of understanding what students have achieved, what they can do on their own, and where their learning is still tentative, requiring the assistance of an "expert"—the teacher. Would that all testing and assessment constructs follow the pattern of designing a framework or theoretical premise for their activity! The IB program states that assessment purposes are formative and summative and explicates these concepts in good detail, not just for its program, but for any interested party. Formative assessments "provide detailed feedback to teacher and their students on the nature of students' strengths and weaknesses, and to help develop students' capabilities." The purposes of summative assessments relate to accountability and certification of student achievement. (IBO, 1994, pp. 3–4)

From Testing Language to Assessing Performance

As educators attempt to make distinctions between testing and assessment, they acknowledge that individual measures may have characteristics of each. However, tests tend to have a cluster of the following characteristics:

- Single right answers
- Short answers with standardized acceptable responses
- Answers capable of machine or automatic scoring
- Security (of the test itself and/or the tasks included)
- Gotcha factor (aim is to see what the test-taker does not know)
- Numerical score or grade
- Occurrence after a unit of instruction

Wiggins (1993) describes tests as

> . . . an evaluation procedure in which responsiveness to individual test takers and contexts and the role of human judgment are deliberately minimized, if not eliminated. This is intended as an observation, not a criticism. There are well-known virtues to standardizing procedure and minimizing bias, drift, and other forms of error in judgment. Most tests accomplish this mechanization of scoring by taking complex performances and dividing them into discrete, independent tasks that minimize the ambiguity of the result. (We can take off points and count up scores easily, in other words.) As a result, most tests tend to be "indirect" (and thereby inauthentic) ways of evaluating performance, because tests must simplify each task in order to make the items and answers unambiguous and independent of one another. . . . we have paid a price for this inauthenticity, irrespective of the indisputable precision gained by using indirect measures. (p. 15)

One can see that through this definition Wiggins begins to construct the argument for more broadly conceived assessments that are inherently more authentic and that recognize the complexity of much of learning.

What "Tests" Are Current in Foreign Languages?

The commercial world of testing is dominated by tests in core disciplines, especially language arts and mathematics. The *No Child Left Behind Act* (NCLB) (2001) has only reinforced this situation; in fact, some jokingly refer to the legislation as the "No Test Developer Left Unemployed" act. NCLB has not mandated testing in foreign languages, although English as a Second Language (ESL) programs are dramatically affected by the pressure to have Limited English Proficient (LEP) students test and be scored on language arts tests in what most educators feel is an unreasonable time frame, especially for students entering the schools in middle or high school grades. An illuminating discussion of the NCLB impact on foreign language programs takes place in the "Perspectives" section of *The Modern Language Journal* with a lead article by Rosenbusch (2005) followed by a number of insightful commentaries. In spite of national standards having been developed by the foreign language profession *(Standards for Foreign Language Learning,* 1996, 1999) and foreign language having been designated a core curricular area under *Goals 2000: Educate America* legislation, no national impetus for student testing has arisen. In those areas subject to the testing demands of NCLB, the tests themselves have been more reflective of discrete-point traditional formats than of the more open-ended multifaceted assessments associated with standards. In that sense, it may be just as well to be outside those constraints so that experimentation with new formats can proceed. In fact, the design and pilot of a Spanish National Assessment of Educational Progress (NAEP), completed in 2004, included some pioneering item types which will be described later in the chapter. Unfortunately, administration of that NAEP has been delayed until at least the year 2012.

Standardized tests in various foreign languages. Relatively few of these exist for world languages in the United States compared to other disciplines. With the demise (in terms of publication, not usage, since a search of the Web indicates that many universities still use these tests which can only be old copies stashed in file drawers) of the *MLA/ETS Cooperative Foreign Language Proficiency Tests for Teachers and Students,* the remaining standardized tests for students would be the *CLEP (College Level Examination Program),* the *SAT II (Scholastic Achievement Test), Advanced Placement* exams, and the *Praxis II Content Knowledge and Productive Skills Tests in French, German, or Spanish.* The first three tests are sponsored by The College Board, are intended for high school through college students, and are produced and scored by Educational Testing Service (ETS). The tests are mainly discrete-point with a mixture of subtests, some of which focus on a skill (for example, listening, reading comprehension) and others which focus on language usage and primarily make use of forced choice, machine-scored items. Movement toward more authentic listening/reading texts has occurred in recent years, yet the items frequently depend upon knowledge of a discrete vocabulary or grammatical item. *Advanced*

Placement and *Praxis* foreign language tests now include productive skill sections that are scored by raters using rubrics. Psychometric issues of reliability and validity require that items be independent of one another, that stimuli be free of prior knowledge, and that statistical measures demonstrate how items discriminate among learners—in essence, they must treat language as unidimensional. It is those very features that cause frustrations among the educators who envision language learning as multi-dimensional, as complex, as a construct that is built upon how individual students assign and create meanings. Given the transitions being made in classrooms and in curriculum toward the goals outlined in the national standards, there is a degree of discontent among stakeholders, that is, teachers, administrators, students, and their parents, as to the alignment or lack thereof. The College Board, through its World Languages Academic Advisory Committee, is in the process of writing a framework intended to guide testing into the next century. One would hope that this project comes to fruition so that new assessments are developed to supplant the current tests, whether for college placement or achievement. As the purposes of assessment in the 21st century are redefined more toward measuring progress and improving student learning, provocative discussions on the role of standardized testing will undoubtedly ensue.

Districts and states. The most innovative assessment programs are being developed at the district or state level, and we shall discuss those later. They represent, however, a thin minority of the kinds of assessments that occur on a daily basis in U.S. world language classrooms. Change has been excruciatingly slow in teaching, in practice, and especially in measurement. The talk about performance testing is highly visible at conferences, yet it has been translated to practice in relatively few places, and, even there, it is but one spoke in the wheel of testing. The other spokes remain discrete-point, convenient paper/pencil tests of vocabulary knowledge and grammatical forms.

The classroom level. Standards and related emphases on communicative goals have pushed world language classrooms toward incorporating more oral activities. Even those classrooms that continue to be based upon a grammatical syllabus pay some attention to orality in the exercises that dominate class time. To a limited extent the grammar topic is tied to some forced communicative end.

And so, the status of "now" consists of lots of "then." Regardless of where a learner's class experience lies on a spectrum of standards-based communication or grammar-driven curriculum, when it comes to assessment, orality is abandoned and paper and pencil come out. Much of classroom assessment continues to be decades-old testing in the form of quizzes and chapter tests with single written right answers. Students receive numerical scores that tell them how many right, how many wrong answers they provided. Items do include listening or reading comprehension *if* the textbook testing package includes these kinds of items. Teacher-made tests tend to be focused on text-covered grammatical items.

How statements of classroom allegiance to communicative goals fall short when it comes to testing is confirmed by observations and surveys. One example comes from a project of the Southern Conference on Language Teaching. The Conference strives to connect researchers and teachers and in the volume *Research within Reach II* took testing as one of the topics. Teachers submit questions that are of concern to them in their practice. While this volume dates from 1995, a year prior to the publication of the national standards, it is positioned well into the decades where the focus has been on communicative language learning. Here are the ten questions that teachers asked about testing at that time (although one suspects that some were edited or planted):

1. Are there ways of testing students other than paper-and-pencil tests?

2. In our schools we hear about "alternative assessment." What does this mean for foreign languages?

3. I am comfortable with achievement tests, but now we hear about proficiency tests and "prochievement" tests. What are the differences?

4. How can I test grammar in a communicative context?

5. How does one assess speaking in a large class?

6. How can listening comprehension be assessed without a lab?

7. What criteria should I use to grade open-ended speaking and writing tasks?

8. What are some ways of testing cultural proficiency?

9. What special testing techniques are most effective at the FLES (foreign language in the elementary school) level?

10. What types of assessment can be easily modified to meet the needs of learning disabled students? (Phillips, 1995).

The questions do reflect that the transition from single-answer, discrete-point tests of grammar and vocabulary is taking place. More recently, in summer 2004, a needs assessment survey administered at the opening of a one-week institute for foreign language teachers in a mid-Atlantic state, contained the following item:

Item: I use the following types of assessment

a. Written tests, quizzes, and compositions

b. Role play or similar techniques to show the ability to communicate in a real life situation

c. Journals, posters, projects

d. Reading or listening comprehension based on authentic materials

e. Other

Results: Raw numbers with percentage in parentheses

A: 84 (98.8%)   B: 1 (1.8%)   C, D, E: 0 (0%)

This is a small sample of teachers; they do, however, represent a spectrum of relatively new to experienced educators who elsewhere on the needs assessment survey indicated a strong knowledge of the standards and an orientation toward communicative language learning. It is discouraging that their assessment practices are so narrowly conceived in practice.

Toward Greater Development and Use of Performance Assessments

As language learning was shifting in the 1970s/1980s toward communicative goals, testing procedures lagged behind. In both classrooms and on larger standardized measures, evaluation continued to consist of discrete-point, convergent-response items or sets of items where the test taker demonstrated control of lexical or grammatical structures. When teachers or external tests proposed to evaluate oral language, purported to have a stronger instructional role, the measures still considered aspects of language such as fluency, pronunciation, accuracy and only peripherally comprehensibility, effectiveness of message conveyance, strategies, and the like as the most important. Students were rewarded, not for daring to communicate the messages they wanted to send, but for sending messages they could send accurately. Taking up challenges beyond one's zone of control could result in a lower score or grade.

By the mid-1980s, academics began to explore how government agencies were measuring oral communication through the Oral Proficiency Interview (OPI). Spolsky's (2000) history of articles on language testing reveals that interest in including speaking on language tests in the U.S. began as early as 1914. Numerous logistic factors compounded by the reality that the instructional focus was grammar-translation preclude advances in that area. The major large-scale measure of speaking in academic terms was a subsection of the *MLA/ETS Foreign Language Proficiency Tests for Teachers and Students*. This test, created in the late 1960s, was innovative in its time for its inclusion of speaking; the test was piloted and used in conjunction with the National Defense Education Act (NDEA) Institutes to assess gains in teacher proficiency among participants in the institutes. The speaking test consisted of a prompt, a four-picture sequence of events, to which the test-taker was to provide a recorded narrative. It was scored by raters at the Educational Testing Service; test takers received a score but no feedback on strengths, weaknesses, nor even what the score represented.

The OPI is an interactive interview based upon a prescribed elicitation procedure, and it is rated according to a proficiency scale, hierarchical in nature. Administration and scoring are done by trained interviewers, and double ratings are used to assure inter-rater reliability. The original scale used by the government was adapted for academic uses by the American Council on the Teaching of Foreign Languages (ACTFL) (1982, 1986; Breiner-Sanders, Lowe, Miles, & Swender, 2000), interviewers were trained, and both the OPI and the *Proficiency Guidelines* (ACTFL, 1982, 1986) precipitated many changes in classroom assessment and instruction. In the ensuing years, both these products have had advocates and critics. Positive change has occurred as a result, but there has also been misapplication as well. The debate over the OPI is more complex than the chapter can address. What can be emphasized is that it advanced an assessment instrument for speaking that had been lacking in a field in which oral communication had been advancing. Consequently, it provided a measurement device that aligned with an instructional goal to a greater extent than had been previously available. In her analysis of the power and the drawbacks of the OPI, Liskin-Gasparro (2003) describes how the assessment created a wash back effect that enabled teachers ". . . to see for themselves the disconnect between students' declarative linguistic knowledge, demonstrated in contexts of controlled production in teacher-centered classrooms, and their more limited ability to communicative in autonomous contexts" (p. 486). This is an example of using an assessment to improve teaching and learning, something that a score on a traditional language test was powerless to do. Many teachers familiarized or trained in the OPI testing procedure and methods derived from it (for example, Simulated Oral Proficiency Interview [SOPI] or Modified Oral Proficiency Interview [MOPI]) never intended to become certified testers. Their initiation into the procedure helped them observe how students used language away from controlled classroom activities and gain a more realistic view of the developmental nature of proficiency. For an extensive review and perspective of the OPI, its history in the academy, advances, and issues that continue to challenge the procedure and its offshoots, the reader is directed to a special issue of *Foreign Language Annals* (Clifford, 2003). One certain outcome of the OPI as a procedure to measure speaking lies in its being an example of a performance assessment in the foreign language field. It pushed the profession toward assessment strategies in other areas of communicative language and culture learning and slowly away from testing of the language system.

Internationally, the *Common European Framework of Reference for Languages* (Council of Europe, 2001) breaks tasks into much smaller, more focused tasks than are covered by the OPI. It has three basic levels of accomplishment: A-Basic user; B-Independent user; C-Proficient user. Each of these levels is further delineated. Within spoken interaction, there are illustrative scales for overall spoken interaction, conversation, informal discussion, formal discussion and meetings, goal-oriented cooperation, transactions to obtain goods and services, information exchange, and interviewing and being interviewed. It would behoove U.S. educators to look for correlations with the U.S. proficiency scales and those of the European Union.

Influences for Assessment from Standards

The federal initiative that evolved around standard setting in most curricular areas in the schools was predicated on two key questions:

- What should students know and be able to do? (Content standard)
- How good is good enough? (Performance standard)

The task force assembled by ACTFL and collaborating professional organizations developed the content standards which were widely endorsed by states and professional associations (National Standards in Foreign Language Education Project [NSFLEP], 1996, 1999). Development of performance standards has been reserved for the states. In many ways, that could result in the reinventing of the wheel, but a number of states have formed coalitions to undertake that charge as we will see later.

An immediate outcome from the standards setting process was to bring performance assessment to center stage. All disciplines began to look at assessment in a significantly broader way than reliance on testing had provided. Colleagues in mathematics led the charge and, in an in-house publication, delineated the shift taking place. In Table 1, substitute the term *foreign language* or *communicative language* for the term *mathematics* [italics added], and the table cogently describes what has been occurring over the last decade.

Practices under the column "AWAY FROM" are more representative of traditional testing in any discipline, as those in the column "TOWARD" represent what is occurring as the shift toward assessment takes place. Wiggins (1993) juxtaposes testing and assessment by claiming that "tests are intrinsically prone to sacrifice validity to achieve reliability and to sacrifice the student's interests for the test makers" (p. 4). Earlier in this chapter, characteristics of testing were set forth. Characteristics of assessment have been addressed by multiple specialists over many years (Cohen, 1994; Cronbach, 1960; Shohamy, 2001; Wiggins, 1993). Wiggins (1993) traces the word *assessment* to its Latin root *assidere,* to sit with. He invites us to think about assessment as something one does *with* a student, not *to* him or her; the assessor assigns value, advises, mentors, and the like. He further defines assessment as a "comprehensive, multifaceted analysis of performance; it must be judgment-based and personal" (p. 13). An assessment may be based upon a series of smaller or more focused assessments that have been evaluated and scored. The final assessment would be more comprehensive. Often the judgment factor is based upon a rubric or scoring guide that describes the performance in terms of expected results. Assessment envisions

- The teacher as a designer of tasks and purposes;
- The teacher as a guide, an interpreter of the performance;

TABLE 1 Major Shifts In Assessment Practice

Toward	Away From
Assessing students' full *mathematical* power	Assessing only students' knowledge of specific facts and isolated skills
Comparing students' performance with established criteria	Comparing students' performance with that of other students
Giving support to teachers and credence to their informed judgment	Designing "teacher-proof" assessment systems
Making the assessment process public, participatory, and dynamic	Making the assessment process secret exclusive and fixed
Giving students multiple opportunities to demonstrate their full *mathematical* power	Restricting students to a single way of demonstrating their *mathematical* knowledge
Developing a shared vision of what to assess and how to do it	Developing assessment by oneself
Using assessment results to ensure that all students have the opportunity to achieve their potential	Using assessment to filter and select students out of the opportunities to learn *mathematics*
Aligning assessment with curriculum and instruction	Treating assessment as independent of curriculum or instruction
Basing inferences on multiple sources of evidence	Basing inferences on restricted or single sources of evidence
Viewing students as active participants in the assessment process	Viewing students as the objects of assessment
Regarding assessment as continual and recursive	Regarding assessment as sporadic and conclusive
Holding all concerned with *mathematics* learning accountable for assessment results	Holding only a few accountable for assessment results

Source: From *Assessment Standards for School Mathematics* (NCTM, 1995, p. 83).

- Tasks that are multi-faceted and simulate real world problems;
- Tasks that allow students to provide the sample of learned material; and
- Transparency so that the learner understands what he/she can do and where there is need for further skill or learning.

Another way of illustrating differences in assessment and testing approaches is to contrast these characteristics in terms of the characteristics of testing identified earlier in the chapter.

Tests	Assessments
Single right answers	Contextualized and individualized responses that differ for the student, by task, and message
Short answers with standardized acceptable responses	Divergent responses with comprehensibility and accuracy a function of learning stage; items that seek information not known to the tester
Answers capable of machine or automatic scoring	Scoring by teacher/tester judgment according to rubric or other criterion guide
Security (of the test itself and/ or the tasks included)	Tasks can be revealed to students prior to assessment; performance based on ability to do the task
Gotcha factor (aim is to see what the test-taker does not know)	Purpose is to see what student can do and where in need of further learning
Numerical score or grade	Evaluation may be score or descriptive; may compare achievement to expectation
Occurrence after a unit of instruction	Occurrence at any time the information is useful to teacher and learner: before, during or after a unit of instruction

A cautionary note on the juxtaposition outlined above: this tends to present these contrasts as black and white. In practice, many assessments will contain aspects of each and operate in a gray area. These definitions of *testing* or *assessment* are not unique to foreign languages, and it has been useful to the profession to be an active part of the educational discussion at large. Frequently, in the past, foreign languages seemed to be set apart by concentrating on how different they were as a discipline from others. As assessment develops specific measures of language and cultures appropriate to the field, the umbrella concerns will be common to the wider spectrum of subject areas.

Tests, with their scores, are limited in the kind of feedback they can give. A student can see what he or she missed on a test and say, "Oh, yes, I see what that word really means," or "Yeah, I got the wrong ending on that verb." But as most classroom teachers confirm, that type of error awareness has little impact on future test performance. As one considers broader and multifaceted tasks for performance assessments, the purposes of evaluation can be met more effectively. Cohen (1994) classifies the purposes of assessment:

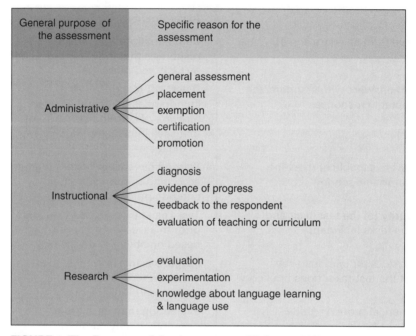

FIGURE 1 The Purpose of the Assessment (Cohen, 1998).

Source: Permission to reproduce Assessing Language Ability in the Classroom 2nd edition, by COHEN, copyright © 1994 Heinle, a division of Thomson Learning, has been granted to Pearson Education for class use. All rights reserved. Aside from this specific exception, no part of this book may be reproduced, stored in a retrieval system, or transcribed in any form or by any means—electronic, mechanical, photocopying, recording or otherwise—without permission in writing from the Thomson Learning Global Rights Group: www.thomsonrights.com, Fax 800-730-2215.

This chart, by helping test developers and users become more specific about the purposes of assessment, forces more thoughtful justification about the form of the assessment and how it will be administered. For example, if an administrative purpose to exempt students from a course is the issue, then a standardized test such as the CLEP may serve that purpose. Even though there is no oral component, which most faculty members would see as a necessary skill developed in the course that students exempt, use of the test over time, with pass rates set locally, has proven to be successful in exempting students from courses and/or in placing them in the appropriate level course. In this case, it may be that the focus of the test listening/reading passages provides a profile sufficient for that administrative purpose. If the purpose is instructional with the intent to provide feedback, diagnosis, or evidence of progress in a class, then a direct assessment of performance might be a preferable choice. In listening, for example, one might ask students to listen to a video clip from a documentary on students with jobs and summarize what they have understood. The teacher can then provide feedback on where they were successful in assigning meaning, discuss where they became misled and how a miscue occurred, and talk about what cultural knowledge was needed for accurate interpretation. The teacher can also account for language that is more of a challenge because it was not within the content focus of the curriculum; students who understood it probably used effective contextual guessing strategies. On the other hand, if a student misunderstood passages with a high degree of "taught" material, then the teacher looks for other explanation (for instance, it was not *learned* or perhaps it was learned in print but not in sound). A research purpose might lead to an interpersonal performance task where students are observed as they concentrate on elaborating their messages in pair work.

In addition to greater awareness of the purposes of assessment, a host of other questions arise for expert test developers, for teachers creating tests and assessments in their classrooms, for consumers of those tests such as guidance counselors, admissions officers, or school boards. Among these:

- Is the assessment a direct measure of performance or an indirect one? (Direct measures draw the sample evaluation from the targeted task: Students prepare a video broadcast and their prepared spoken language is evaluated. Indirect measures sample through an alternative means: Students fill in missing items on a script of a TV broadcast to show they know the vocabulary and grammatical structures needed.)

- How is it scored, objectively or subjectively? Who scores it? Who receives the results?

- Does it reflect a particular course/curriculum, or is it independent of curriculum?

- Has a framework been designed to guide the construction of the assessment?

- What standards of reliability and validity have been met? (*Reliability* refers to the accuracy of the measure in terms of whether the same result would be achieved if administered to the same group a second time. *Validity* refers to the extent the test measures what it purports to measure and may be of several kinds: content, criterion-related, construct, systemic, and face. See Cohen, 1994, pp. 36–43, for a clear discussion of these concepts with language examples.)

- Is the student performance sample gathered from one instrument or several? If the latter, are the samples integrated (interdependent) or a collection (e.g., portfolio)?

- Will the assessment be used as a snapshot of a performance at a decision point or as a measure of progress toward a goal?

Whether one is creating, administering, reflecting, or reporting on results, performance assessments are complex and require greater insights than the tests prevalent in the past. Let us look at some of the newer assessment products and strategies being explored in language education today at the national, state, district, and classroom levels. The developers of most of these assessments consider them to be works in progress. The listing is not comprehensive: it is but a sample, since at this stage the literature has not been developed and most information is communicated at conferences and meetings.

World Languages/Spanish NAEP (National Assessment of Educational Progress)

When the National Assessment Governing Board (NAGB) approved the development of a NAEP in foreign languages, many saw it as an opportunity to assure placement of the discipline within the core curriculum. Accountability plays such a strong role in schools that supervisors and district administrators felt it to be critical for foreign languages to be "on" the Nation's Report Card, the nickname for NAEP results. The original date for a NAEP 2003 was pushed back at least twice and is not slated for 2012. In spite of the disappointment in this delay, the process that went into creating the NAEP and piloting the assessment produced some important innovative products.

The framework. All NAEP assessments require a consensus-building phase that leads to the construction of a framework. While the foreign language profession experienced a successful consensus-building effort for the national standards, this was another opportunity to do so and, more importantly, to create a framework for a national test. This direct connection between a framework derived from consensus of a representative group of foreign language educators and an assessment is a first. Certainly, professionals have used various frameworks as the justification for instructional or curricular approaches (for example, communicative competence model, Canale & Swain, 1980), and test developers designed parameters for standardized tests. A requirement for this framework from NAGB is that it reflect the standards of the discipline and that the test items to be developed be explicitly linked to the framework. The NAEP development was contracted to a collaboration of four organizations: ACTFL, American Institutes for Research (AIR), Center for Applied Linguistics (CAL), and Educational Testing Service (ETS). CAL was charged with the consensus building and the framework, and the other groups would each be part of the test development itself. Intensive discussion and presentation of progress to the profession generated the Framework.

A few explanatory background notes about the NAEP can contribute an understanding of this assessment. First, it is a low-risk test for students. Their scores are not attributed to them by name; the intent of the test is to report on the status of

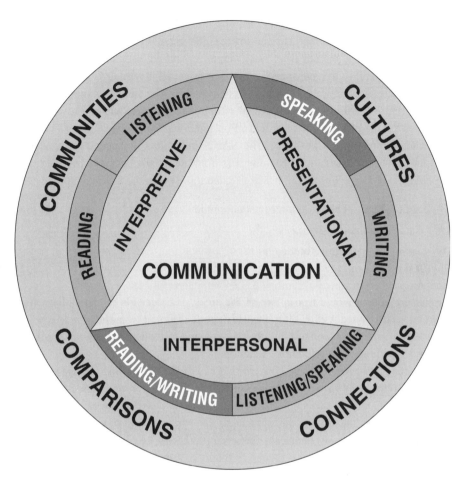

FIGURE 2 NAEP Framework.

learning in the targeted discipline at large. No student is promoted, rewarded, or punished for performance on the NAEP. Consequently, the test can be forward-looking, innovative, with direct measures, while meeting statistical standards of reliability and validity, for which assurances are run during the test development and pilot stages.

For almost a century, foreign language abilities had been defined in terms of the four skills of listening, speaking, reading, and writing. The advent of the standards presented these skills within three contexts for communication, or modes. The Framework of Communicative Modes (NSFLEP, 1996, p. 33) acknowledged that each skill exists in the real world in one of two modes at a given time. For example, listening can occur in face-to-face communication or it can be done with recorded material or as eavesdropping. For the learner, the strategies and the comprehensibility are dramatically different. In face-to-face, the listener can ask for repetition or for rewording, can gain cues from body language, and the like. When listening to a broadcast, the ability to have speech slowed or repeated is only possible with available technology, which might not always be possible. The standards then classified communication as Interpersonal (speaker/listener or reader/writer), Interpretive (Listener/Reader of a document or text), Presentational (Speaker or Writer in a context where preparation is possible). The NAEP Framework embedded the modes in its approach to the assessment—another first for a nationally designed test. Because the NAEP had a time limitation, it was decided to assess in the following modes:

- Listening and speaking in interpersonal mode;
- Listening in interpretive mode;
- Reading in interpretive mode; and
- Writing in presentational mode.

Any given student would test in two of the areas. The decision to test skills within the modes designated will result in measures quite different from the typical reading or listening comprehension test and from a speaking test where the test taker talks to a recorder without an interlocutor's reaction.

A second aspect of the framework worth noting is the effort to incorporate standard goal areas other than that of "Communication." At this point in time, direct testing of goal areas of Culture, Connections, Community was unlikely for several reasons. The time constraint for the test and the fact that NAEP is independent of a specific curriculum are two main reasons; another is that, as a profession, our experience testing culture has consisted of random "factoids" without consensus on what cultural perspectives should be assessed. Maybe by 2012 the assessment can tackle that. What the NAEP framework did propose was to build into the communicative tasks contexts and content that related to the other "Cs." It was agreed that seniors in high schools shared sufficient background knowledge in areas of daily life, school, and work that these topics would not disadvantage the student. The authentic materials that would serve as interpretive listening and reading prompts, the topics for presentational writing, and the context for the interpersonal interview would all be grounded in these areas and build upon cultural and interdisciplinary subjects, as well as community content.

Other logistical constraints limited the NAEP to one language, Spanish, and to one grade level, twelfth. The other languages would be included in an extensive background questionnaire, one for students and one for teachers. The student questionnaire contained a self-assessment instrument. Had the NAEP gone forward as planned, the background questionnaire would have generated much data for analysis.

Test parameters. Given the delay in the Spanish NAEP, it may mean that the process will need to begin all over with a new framework and new test batteries. If that occurs, it may be possible to release the items developed for the 2003 NAEP to the profession. Access to those items which were submitted to revision and piloting would permit other developers to move forward with new assessments more quickly. What were some of the innovations in the assessment? Because the test has not been released, this description is based upon public presentations during the development period.

- **Listening and speaking in interpersonal mode**. ACTFL and CAL worked on this part of the assessment. This was not just a speaking test, but it was also an interpersonal telephone interview. Students were presented with a task that had them talk with a teacher from a South American country who was interested in establishing an exchange. Prior to the call, students had an opportunity to peruse a dossier about the school, its student body, location, and so forth. They knew that in the interview, they would be asked for information about their school and have an opportunity to ask questions of the teacher. In the pilot, the interviewer playing the teacher was also briefed so that responses to student questions were reality based. The pilot demonstrated (a) that high school students are not bothered by talking on the phone as an interpersonal task; (b) that ratable language samples could be drawn; (c) that interviewers could be trained to play the role required; and (d) that the samples could be rated with a reasonable training commitment. Of course, the interview required some set-up time, but with advances in technology this should become even less of a constraint. The future will see Internet phone, Webcams, and the like make the logistics easier. The bottom line was that one could sample oral interpersonal communication and not have to settle for recorded prompts with students presenting but not interacting.

- **Reading / listening in interpretive mode**. A key word for the development was *interpretation* to replace *comprehension*. As with the standards, there was keen interest in having the prompts be authentic and worth the student's effort to interpret, react, and read between the lines. Drawing from materials that treated of daily life, school, and work narrowed the field. Passages were chosen, reviewed, dismissed, and ultimately selected. These passages represented readings that ranged from realia to short passages to essays. Instead of being designated according to narrowly defined levels, these readings were divided into three overlapping groups: novice/early level, an intermediate level, and a more advanced level. All readings were presented with a pre-reading context. This was an innovation and was meant to simulate the pre-reading instructional activity that occurs in classrooms. Answer formats consisted of multiple choice, short answer, and extended answer. This variety allowed for assessing the student's ability to interpret and provide meaning beyond what was understood in the passage. Some passages had only one type response, whereas others might have two: for example, a passage might have two multiple-choice items and a short answer.

Short answer and extended answers could be done in English, and scorers received sets of probable possible answers. While not as quick as machine-scoring, the scoring proceeded relatively quickly. Again, this assessment parallels recommended instruction in a standards-oriented communicative classroom. Listening was similar in construct, except that the materials were not authentic; this was because of the financial and administrative concerns involved with having video materials. All recorded materials were audio only and recorded in studios. With the postponement of the NAEP, this may be a factor that could be ameliorated in future testing. Web-based video prompts are more accessible now in more schools than at the time of the test development.

- **Writing in presentational mode.** Two instructional parallels were built into the writing task: an ungraded prewriting phase and authentic tasks that designated genre and audience for the writing sample. The prewriting prompt sometimes presented a chart or gave guidance on how to assemble thoughts. Data gathered from the prewriting and drafts will provide rich information for researchers into the writing process.

In sum, the NAEP assessment has numerous instances of the best of performance assessment. It reflects instructional approaches without tying to a specific curriculum. It gives the test taker fewer tasks, but these are ones to which the student can respond with thoughtfulness while demonstrating strategies as well as established knowledge. Students respond to several items per prompt, a format which allows them to follow through. It attempts to meet the parameters of authentic assessment by giving students tasks that reflect real-world activities. The test developers from AIR and ETS responded to the concerns of the foreign language educators who wanted an assessment that they could "buy into"—the developers listened and found ways to respond to psychometric issues rather than by saying "that can't be done." The best news for the profession and for future work with assessment would be the release of the test bank now, since by 2012 much will need to be changed.

Integrated Performance Assessment (IPA)

The attempt to make assessments more authentic in the tasks presented and the recognition of a constructivist approach to language learning has encouraged teacher and test developers to break with a testing system that required that each item be independent of the others. The Integrated Performance Assessment (IPA) project was funded by a federal grant to create a prototype that was capable of assessing student progress in the various modes of communication. Like the NAEP, it began with a descriptive framework that spells out principles of assessment and instruction and the nature of guidance and feedback to learners:

- Performance is effectively assessed within tasks that test learners' knowledge and skills in real-world situations, i.e., in "authentic" contexts in which students use the language in their lives both within and outside the classroom;

- Performance-based tasks require students to "do something with the language" (complete a task) and not merely "recite";

- Performance-based situations provide opportunities for students to use a repertoire of skills, areas of knowledge, and modes of communication in order to negotiate tasks; therefore the IPA features an integrated sequence of tasks reflecting the interpretive, interpersonal, and presentational modes of communication within a specific area of content (e.g., health);

- In order for students to be successful in performance assessment, they need to be aware of what their performance should look like; i.e., students should be given models of the standards we expect them to achieve;

- Performance-based assessment blends classroom instruction and experiences; i.e., it features a cyclical approach in which learners receive modeling, engage in practice, perform the assessment task, receive feedback from the teacher, engage in additional practice, perform another task, etc.;

- Assessment can improve performance if students receive feedback in their attempts to complete tasks; i.e., teachers' feedback enables students to improve their performance;

- Teacher feedback of high quality is that which provides learners with information regarding their performance as compared to model performance. Based on clearly defined criteria, teacher comments address whether the student performance "meets" the expectations for level, "exceeds" the expectations, or "is not there yet." Comments do not consist of judgmental statements such as, "That was good." (Glisan, Adair-Hauck, Koda, Sandrock, & Swender, 2003, pp. 9–10)

This set of principles encompasses many of the dimensions of performance assessment with the ultimate goal of improving student learning. In this model, teachers do "sit with" students to provide feedback, they make judgments, it is personal, criteria are given through rubrics to the student in advance, and the tasks are as authentic as one can accomplish in a classroom setting.

The IPA is based upon two essential processes. The first involves a cyclical approach (Figure 3) in which one task is being constructed from a previous one. The statistical contamination of concern in traditional tests is prevented through the feedback mechanism after each stage. Basically the cycle has the student interpret (read or listen to a text), engage in interpersonal discussion of a topic related to the text, and then present, orally or in writing, on the topic. The second process is one of building in at each stage the phases of modeling, practicing, performing, and feedback advocated by Wiggins and McTighe (1998). If the student does not adequately

> **I. Interpretive Communication Phase**
> Students listen to or read an authentic text (e.g., newspaper article, radio broadcast, etc.) and answer information as well as interpretive questions to assess comprehension. Teacher provides students with feedback on performance.

> **III. Presentational Communication Phase**
> Students engage in presentational communication by sharing their research/ideas/opinions. Sample presentational formats: speeches, drama skits, radio broadcasts, posters, brochures, essays, websites, etc.

> **II. Interpersonal Communication Phase**
> After receiving feedback regarding Interpretive Phase, students engage in interpersonal oral communication about a particular topic which relates to the interpretive text. This phase should be either audio- or videotaped.

FIGURE 3 Performance Assessment Units: A Cyclical Approach (Glisan et al., 2003, p. 18)
Source: ACTFL Assessment Project 1998

interpret the text, the feedback provided enables him or her to move on to the interpersonal task.

Finally, the IPA is a model; although the manual provides content examples, individual teachers can create their own IPAs based on course content and student interests. Teachers would assess with IPAs judiciously at key points in a semester. IPAs are time-consuming to create and to conduct, but the payoff for students is the insight they gain into their performance. A video example of students participating in an IPA can be accessed through the Teaching Foreign Languages K-12: A Library of Classroom Practices (Annenberg Learning Channel, 2004). The Video on Demand program shows third-year French students of Nancy Gadbois, Springfield (MA) School District, doing the Interpretive and Interpersonal segment of an IPA. On the Web at <http://www.learner.org/resources/series185.html>, the program can be accessed at the "Program 3, Assessment Strategies" link.

State, District, College/University Assessment Efforts

A number of states are in the process of developing assessments for their state standards. In many ways, this is an ideal place for new assessments to take root. A key factor is that states can assure that the necessary professional development accompanies their efforts. Assessments require teacher training in ways that standardized tests do not. The most a teacher can do with a standardized measure is to gain awareness of the coverage of the test either through reports from students after the test or through the sample or practice test items often released after a version of the test has been given (for example, College Board programs provide this information to teachers and students in print and on their Web site). With performance assessments, the teachers must do the observation and make the judgments according to the rubrics and scales provided. They are intimately involved in the administration and evaluation process, and they see the students' performances as they take place. The Minnesota Articulation Project (MNAP) sponsored by the Center for Advanced Research on Language Acquisition (CARLA) is one of the earliest efforts to create proficiency tests that could be used to ameliorate the transition from high school to college. It has produced a battery of tests at two levels (Intermediate Low and Mid/High on the ACTFL scale) in French, German, and Spanish. The project also published a handbook for teachers so that assessment practices in daily classrooms prepared students for the state assessment. Lentz (2005) reports that incorrect placements at the University of Minnesota have been virtually eliminated. It must be noted that the success of this effort can be traced to the collaboration and participation in development of faculty from the schools and higher education institutions.

Connecticut, New Jersey, Wisconsin, and Indiana are but a few of the states taking steps to develop assessments, to provide professional development on the topic to teachers, and to publish handbooks with samples of student work and scoring guidelines. For example, Connecticut's assessment project is one of the first to delve beyond evaluating just the communication outcomes for standards. It plans to assess culture in conjunction with social studies content and to assess connections through linkages with language arts. As the assessments are developed, the plan is to have all K-7 students have a digitized portfolio to take with them as they advance (Brown, 2005). Dissemination of state projects is generally provided on Web sites that are effective ways of sharing progress. A number of states realize that there is not a need for fifty different assessments and that duplication is a waste of time and money. Some have entered into a consortium for development of assessments; some are collaborating with National Foreign Language Centers, such as the Center for Applied Second Language Studies at the University of Oregon, or, for elementary school assessments, with CAL.

A number of large districts have received grant money to further their efforts at district-wide assessment. A key player in these cases is the presence of a district foreign language specialist, without whom the expertise is lacking. Fairfax County (VA) has developed a set of rubrics, Performance Assessment of Language Students (PALS), as well as a version for elementary age learners, Language Immersion Student Assessment (LISA). The PALS rubrics cover Speaking, Writing, Interactive, Presentational Tasks for four levels; there is also a rubric for "Fluent Speakers of Spanish." These rubrics are detailed, and for each category there are holistic and analytical rubrics, an explanation of the rubric, and a scoring guide for the analytical task. Teachers are also shown how to convert a rubric score to a grade. All information is posted on the district Web site: <http://www.fcps.edu/DIS/OHSICS/forlang/PALS/index.htm>.

In the Edison School District (NJ), Smith (2005) has used a Foreign Language Assistance Program (FLAP) grant from the federal government to develop district-wide tests on thematic units. Teachers receive stipends for summer work and have developed sets of assessment materials tied directly to their curriculum. As these are shared, they can be easily adapted by other teachers using the same text-book series or covering similar topics. However, one must caution that it is the direct involvement of the end user in the development process that is often a key to success.

In higher education, the traditional focus on wide-scale testing has been for pur-poses of placement. That has been eased with the availability of Web-based delivery systems and computer-adaptive tests with instantaneous scores that are quicker to ad-minister. The newer challenge in higher education emanates from external pressures, specifically accreditation agencies, both regional agencies (that is, Northwest, Mid-Atlantic) and the National Council on Accreditation of Teacher Education (NCATE). All the regional accrediting agencies have a standard that addresses outcomes assess-ment for majors, and institutions must meet that standard. Colleges and universities are charging faculties with developing an assessment system that is broader than grades and grade point averages. In some cases, institutions have developed a template for departments; in others, it is left to the individual discipline. To cover the various outcomes in foreign language and literature departments, the portfolio seems to be the more common choice since it lends itself to collecting data on language performance as well as literature, culture, and the like. For a description of one department's expe-rience with outcomes assessment, see Mathews and Hansen (2004). The new foreign language NCATE process begun in 2004 has been a challenge to programs preparing teachers of foreign language. The *ACTFL/NCATE Program Standards for the Prepa-ration of Foreign Language Teachers* (2002) were new to the profession when adopted. Shortly after the first programs undergoing accreditation used them, NCATE changed the program report system. Presently, departments are experiencing a double challenge: using the new standards in a new process. The process requires that all in-stitutional information be submitted through the lens of assessment. Each program submits data on seven to eight assessments. Some of the assessments are required in all disciplines (e.g., data on how teacher education candidates plan instruction); some are unique to ACTFL (e.g., evidence on teacher education candidate oral proficiency). One of the required assessments for all teacher education candidates focuses on as-sessment itself and reads:

> Required Assessment # 5: EFFECTS ON STUDENT LEARNING: Assessment that
> demonstrates candidates' knowledge, skills, and dispositions are applied in practice.
> (From the NCATE template, Section IV at <www.ncate.org>)

The six ACTFL/NCATE standards also devoted one standard to assessment in foreign languages. Standard 5: Assessment of Languages and Cultures has three supporting standards that read:

> **Standard 5.a.** Knowing assessment models and using them appropriately.
>
> **Standard 5.b.** Reflecting on assessment.
>
> **Standard 5.c.** Reporting assessment results.

Departments of foreign languages who prepare teachers need to incorporate these standards into their teacher education programs, to gather samples of good assessments, and to create templates that can be adapted for institutional use. This is a huge challenge, yet meeting it should improve the performance of new teachers in our nation's classrooms.

Classroom Teachers and Performance Assessment

For those teachers participating in state or district assessment projects, the wash back effect on their classroom assessment activity is evident. They gain confidence in making subjective evaluation fair to the student by giving constructive feedback. They understand that written tests are not the only form, or even the best form, of assessment for the outcomes they are seeking. Teachers who gain competencies in understanding what the standards really mean and who go beyond a superficial acceptance of them realize the importance of aligning assessments. Several of the useful instructional approaches they adopt are building thematic units and creating and using rubrics. Thematic units enable content to be contextualized so that performance tasks have consistency, flow, and linkage of ideas. The literature now is rich in helping teachers develop these, and the CARLA Web site <http://www.carla.umn.edu/assessment/vac/CreateUnit/e_1.html> provides a particularly clear and uncomplicated guide: Creating an Assessment Unit (n.d.). The step-by-step approach advises and explicates:

> Step 1: Review the Standards
>
> Step 2: Choose a Theme
>
> Step 3: Identify goals and objectives
>
> Step 4: Develop a performance assessment
>
> Step 5: Identify structures and functions
>
> Step 6: Identify vocabulary
>
> Step 7: Choose the instructional strategies

Note that this is in opposition to the way units were developed in the past where the syllabus began with the vocabulary and grammar to be taught and then appended a topic. This process reflects Wiggins and McTighe's (1998) backward design where

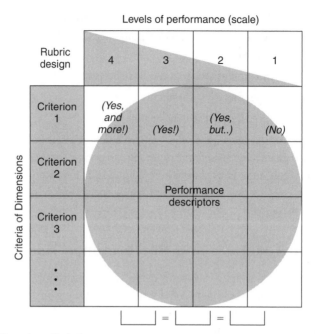

FIGURE 4 Creating Rubrics.
Source: Reproduced from CARLA Web site.

teachers need to make decisions about outcomes first and tie the language components to what is required for the performance task.

Performance assessment also requires familiarity with rubrics. For teachers who
might want to start with less complicated rubrics than those in the Fairfax County
PALS program, many examples are provided in textbooks, in curriculum guides,
and on Web sites. Teachers wanting to design their own can start with the template
(Figure 4) provided on the CARLA Web site, Creating Rubrics: <http://www.carla.
umn.edu/assessment/vac/Evaluation/p_7.html>. Full and concrete discussion helps
the teacher create a rubric appropriate to his/her students. Experimentation with
rubrics is a given, and teachers have to be prepared to revise if the students do not
understand the rubric or if the teacher finds that the rubric does not consistently
document student performance.

Keeping the Momentum: Where Might We Be in 2015?

At a two-day summit convened in spring 2005 by New Visions in Action Project in
collaboration with ACTFL and the MLA (Modern Language Association), the discussions about assessment were rich, provocative, and almost overwhelming in

terms of trying to set an agenda. Some of the priorities for a two-year plan (which will probably be a ten-year reality) included the need for assessment literacy for teachers; databases for assessment models and practices; anchors/models generated from research and pilot projects; multiple measures of assessment; research with the potential to impact policy; assessments to assist articulation at all levels; and advocacy so that assessment results support programs. The plan is for a white paper to come from the summit.

At approximately the same time as the summit, ACTFL received news of a grant award from Title IV: International Research and Studies Program. The proposal, ACTFL Assessment for Performance and Proficiency of Languages, includes in its objectives the following:

- Articulate a blueprint to assess performance and proficiency in languages on a national scale across the educational spectrum K-16;
- Create a framework appropriate for a national test;
- Develop a prototype with language-specific items; and
- Disseminate information on the project in order to inform the profession and build consensus through collaboration.

With this project and advancements at the national, state, district, and classroom levels, what might language learners experience in the year 2015?

Might students who begin their language study in the elementary schools, whether content-based FLES or immersion, exit those programs with a DVD portfolio that captures their interpersonal performance with recordings of their conversational exchanges with peers, the teacher, and a visiting native speaker? Might the DVD contain a clip of the students reading a children's book with the teacher and interpreting what it means to them? Might we see on the DVD some samples of a story they invented and a presentation they did on parents' night on a cultural celebration in a country where the language is spoken? Might the DVD contain a clip of the class during a science or geography lesson that shows they can acquire content knowledge through L2? Could this DVD be used by the middle school teacher as evidence of individual and class performance? Might students continue to build that electronic portfolio during their subsequent study of that language or create a new one as they progress through middle school, high school, and on into college?

In 2015, might there be a nationally available assessment, an outgrowth of the NAEP, but one that enables students to be articulate about their own performances in another language? Might students have experienced assessments where the results are transparent and comprehensible to them? Might they be able to say, as European language learners can with the scales available to them, "I can interact in Russian at the B2 level (Independent/Vantage stage). That means that in turn-taking, I can intervene appropriately in discussion, initiate, maintain, and end discourse appropriately although not always elegantly, that I can use stock phrases to gain time and keep my turn while determining what to say" (Council of Europe, 2001, p. 86). Might students recognize that their language instruction was built upon assessment processes consistently aimed at helping them improve regardless of communicative mode or content area?

In 2015, will the transitions between elementary, middle, high school, college, and graduate programs be smoother because of better assessments and better collaboration and increased respect among the teachers at each level? Will students interested in advanced studies or in using their language in careers have the opportunity to specialize in content areas of interest, for example, medical fields or journalism? Will our new teachers have gained the proficiency needed to teach in the language, to be comfortable using authentic materials with their students, to be culturally sensitive and aware so that they can pass on those attitudes to their students?

In 2015, will the teacher concerned with developing a theme that interests students, but for which he or she has minimal knowledge, be able to go to the Web, find a thematic unit developed by a colleague across the nation and adapt it and the accompanying performance assessment? Will the teacher who wants to find a more effective way of assessing the students' ability to read independently be able to find an assessment or a template to help in the creation of a new measure? Will there be a database of best assessment practices so that each individual, district, state does not duplicate unnecessarily?

The answer to all these questions is a tentative "maybe"! A decade after the publication of the national standards, there is widespread recognition but also uneven implementation. In many places the evidence of influence on curriculum and instruction is strong; in other places, it is superficial.

Responsible Assessment in 2015

Assessment will play an even greater role as forces for accountability and for improved learning intensify. It might be fitting to conclude this chapter with a philosophical look at what assessment means to learners and to test-makers. Wiggins (1993) and Shohamy (2001) have taken this larger perspective to insure that in the throes of creating new tests, the larger issues are not lost. Wiggins proposes an "Assessment Bill of Rights" (p. 28). He proclaims that

All students are entitled to the following:

1. Worthwhile (engaging, educative, and "authentic") intellectual problems that are validated against worthy "real-world" intellectual problems, roles, and situations

2. Clear, apt, published, and consistently applied teacher criteria in grading work and published models of excellent work that exemplifies standards

3. Minimal secrecy in testing and grading

4. Ample opportunities to produce work that they can be proud of (thus, ample opportunity in the curriculum and instruction to monitor, self-assess, and self-correct their work)

5. Assessments, not just tests: multiple and varied opportunities to display and document their achievement and options in tests that allow them to play to their strengths

6. The freedom, climate, and oversight policies necessary to question grades and test practices without fear of retribution

7. Forms of testing that allow timely opportunities for students to explain or justify answers marked as wrong but that they believe to be apt or correct

8. Genuine feedback: usable information on their strengths and weaknesses and an accurate assessment of their long-term progress toward a set of exit-level standards framed in terms of essential tasks

9. Scoring/grading policies that provide incentives and opportunities for improving performance and seeing progress against exit-level and real-world standards

Would acceptance of these premises not change assessment in 2015?

For the test maker, Shohamy (2001, pp. 146–149), in her concern for how tests are sometimes used in society, outlines five responsibilities that would result in what she calls "democratic perspectives of testing."

- *Ethical perspective*: Quoting Davies (1997), she argues for professional morality to assure that social consequences of testing are taken into consideration.

- *Making others aware*: The tester must point out to society the intentions, effects, and consequences of tests in an effort to avoid the misuse and abuse of tests.

- *All consequences*: The tester must accept responsibility for all consequences of which he or she is aware.

- *Impose sanctions*. The tester is responsible for the product and therefore must bring attention to misuse and even punish those who violate professional standards.

- *Shared responsibility and shared discourse*. Power should not remain in the hands of test makers but the test takers, test givers must enter into dialogue about issues of fairness and consequences.

Assessment plays a critical role in the lives of today's learners, today's teachers, and all the other stakeholders. The nature of the transition as we build toward more powerful performance assessments that inform us all in more significant ways will consist of steps forward and steps back—but more forward than back. The hope is that the coming decade will see advancements within a paradigm of ethical research and practice.

References

American Council on the Teaching of Foreign Languages. (1982). *ACTFL provisional proficiency guidelines.* Yonkers, NY: Author.

American Council on the Teaching of Foreign Languages. (1986). *ACTFL proficiency guidelines.* Yonkers, NY: Author.

American Council on the Teaching of Foreign Languages. (2002). *Program standards for the preparation of foreign language teachers.* Yonkers, NY: Author.

Breiner-Sanders, K. E., Lowe, P., Jr., Miles, J., & Swender, E. (2000). ACTFL proficiency guidelines—speaking, revised. *Foreign Language Annals, 33*(1), 13–18.

Brown, C. (2005). Presentation at the New Visions in Action National Assessment Summit. Alexandria, VA.

Canale, M., & Swain, M. (1980). Theoretical bases of communicative approaches to second-language teaching and testing. *Applied Linguistics, 1*(1), 1–47.

Clifford, R. T. (Ed.). (2003). Oral proficiency testing [Special issue]. *Foreign Language Annals, (36)*4.

Cohen, A. D. (1994). *Assessing language ability in the classroom* (2nd ed.). Boston: Newbury House/Heinle & Heinle.

Council of Europe, Council for Cultural Cooperation. (2001). *Common European framework of reference for languages: Learning, teaching, assessment.* Cambridge, UK: Cambridge University Press.

Cronbach, L.J. (1960). *Essentials of psychological testing* (2nd ed.). New York: Harper Collins.

Davies, A. (1997). Demands of being professional in language testing. *Language Testing, 14*(3), 328–39.

Glisan, E.W., Adair-Hauck, B., Koda, K., Sandrock, S. P., & Swender, E. (2003). *ACTFL integrated performance assessment.* Alexandria, VA: American Council on the Teaching of Foreign Languages.

International Baccalaureate Organization. (2004). *Diploma programme assessment: Principles and practice.* Cardiff, Wales: Author.

Lentz, U. (2005). Presentation at the New Visions in Action National Assessment Summit. Alexandria, VA.

Liskin-Gasparro, J. E. (1996). Assessment: From content standards to student performance. In R.C. Lafayette (Ed.), *National standards: A catalyst for reform* (pp.169–196). Lincolnwood, IL: National Textbook.

Liskin-Gasparro, J. E. (2003). The ACTFL proficiency guidelines and the oral proficiency interview: A brief history and analysis of their survival. *Foreign Language Annals, 36*(4), 483–490.

Mathews, T. J., & Hansen, C. M. (2004). Ongoing assessment of a university foreign language program. *Foreign Language Annals, 37*(4), 630–640.

National Assessment of Educational Progress. (2003). *Executive summary from the framework for the 2003 foreign language national assessment of educational progress.* Retrieved from the Center for Applied Linguistics Web site: <http://www.cal.org/flnaep/page3.html>.

National Council on the Teaching of Mathematics. (1995). *Assessment standards for school mathematics*. Reston, VA: Author.

National Standards in Foreign Language Education Project. (1996). *Standards for foreign language learning: Preparing for the 21st century*. Lawrence, KS: Allen Press.

National Standards in Foreign Language Education Project. (1999). *Standards for foreign language learning in the 21st century*. Lawrence, KS: Allen Press.

No Child Left Behind Act, PL 107-110 (2001). Retrieved from <http://www.ed.gov/policy/elsec/leg/esea02/index.html>.

Phillips, J. K. (1995). Testing. In V. Galloway & C. Herron (Eds.), *Research within reach II* (pp. 161–174). Valdosta, GA: Southern Conference on Language Teaching.

Rosenbusch, M. H. (2005). *The No Child Left Behind Act* and teaching and learning languages in U.S. schools. *Modern Language Journal, 89*(2), 250–261.

Schulz, C, (1979). *Peanuts*. New York: United Feature Syndicate.

Shohamy, E. (2001). *The power of tests: A critical perspective on the uses of language tests*. Essex, UK: Pearson Education.

Smith, M. J. (2005). Poster session presented at the Northeast Conference on the Teaching of Foreign Languages, New York.

Spolsky, B. (2000). Language testing in *The Modern Language Journal*. *Modern Language Journal, 84*(4), 536–552.

Vygotsky, L. (1978). *Mind and society: The development of higher psychological processes*. Cambridge, MA: Harvard University Press.

Vygotsky, L. (1986). *Thought and language*. Cambridge, MA: MIT Press.

Wiggins, G. P. (1993). *Assessing student performance*. San Francisco: Jossey-Bass.

Wiggins, G. P., & McTighe, J. (1998). *Understanding by design*. Alexandria, VA: Association for Supervision and Curriculum Development, 1998.

6

Teacher Leadership in a Learning Community

Anne Conzemius

Introduction: **Why Teacher Leadership? Why Now?**

Why the sudden interest in teacher leadership? Don't teachers have enough to do? Isn't a teacher's time supposed to be spent teaching? How can teachers possibly find another minute in the day to take on yet another set of responsibilities? After all, isn't leadership the job of the principal?

These are questions that are typically raised at the first mention of the idea of *teacher leadership*. They are logical concerns that reflect the prevailing paradigm of school organization and culture—that of the traditional hierarchy of management and labor. In the traditional model, one person (the principal) is in charge of making all the decisions and it is the job of the rest of the people (the teachers) to do their best to carry those decisions out within their individual classrooms. This model has actually been quite successful in the past. However, given the dramatic changes being experienced in today's educational, economic, political and social arenas, this model simply will not work anymore.

When we think about the demands facing educators today, it is easy to see why people are feeling tugged and pulled in all directions. As a system, we accept a myriad of responsibilities that extend well beyond expectations of prior decades.

"Consider the enormity of the task:

- **We must educate the whole child**—Assuring that children can read, write, and compute; know basic scientific facts and processes; are knowledgeable about history, languages, cultures, geography, social, civic, and economic issues and events; learn and apply creative expression through art, music and dance; and are physically, socially and emotionally healthy.

- **We must attend to children's daily needs**—Feeding and transporting them, providing a safe environment in which to learn, disciplining them, teaching them, and even attending to their most basic physical needs when they are not yet skilled to do so for themselves.

- **We must prepare children for all possible futures**—Preparing them to be good workers, good parents, good citizens, and good selves: they need to learn technology skills, organizational skills, communication, teamwork and conflict-resolution skills.

- **We must meet the needs of *all* children**—Educating and caring for all the children who come to school representing a full spectrum of abilities, ages, attitudes, interests, economic conditions, and experiences, including those who speak different languages and come from diverse cultural backgrounds.

- **We must meet the needs of multiple stakeholders with differing expectations**—Satisfying the needs and desires of parents, grandparents, community members, social service agency employees, politicians, and journalists, those in higher education and business, and taxpayers.

- **We must be accountable to our government**—Meeting the continuous onslaught of new initiatives and requirements that come from state and federal mandates (mostly unfunded) whether we believe they are in the best interests of the children or not." (Conzemius & O'Neill, 2002, pp. 1–2)

When viewing these demands as a whole, it is no wonder that teachers would resist what appears to be one more thing on their plates. But this list of new and emerging responsibilities also demonstrates why a new and better way to educate our children is essential. The ability to meet these demands and to sustain ongoing improvement in the face of constant change is well beyond the capacity of most current educational systems. Lambert (2002) notes, "The old model of formal, one person leadership leaves the substantial talents of teachers largely untapped. Improvements achieved under this model are not easily sustainable . . ." (p. 37).

There is a better way. Current educational dialogue seems to be converging on a powerful notion about what it means to live, learn and lead in a constantly changing world. That powerful idea is called the *learning community*. Teachers and administrators alike are talking about learning organizations, professional learning communities, collaboration, and teamwork. Oddly, these age-old concepts (some of them put forth by John Dewey) are relatively new to education, at least in terms of practice.

What Is a Learning Community?

A learning community is not a place or a thing, but a set of actions. Those actions are informed by the community's shared vision, common purpose, and goals, and they are guided by the learning that occurs when the professionals who comprise the community share their knowledge, examine and reflect upon meaningful data, and engage in dialogue meant to build common understanding. Learning communities are not defined by political jurisdictions, geographic regions, organizational by-laws, or even by structural divisions that have been created to define organizational boundaries (for example, grade levels or content areas). Learning communities are self-established, self-powered, and self-actualizing.

What differentiates a learning community from just another team? Whereas a team might define a set of behavioral norms to guide its work, the very foundation of a learning community is based on a set of core values and beliefs that not only guides the actions and behaviors of the individuals but defines the essence of the relationships within the community. Though the words may differ from one group to the next, learning communities by their very nature share responsibility, operate out of mutual respect, and bring together individuals who care deeply about one another and who put their common purpose ahead of individual need or gain. The truest test of community is how the values and beliefs are brought to life through action. For example, when the values of democracy are alive and well in schools, you can see it, feel it, and hear it in the hallways, office, and classrooms. For the adults in the community, that means active engagement in the governance and decision-making that affects what happens in their work. For the students, it means that they are authentically engaged and taking ownership for their learning and their behavior. They have learned skills for working together and adhere to a set of norms they were a part of creating. Thus, the impact of the learning community philosophy on both adults and students is direct and profound.

A learning community is not a structural entity that becomes part of yet another reform initiative. It is the venue in which teacher leadership is exercised. In a learning community, everyone is a leader and everyone is a learner. Lambert (1998) talks about leadership as energy flow, a continuous give and take of ideas and learning. "Leadership is broader than the sum total of its leaders, for it also involves an energy flow or synergy generated by those who choose to lead. It is this wave of energy and purpose that engages and pulls others into the work of leadership." (p. 5)

"Teacher leaders are those whose dreams of making a difference have either been kept alive or have been reawakened by engaging with colleagues and working within a professional culture." (Lambert, 2003, p. 33)

Lambert (1998) defines leadership as "the reciprocal learning processes that enable participants to construct and negotiate meanings leading to a shared purpose of schooling" (p. 9). Given this definition of leadership, the common purpose of the community determines the activities in which the community must engage. In high-performing, dynamic, and changing schools, the purpose of teacher leadership is improvement of student learning. Keeping students at the center of our learning and keeping us at the center of their learning is what this is all about. It is not about collaborating because we like each other or because it feels good to collaborate. If collaboration is not focused on this purpose, then it is nothing more than another time-waster on already too-full plates.

Clearly, the notions of leadership, learning, and community go hand in hand. When thought about in this way, anyone can step into the work of leadership at any time. This means that there are limitless possibilities for communities to form, and that means limitless opportunities for leadership to emerge.

The Will and Skill of Teacher Leadership

In their seminal report entitled "Successful School Restructuring," Newmann and Wehlage (1995) synthesized the results of five years of research that included more than 1500 schools across North America and field research in 44 schools in 16 states. The focus of their analysis was to determine which, if any, school restructuring initiatives made a difference in student achievement. They examined a variety of reform initiatives that included structural changes such as site-based management and teachers working in teams as well as instructional changes such as multiyear placements, various grouping strategies, and choice options for parents and students. Here is what they found:

> "While each of these reforms has some potential to advance student learning, none of them either alone or in combination, offers a sure remedy. The quality of education for children depends ultimately not on specific techniques, practices or structures, but on more basic human and social resources in a school, especially on the commitment and competence (the will and skill) of educators, and on students' efforts to learn." (Newmann and Wehlage, 1995, p.1)

"Technique and ability alone do not get you to the top—it is willpower that is the most important. This willpower you cannot buy with money or be given by others—it rises from your heart." (Junko Tabei of Japan, after becoming the first woman to climb Mt. Everest in 1975.)

Let's start with the *will*, or the commitment of educators. There is no doubt that educators as a whole come to the profession because of a strong desire to affect the lives of children in positive ways. This commitment is unwavering. But what is it that compels commitment to engage in leadership for improved student learning?

In our traditional model, it is the principal who either appoints a leader (for example, team leader, committee chair, or project coordinator) to head up a team effort. The team or committee is then charged with a series of tasks or a goal that has been set for them. Additionally they may or may not have the authority to actually make a final decision or to implement the set of recommendations they create. As Rick DuFour so cleverly states in his presentations, "If YOU build it, they will NOT come." This is why one reform effort after another has failed to sustain improvement over time. The leadership model is flawed. Even a well-intentioned and carefully constructed appointment with clearly defined tasks set out for a smart group of professionals will not guarantee the level of commitment and shared responsibility that is needed for substantial, sustained improvement.

"If schools want to enhance their organizational capacity to boost student learning, they should work on building a professional community that is characterized by shared purpose, collaborative activity and collective responsibility among staff." (Newmann & Wehlage, 1995, p. 37)

We all know that we cannot mandate leadership. We also know that some people are more inclined to step into leadership than others. Why do some teachers take initiative while others hold back and wait to be told what to do, or even resist when invited to participate? What is it about natural leaders that drives them to pursue leadership roles in spite of time constraints, setbacks, and frustrations? Are leaders born or can they be made?

"It is true that some individuals have particular personalities that lead them to take a world view different from those who choose not to lead. Research on the differences between optimists and pessimists make that clear" (Conzemius & O'Neill, 2002). Gabriel (2005) puts it this way, "There will be those who rise to the challenge and those who attempt to knock them down" (p. 21). But we need to remember that most teachers who do opt to engage in leadership find the intrinsic rewards well worth the effort: "they derive a sense of self-worth from having their voices heard, developing vision, or serving their students and colleagues" (p. 21). The challenge for the system is to create the environment where more and more teachers are experiencing these rewards on a systematic basis throughout their careers.

There is an interesting symbiotic relationship between *will* and *skill* when it comes to leadership. At a very simple level, one can see how either one without the other is not sufficient to enact effective leadership. The relationship is interdependent and is best illustrated by the literature on self-efficacy. Goleman (1995) writes,

> Developing a competency of any kind strengthens the sense of self efficacy, making a person more willing to take risks and seek out more demanding challenges. And surmounting those challenges in turn increases the sense of self-efficacy. This attitude makes people more likely to make the best use of whatever skills they may have—or do what it takes to develop them. (pp. 89–90)

The phenomenon is not unlike the proverbial chicken and egg discussion. As Fullan (1991) states, "when the changes involve a sense of mastery, excitement, and accomplishment, the incentives for trying new practices are powerful" (pp. 128–129). For the purpose of this argument, *new practices* include both instructional practices for improvement and leadership practices and opportunities.

The Work of Leadership in Community

The work of leadership in community is both broad and specific, requiring a unique set of skills, attitudes, and abilities. Whether leading grade level teams, a department, a school, or a professional organization, the work is the same. Leadership in a learning community requires the ability to

- Facilitate the creation of clear and compelling statements of vision and mission that reflect the core values and beliefs of the community.
- Lead effective meetings that engage the full range of talents and perspectives of the team.
- Facilitate the collaborative development of results-based goals and monitor them on an ongoing basis.
- Work with others to gather and make meaning of qualitative and quantitative data on student performance and staff and student satisfaction.
- Bring promising new curricular, instructional, and assessment practices to the group for consideration, study, and implementation.
- Surface underlying assumptions and causes at the root of conflicts that may keep the community from being effective.
- Build leadership capacity in others by coaching, modeling, mentoring, and providing opportunities for them to step into leadership roles.

Vision, Mission, Values, and Beliefs

Educators can no longer think only in terms of what is good enough for now. Part of becoming a learning community is being clear about where we are going together. Skillful teacher leaders facilitate the dialogue about vision and in doing so create the motivation that compels the team to pursue it. It is not an exercise in predicting the future, but one of aspiring beyond today's reality. The very act of considering possibilities and thinking about a new future generates enthusiasm and optimism. It is a positive and creative endeavor as opposed to a problem-solving endeavor. When a group is creating, they are bringing into reality that which they collectively value (Senge, 1990). This is at the heart of leadership in a learning community, and it is what will move the learning community to higher and higher levels of success in the long run.

Broadly, the mission of any school's learning community is to improve student learning. Though this statement is elegant in its simplicity, it represents a complex and difficult purpose. Thus, it is rarely enough to simply have a mission statement. The power of the mission is in its interpretation every time the community is confronted with a choice. Every discussion, every decision, and every resource expended by the community is judged against this common purpose. Thus, the leadership challenge is to keep the mission constantly in the forefront of the group's thinking and to continually test the way in which it is interpreted and operationalized by the decisions that are made.

Finally, the work of the learning community is guided by a set of core values and beliefs about "what is good enough" and "what we truly believe is possible." These values and beliefs shape the vision and guide the actions of the community. When setting its goals, the community will refer back to these values and beliefs. When faced with difficult decisions, the community will rely on its values and beliefs. And when forced to choose between maintaining the status quo and implementing a change, the values and beliefs will prevail. These are powerful discussions that cannot be taken lightly. Once the community has agreed upon its values and beliefs, it must live by them. Everyone will be watching.

Goals

We use the acronym SMART (Strategic and specific, Measurable, Attainable, Results-oriented and Time-bound) to define learning community goals. This simple formula keeps the conversation centered on student results and builds in a natural cycle for monitoring and adjusting professional practice. SMART goals incorporate the use of appropriate, accurate data, gathered from both formative and summative measures. Clear, measurable goals that are monitored on a continuous basis are the change drivers of the community's improvement efforts. Done with integrity and skill, the use of goals and data to guide collaborative improvement of instruction takes advantage of the most powerful set of tools a learning community can have.

Data

The use of data as a routine resource for teachers is still a relatively new concept. In a learning community, it is data that provide the fuel for improvement. By reflecting on data collaboratively, the learning community can make better decisions about what is working well or not and will have a more accurate picture of the impact they are having on student learning. The leadership challenge is in keeping the community focused on the right data and not jumping to conclusions or over-analyzing the results. Consequently, the skilled teacher leader will need knowledge of data sources and analytical processes, appropriate graphing and reporting techniques, and the facilitation of data dialogue as a tool for collective inquiry.

Promising Practices

Effective leadership does not mean that the individual leader must know all there is to know in the domain within which he or she leads. The best teacher leaders work with others in their community to research and experiment with new and promising instructional and leadership practices. This might include practices that are being proven effective in the classroom right next door. It also includes being willing to share the practices that are working or not working in one's own classroom. And finally, it means bringing in new resources that the group can study, discuss, and try on a limited basis rather than going full steam ahead on implementing the latest, greatest new fad. Patient, professional, and focused improvement efforts will pay large dividends in the long run. It is up to the learning community to make sure that the improvement efforts are translating into improved results.

Dialogue

Dialogue is a unique form of conversation that is characterized by a balanced flow of ideas and wonderment. The purpose of dialogue is to stimulate thinking around a variety of perspectives and to deepen the meaning of any idea before a decision is made or a solution is sought. In fact, it may be that no right answer emerges from the dialogue, but instead that a whole new series of questions, ideas, and inquiries is generated. Dialogue is an exploration of meaning through words. It is the primary vehicle for the reciprocal learning that characterizes how communities function and grow.

One useful application for dialogue is in the resolution of conflict. Dialogue balances two forces of communication, advocacy, and inquiry. Through dialogue, underlying assumptions are brought to the forefront of learning and are examined by the members as a means for better understanding each individual's perspective on any given topic or idea. Once the assumptions are surfaced, the group can see where the root of conflicts or misunderstandings might have germinated. The leadership act associated with dialogue is in modeling and using it as a tool for helping the team resolve its own issues so that it can move forward.

Effective Meetings

Time is a precious resource in schools as it is in any organization. One of the biggest time wasters in organizational life is poorly run meetings. Everyone has experienced them and can articulate what *not* to do, but it is another major step to take what we know is not working and make changes for the better. In a high-performing learning community each and every person is responsible for the meetings going well. This may not be the case at the early stages of the team's existence, but with excellent modeling and persistence on the part of the teacher leader, the group will evolve into a self-facilitating community that uses its limited time wisely. Teacher leaders who are natural facilitators will find ways to engage the entire group, balance the participation so that all voices are heard, manage the time and tasks so that there is a sense of real accomplishment, and keep the meeting focused on the essential few things that will have the greatest impact on the goals of the community.

Capacity Building

O'Neill and Conzemius (in press) examine the place of capacity building in the context of leadership in a learning community:

> Lambert (1998) defines leadership capacity as broad-based, skillful participation in the creation and fulfillment of a vision focused on student learning. High leadership capacity schools are characterized by many opportunities for everyone to engage in leadership; everyone sharing high levels of skillfulness in leadership; coordinated, aligned programs and activities; and a constant focus on improvement. The question for the emerging teacher-leader is "What can I do to contribute to building leadership capacity in my school?" Lambert outlines specific benchmarks teachers can attend to, that will grow not only their own leadership but leadership capacity in the school. Teachers should:

- Initiate new action by suggesting other ways to accomplish tasks or goals.
- Solve problems instead of asking permission and assigning blame.
- Volunteer to take responsibility for issues or tasks.
- Invite other teachers to work with them, share materials, and visit classrooms.
- Listen to each other, and particularly to new members of the staff.
- Admit to mistakes and unsolved instructional issues and ask for assistance from colleagues.
- Talk about children in a way that suggests that all children can learn.
- Become more skillful in conversations, facilitation, asking inquiry questions, and teaching.

Bringing Others Along

Peter Scholtes (1995), author of *The Team Handbook*, posits that people do not resist change so much as they resist being changed. Lambert puts it another way—people must *learn themselves* through change. Change is a learning process. It takes time and full engagement in the process to make any change happen. The question is not how we implement the change, but rather how we build a system of learning that nurtures change as a natural result of our collaborative work. If it is not already apparent, that is the work of learning communities.

Seymour Sarason once said, "Change depends on what teachers do and think; it's as simple and as complex as that" (Fullan & Stieglebauer, p. 117). "What teachers do and think is very much connected to belief systems, and belief systems in turn are shaped by evidence of effectiveness" (Conzemius & O'Neill, 2002). Michael Fullan (1991) offers a slightly more pragmatic view: ". . . personal costs in time, energy, and threat to sense of adequacy, with no evidence of benefit in return, seem to have constituted the major costs of changes in education over the past 30 years" (p. 128). Many so called *resistors* or *non-leaders* may have invested significant time and energy in previous change initiatives with poor or inadequate results and are now choosing to sit it out. The culture of the school and its support for teacher leadership clearly has a significant impact on whether it is possible to reengage those who may have opted out.

One of the significant and challenging roles of the teacher leader is that of building the community vision and belief systems that will ultimately lead to successful changes in professional practice. Facilitating broad-based participation in the change and using data to provide feedback on the effectiveness of the change will help to sustain the learning community over time. But what can teacher leaders do to pull people into the work initially? Here are some suggested strategies:

1. Start with relationship building. Initiate conversations and listen respectfully. Listen deeply to hear beyond the words. Acknowledge people's busy schedules, their fears, and their hesitations.

2. Talk enthusiastically about the vision. Help members of a group to see themselves in the vision and talk about their value as members of the learning community, being specific about what each has to offer.

3. Find the good and praise it. Recognize all the good things that have already happened as a result of each person's contribution to the school. Help all to see how engaging in a learning community can magnify their impact.

4. Share literature, books, and stories that illustrate the power of learning communities and shared responsibility for leadership.

5. Volunteer to do something for the individual that will save him or her time during the transition.

Once the learning community is established, the challenge will be in maintaining enthusiasm in the face of multiple, competing priorities. It is imperative that the leader take an active role in nurturing the ongoing development of relationships. Gabriel (2005) states, "Establishing a sense of connection, belonging, interdependence and growth will make a group more cohesive and develop community, another factor essential to your success as a leader and their efficacy as a team" (p. 108).

To nurture the growth of a team, the teacher leader can make use of the following practices:

1. Model leadership skills and behavior, model willingness to change, and model reflective practices.

2. Facilitate conversations and meetings skillfully and encourage participation.

3. Do team-building exercises (be sure there is a point to them so they are not viewed as time-wasters).

4. Ask others for specific feedback on your leadership. Make changes when they are warranted.
5. Bring food to meetings.
6. Say "thank you" often.

These are simple things that are too often taken for granted. What we sometimes forget is that teachers are human beings with real needs—both professionally and personally. We all need to feel competent in our work and to be recognized for our accomplishments. We need to feel as though we not only belong but are valued members of our community. We need to know that what we do matters. These are fundamental needs that cannot be met by getting a paycheck. They are the intrinsic motivators that keep us believing in what we do and coming back for more despite the many challenges we face each day. Palmer (1998) wrote, "If a work is mine to do it will make me glad over the long haul despite difficult days."

Summary

Leadership in the learning community brings promise of great rewards for both teachers and students alike. Organizational cultures and environments that recognize and value the leadership and learning connection will provide nourishment for teacher leadership to grow. To be effective as leaders, teachers will need to become more self-aware and more intentional about their role as teacher leaders. If they are to have significant impact on student learning, they will need to develop the will to lead by identifying a clear vision of *leadership* and clear goals for getting there. They will also need to develop the skills to lead. As Gabriel (2005) so aptly states, teachers are perfectly "positioned where all the fulcrums of change" exist in schools (p. 1). They are at the heart of the learning process; they have the most powerful perspective in terms of what changes need to occur; and they have the intrinsic drive to do what's best for kids.

References

Conzemius, A., & O'Neill, J. (2001). *Building shared responsibility for student learning.* Alexandria, VA: Association for Supervision and Curriculum Development.

Conzemius, A., & O'Neill, J. (2002). *The handbook for SMART school teams.* Bloomington, IN: National Education Service.

DuFour, R., & Eaker, R. (1998). *Professional learning communities at work.* Bloomington, IN: National Education Service.

Fullan, M., & Stieglebauer, S. (1991). *The new meaning of educational change.* New York: Teachers College Press.

Gabriel, J. (2005). *How to thrive as a teacher leader.* Alexandria, VA: Association for Supervision and Curriculum Development.

Goleman, D. (1995). *Emotional intelligence.* New York: Bantam

Lambert, L. (1998.) *Building leadership capacity in schools.* Alexandria, VA: Association for Supervision and Curriculum Development.

Lambert, L. (2002). A framework for shared leadership. *Educational Leadership, 59*(8), 37–40.

Lambert, L. (2003). *Leadership capacity for lasting improvement.* Alexandria, VA: Association for Supervision and Curriculum Development.

Newmann, F., & Wehlage, G. (1995). *Successful school restructuring.* Madison: Center for Organization and Restructuring of Schools.

Conzemius, A. & O'Neill, J. (2002). *The Power of SMART Goals: Using Goals to Improve Student Learning.* Bloomington, IN: National Education Service.

Palmer, P. (1998). *Courage to teach.* San Francisco: Jossey-Bass.

Scholtes, P. (1988). *The team handbook.* Madison: Joiner Associates/Oriel.

Senge, P. (1990). The fifth discipline: *The art and practice of the learning organization.* New York: Doubleday.

7

Foreign Language and Special Education

Sandra Brunner Evarrs
Steven E. Knotek

Special education is an outcome of a century-old legal and reform movement that came to fruition in public schools with the passage by Congress in 1975 of the Education of All Handicapped Act, PL 94-142. Special education is, simply put, focused education that arose out of a legal directive for schools and teachers to instructionally meet the educational requirements of students within ten core categories of special needs. This array of special needs is expansive, ranging from narrowly defined learning issues to visual sensory impairment to cognitive delays.

When the average person thinks of attributes that define a special education student, what terms come to mind? For many people a range of terms describing various deficits will surface, including, perhaps, *impaired*, *slow*, *dependent*, and *behavior problem*—but certainly not the word *capable*. People often see students with special needs through a black-and-white lens: either they are special education and limited, or they are regular education and competent. The reality of the situation is of course far more complex; all students have strengths and all students have areas that may benefit from improvement.

Almost all teachers make modifications to some extent so that their instruction will better fit individual students' educational needs. Teachers are often comfortable with some degree of difference among their students and make adjustments accordingly. For example, a first-grade teacher may target reading instruction so that some students receive more instruction in acquiring reading fluency, while other students receive more instruction in comprehension strategies. Likewise, students who receive special education services are not an undifferentiated amalgam of humanity. Rather, they are individual children whose unique attributes have been mandated to be taken into account when instruction is being planned. All of our students should be so lucky.

Foreign language teachers should keep the following points in mind about teaching students who receive special education services: (a) Special education is a broad legal mandate designed to impact the delivery of education to a wide variety of students, and (b) the vast majority of students receiving special education services have their core language skills intact. This chapter will review specifics of special education legal concerns, describe some of the general learning issues associated with some prominent special education categories, and offer suggestions for possible accommodations to support students' acquisition of foreign language.

117

Special Education and Legal Requirements

The Individuals with Disability Education Act (IDEA) is federally funded to assist schools to guarantee and ensure that all students with special learning requirements have access to fair and appropriate education programs. IDEA has categorized thirteen different disabilities that qualify for special education services. Despite these children's deficits they are all capable of learning and have many abilities. Students who fall under the IDEA disability spectrum comprise approximately 12% of the general school population. Of the students identified with a disability, approximately 50% of them have a learning disability (Jones, Apling, Mangan, & Smole, 2004). Key elements of IDEA are Free and Appropriate Public Education (FAPE) and the Individualized Education Plan (IEP).

Free and Appropriate Public Education

Under the IDEA all children who receive special education services are entitled to an appropriate education at no cost as directed by their individualized education program. Under the laws and court decisions, FAPE requires that an *educational benefit* be conferred upon the child. Educational benefit should be measured through both academic and social progress.

Individualized Education Program

A critically important feature of the law governing special education specifies that regular teachers, a designation which can include foreign language teachers, will be part of the team that develops each child's Indvidualized Education Program (IEP). This is especially important since the law removes barriers to placing disabled children in regular classroom settings and ties the education of children with disabilities more closely to the regular education curriculum. The current educational policy of inclusion which has been adopted in the general curriculum includes areas such as math, language arts, and science and should also include foreign language instruction.

An Individualized Education Program is a plan developed for each child receiving special education services. An IEP must include an evaluation of the child's academic performance and learning characteristics, social and emotional performance, health and physical development, annual goals, short-term objectives to meet those goals, school environment and service recommendations, a detailing of the extent to which the student will participate in other school activities, any related service recommendations, and a detailing of the extent to which the student will participate in state and citywide assessments, either with or without modifications. IEPs can be reviewed at any time upon request from any of the interested parties, and by law these must be reviewed at least once a year.

Section 504 of the Rehabilitation Act of 1973

Section 504 of the Rehabilitation Act of 1973 prohibits discrimination against students with physical and mental disabilities who attend public school (Smith, 1998). This section protects students whose physical or mental impairments substantially limit one or more *major life activities*, for example, caring for themselves, seeing, breathing, walking, and learning. This statute protects both children with physical and mental disabilities who are not and should not be receiving special education services and children receiving special education services. Section 504 requires school districts to develop and implement standards and procedures for identifying, assessing, and assuring appropriate placement of eligible students; ensure the provision of necessary individualized services and support; and train teachers and support staff to perform services or make accommodations in the classrooms. Section 504 can require administration of medication, monitoring students' physical well-being, provision of accessible facilities, use of equipment like tape recorders and calculators, counseling, and test modifications or accommodations. Both Section 504 and IDEA are available to assist students with learning problems.

Foreign Language Learning Difficulties

Many students, identified for special education services or not, have some difficulty acquiring a foreign language. Numerous theories provide possible explanations for students' learning issues; these explanantions run the gamut from auditory ability, anxiety, memory, subaverage reading ability, inability to maintain focus, and difficulties with the student's first language.

Auditory Ability

In the 1960s Paul Pimsleur, a foreign language researcher, and his colleagues found that students who experienced difficulty in foreign languages often would have deficits in *auditory ability*. This auditory ability refers to the skills in learning sound/symbol correspondences and sounds that are required to succeed in acquiring a foreign language (Pimsleur, 1968; Pimsleur, Sundland, & McIntyre, 1964). These skills are required when repeating sounds and phrases and when encoding from auditory stimulus. Difficulty with auditory rehearsal may also interfere with foreign language development. If a student is unable to distinguish phonemes, foreign language acquisition may be compromised and accuracy will be weakly developed.

Language Skills

Another theory addressing the question of why students experience foreign language learning difficulties is that the basic language skills are below grade level. Drinklage (1971) studied cases at Harvard University and hypothesized that students exhibiting differences in the foreign language requirement demonstrated a similar learning profile as individuals with dyslexia. These learning struggles included problems with discrimination of sounds and syllables, verbal memory, reading, and spelling. Symptomatology of dyslexia can cause severe learning problems in the student's first language and, in turn, will negatively affect a student's acquisition of a second.

Other Possible Causes for Foreign Language Learning Difficulties

Some of the learning deficits that may negatively impact foreign language learning are memory difficulties, high anxiety, distractibility, poor reading skills, and inability to mimic (Arries, 1999). Although an anxious student may have the abilities to acquire a foreign language successfully, the anxiety symptoms negatively impact the student's learning.

IDEA Disabilities and Foreign Language Expectations

It has been established that not all students learn foreign languages with the same ease or to the same degree of success as their peers. Differentiation of students' foreign language abilities can be further described within the range of categorical definitions found within IDEA.

These federal definitions guide how states define who is eligible for a free appropriate public education under IDEA. The definitions of disability terms and guidelines for foreign language production expectations are as follows:

Autism

Autism is a developmental disability significantly affecting verbal and nonverbal communication and social interaction, generally evident before age of three, which adversely affects educational performance. Characteristics often associated with autism are engagement in repetitive activities and stereotyped movements, resistance to changes in daily routines or the environment, and unusual responses to sensory experiences. Because of autism's negative impact on verbal and nonverbal communication, acquisition of foreign language will most likely be compromised. Some children with autism may exhibit signs of echolalia which is a repetition of sound, words, or phrases in a perseverative manner. Teachers should use caution when interpreting echolalia, as there is often a lack of purposeful meaning associated with this autistic characteristic.

Deaf-Blindness

Deaf-Blindness is concomitant hearing and visual impairments, the combination of which causes such severe communication and other developmental and educational needs that these cannot be accommodated in special education programs designed solely for children with deafness or children with blindness. These students diagnosed with Deaf-Blindness will have compromised ability to fully learn a foreign language. These students will more likely have their program concentrated on general communication and adaptive abilities.

Deafness

Deafness is a hearing impairment so severe that a child is impaired in processing linguistic information through hearing, with or without amplification, which adversely affects educational performance. The inability of these students to hear will significantly impact their foreign language acquisition. In most cases these students and their families choose to focus their educational programming within the general education curriculum.

Emotional Disturbance

An Emotional Disturbance is a condition exhibiting one or more of the following characteristics over a long period of time and to a marked degree that adversely affects a child's educational performance:

a. An inability to learn that cannot be explained by intellectual, sensory, or health factors.

b. An inability to build or maintain satisfactory interpersonal relationships with peers and teachers.

c. Inappropriate types of behavior or feelings under normal circumstances.

d. A general pervasive mood of unhappiness or depression.

e. A tendency to develop physical symptoms or fears associated with personal or school problems.

Students diagnosed with an Emotional Disturbance will most often be able to learn a foreign language with appropriate accommodations, modifications, and support. These students will often have behavior intervention plans and reinforcement programs which require utilization in every school environment, including the foreign language class.

Hearing Impairment

A Hearing Impairment is an impairment in hearing, whether permanent or fluctuating, that adversely affects a child's educational performance but that is not included under the definition of *deafness*. Students with hearing impairments can often still be included in the general foreign language courses. These students may require FM devices or monitoring of hearing assistive devices. The production of proper sound formation in foreign languages may be difficult as a result of the weakened ability to hear and mimic sounds and enunciations.

Mental Retardation

Mental Retardation is a significantly subaverage general intellectual functioning, existing concurrently with deficits in adaptive behavior and manifested during the developmental period, that adversely affects a child's educational performance. Mental retardation will negatively impact the student's ability to fully fulfill the typical requirements of a foreign language program. General language development is usually significantly delayed in these students. These students should not automatically be excluded from the foreign language curriculum simply due to their limited intellectual capacity. Often students can learn basic vocabulary and concepts with repetition and review. Teachers can choose to teach the most important words and concepts in lieu of the entire curriculum which general education students would complete.

Multiple Disabilities

Multiple Disabilities is concomitant impairments (such as mental retardation-blindness, mental retardation-orthopedic impairment, and similar co-occurring impairments), the combination of which causes such severe educational needs that these cannot be accommodated in a special education program solely for one of the impairments. Students with Multiple Impairments will most likely experience tremendous difficulty, and often teachers and parents choose to focus the student's education on more basic skills rather than have the student attempt a foreign language.

Orthopedic Impairment

An Orthopedic Impairment is a severe impairment that adversely affects a child's educational performance. The term includes impairments caused by congenital anomaly impairments, by disease, and by other factors. Most often an Orthopedic Impairment does not affect a student's intellectual and academic performance within a classroom with the exception of confounding secondary disabilities such as a Mental Impairment. These students can enroll in foreign language with very few curriculum accommodations, but they may require support in order to access appropriate equipment such as chairs, desks, keyboards, slant boards, and the like. Each student with an orthopedic impairment requires unique accommodations directly related to the specific needs.

Other Health Impairment

Other Health Impairment (OHI) is having limited strength, vitality, or alertness, including a heightened alertness to environmental stimuli that causes limited alertness with respect to the educational environment, resulting from chronic or acute health problems (for example, a heart condition, asthma, attention deficit hyperactivity disorder, epilepsy, hemophilia, leukemia, rheumatic fever, sickle cell anemia, and diabetes) and adversely affecting a child's educational performance. Due to the extreme variability of skills and deficits of these students, a general expectation regarding their foreign language production cannot be made. Most often students with OHI simply require environmental and/or medical accommodations. Each student's needs are different, and the IEP should reflect these distinctive needs.

Specific Learning Disability

A Specific Learning Disability is a disorder in one or more of the basic psychological processes involved in understanding or in using language, spoken or written, that may manifest itself in an imperfect ability to listen, think, speak, read, write, spell, or do mathematical calculations. The term includes such conditions as perceptual disabilities, dyslexia, and developmental aphasia. The term does not include learning problems that are primarily the result of visual, hearing, or motor disabilities; of mental retardation; of emotional disturbance; or of environmental, cultural, or economic disadvantage. It is important to remember that students diagnosed with learning disabilities must have at minimum an average intellectual capacity. As a group, students with diagnosed learning disabilities vary greatly in their expected foreign language production. For example, a student with a learning disability in the area of math computation may not exhibit any signs of foreign language learning difficulties; however, a student diagnosed with a reading decoding learning disability may experience tremendous difficulty in learning a foreign language. When teaching a student diagnosed with a learning disability, it is imperative that teachers learn about the student's specific learning needs, processing deficits, and strengths.

Speech or Language Impairment

A Speech or Language Impairment is a communication disorder such as stuttering, impaired articulation, language impairment, or a voice impairment that adversely affects a child's educational performance. Students with this disability will probably require some consultation between the foreign language teacher and the speech language therapist. Techniques and strategies used in speech language sessions can often be transferred to foreign language instruction. The speech language therapist can also assist the foreign language teacher in the understanding of the student's processing deficits and the overall effect of these on language production.

Traumatic Brain Injury

Traumatic Brain Injury is an acquired injury to the brain caused by an external physical force, resulting in total or partial functional disability or psychosocial impairment or both, that adversely affects a child's educational performance. The term applies to open-or closed-head injuries resulting in impairments in one or more areas, such as sensory, perceptual, and motor abilities, cognition, language, memory, attention, reasoning, abstract thinking, judgment, problem-solving, psychosocial behavior, physical functions, information processing, and speech. The term does not include brain injuries that are congenital or degenerative, nor does it include brain injuries induced by birth trauma. Often these students will exhibit an uneven language development trajectory, which may create struggles in learning a foreign language. Students who fall in this disability category can vary greatly in their intellectual abilities and academic performance; therefore students must be addressed according to their own specific abilities and deficits. Memory is often weak in these students, a weakness which in turn will impair both long-term and short-term memory retention. Accommodations and modifications applied in the general education classroom should be implemented within the foreign language environment; however, these may require some reconfiguring as a consequence of the novelty and lack of background knowledge of the specific foreign language.

Visual Impairment Including Blindness

A Visual Impairment Including Blindness is an impairment in vision that, even with correction, adversely affects a child's educational performance. The term includes both partial sight and blindness. These students have their hearing intact and therefore will be able to fully learn a foreign language with a few exceptions. Reading a foreign language will obviously be very difficult for these students. The foreign language curriculum will need to be modified in order to meet these students at their instructional level. It is most likely that students with a visual impairment will learn a foreign language through a more auditory mode of instruction.

Individualized Education Plans and Disabilities

Students can qualify for special education services under a variety of categories. When teaching a foreign language to a student who receives special education services, the teacher may find it useful to consider how aspects of the student's categorical definition can inform foreign language instruction. In fact, instructional issues related to a student's disability can be addressed within his or her IEP.

Students diagnosed with one or more of the thirteen disabilities as defined by IDEA must have an Individualized Education Plan which delineates the annual goals, accommodations, and modifications. This IEP must be reviewed at a minimum of once a year in order to update the learning goals, teaching strategies, and other elements included there. Foreign language teachers can be included as part of these annual meetings in order to provide feedback as it relates to foreign language study.

Although students may have a disability diagnosis, this identification does not define and outline their educational program. The individual's learning characteristics should guide the learning program, accommodations, and modifications. The following will review the accommodations and modifications which may be used for each developmental level. It is important to note that there are numerous students without a defined disability who would also greatly benefit from these accommodations and modifications. Delivering an academic program to a room full of unique students is a challenge. Implementing some of the listed strategies will provide a comfortable learning place for all students regardless of their academic and intellectual abilities.

Accommodations and Modifications at the Elementary/Middle School Level

Students enrolled in a second language at the elementary and middle school levels can benefit greatly from accommodations and modifications. For elementary and middle school students, these may include assessments in a distraction-free environment, provision of verbal and visual cues for vocabulary, extended wait time, opportunity for extra rehearsal of verbal responses, and allowances for poor spelling,

Accommodations and Modifications at the High School Level

Accommodations and modifications for high school students may include allowances for poor spelling, advance notice for lengthy reading assignments, extra time for reading tests, allowance of extra time for written responses, access to teacher or student lecture notes, and testing in a distraction-free environment. Transition plans from high school to college are necessary in order to continue accommodations and modifications at the college level for students with a diagnosed learning disability.

Accommodations and Modifications at the Post-Secondary Level

Students of public schools, colleges, and universities are often obligated to demonstrate a foreign language competency before they confer a degree. This institutional requisite can be very difficult and frustrating for many students demonstrating a foreign language learning deficit (Freed, 1987). These students include those with cognitive ability in the average to above average range who do not exhibit weaknesses in their other courses such as math, science, and so forth.

Section 504 of the Rehabilitation Act of 1973 protects students from discrimination in admission to college activities and programs. Colleges and universities have varied greatly in their implementation of accommodations governed by the Section 504 Act. Reportedly, college faculty noted that students with difficulties in foreign language experienced most of their problems with taking notes, completing written assignments during class, and presenting and interpreting ideas orally in class (Ganschow, Philips, & Schnieder, 2001).

There is a broad continuum of supportive services given to college students. Programs and services may include diagnostic learning assessments, advocacy, trained tutors, study skills courses, counseling, and course advising with a special services coordinator. Accommodation letters for professors are often created by the university after it has reviewed testing findings and past IEPs or 504 Plans. Additional accommodations and modifications at the college level may include picture cues, labels, modified worksheets and learning materials, allowances for mechanical errors in written work produced in class, the option to tape record lectures, the use of computer for essay tests, and testing in a separate area with minimal auditory and visual distractions.

Accommodations and Student Needs

The following accommodations and modifications can also be adapted to most developmental, grade, and intellectual levels. The foreign language teacher should choose the supportive services which would best meet the student's needs.

Classroom Environment

Classroom environment accommodations and modifications can be implemented for students demonstrating distractibility, impulsiveness, organization, and inattention. Teachers may select from the following accommodations and modifications: seat student in an area free from distractions, eliminate all unnecessary materials from student desk to reduce distractions, allow the student frequent breaks, reduce visual distractions, keep a supply of extra pencils, books, and paper in the classroom, create a checklist to help student organization, provide a study carrel or designated area when necessary, and develop an agreed upon cue for the student to leave the classroom.

Time Management and Transitions

Time management and transitions can be integrated into a student's foreign language learning program when the deficits exhibited include extended wait time, slow processing abilities, and weaknesses in listening comprehension. To address transition and time management concerns, the teacher can allow extra time for homework completion, reduce the amount of work from assignments, provide additional time to complete assignments, space short work periods with breaks, inform the student with several reminders several minutes apart before changing from one activity to the next, and provide a specific place for turning in assignments.

Presentation of Materials

A variety of presentation styles will assist students with foreign language learning difficulties who may become easily overwhelmed or distracted by large amounts of information or material. Teachers can choose from the following modifications and accommodations: provide a model of end product; number and sequence steps in a task; break long assignments into small sequential steps, monitoring each step; break assignments into segments of shorter tasks; provide written and verbal direction with visuals; check that all homework assignments are written correctly in some kind of an agenda/homework book; give alternative assignments in lieu of long written assignments; and alert student attention to key points within the written directions of the assignment through highlighting. Additionally, teachers can provide outlines, study guides, and copies of overhead notes; limit the number of concepts presented at one time; provide incentives for beginning and completing material; allow oral administration of tests; check for the student's attentiveness before beginning a lesson; explain learning expectations to the student before beginning a lesson; and allow the student to use tape recorders, computers, calculators, and dictation to obtain and retain assignment success.

Assessment, Grading, and Testing

Many students without a diagnosed disability will benefit from various modes of testing, grading, and assessment. It is important to assess what the students have learned overall and not how well they have mastered their test-taking skills. The following are suggestions for assessment grading and testing: permit retaking the test, divide the test into small sections, allow as much time as needed for completion, provide monitored breaks from the test, grade spelling separately from content, avoid timed tests, change percentage of work required for passing grade, provide a quiet setting for test taking, allow tests to be scribed if necessary, and allow oral responses. When foreign language teachers report the grade of students who have had modifications or accommodations, it is important that they clearly define the circumstances under which the student received his final grade.

Behavior

Behavior concerns are an area which all teachers, foreign language or otherwise, constantly are required to address in their classrooms. With a few clear and consistently applied interventions in place, a foreign language classroom with behavioral issues can become a positive and productive learning environment. Behavior concerns can be addressed through the following examples of intervention strategies: develop a behavior intervention plan that is realistic and easily applied, ignore attention-seeking behaviors that are not disruptive to the classroom, provide an appropriate peer role model, develop a code of conduct for the classroom and visually display it in an appropriate place where all students can see it, review the code of conduct frequently, avoid confrontations and power struggles, develop a system or code that will let the student know when behavior is not appropriate, and provide immediate reinforcers and feedback.

Teaching Approaches and Language Development

Not only can teachers support students by managing the particulars of the classroom environment, they can also adopt pedagogical approaches that allow for targeted instruction. Instructional approaches that may be useful include differentiation, inclusion, direct teaching of language form, attention to a student's learning styles, and consideration of the student's multiple intelligences.

Differentiating Instruction

Differentiation of instruction identifies each student's learning preferences and the best learning strategies to meet the student's learning needs. An instructional match is met when the curriculum and the mode of instruction are adapted to the learner so that learning can be established. Differentiation is a process that enables teachers to improve student learning by matching students' individual learning characteristics to the curriculum. Differentiation requires teachers to anticipate and acknowledge the differences in each student's readiness, interests, and learning styles. Teachers can then effectively engage students in meaningful and challenging work. Classroom teachers can challenge every student to think, work, and produce at a high level while simultaneously targeting the specific learning needs of all students.

Inclusion

Inclusion is a term often used to describe a *least restrictive environment* method of educating children who need special programming in a general education classroom in the school they would have attended if not disabled, with age appropriate peers, and with appropriate supports and services. Inclusion has brought about a change in the student composition of general education classrooms. Students with disabilities are now included in the general education classroom with their nondisabled peers as much as possible. This in turn creates a broader spectrum of abilities in a general education classroom.

Explicit Instruction and Whole Language

Overt teaching of language form was until recently considered the primary integral component of foreign language teaching curricula as reported by Stern (1983). This explicit teaching would include instruction in grammatical, sound, and sound-symbol rule systems. Teaching a foreign language through natural communication emphasizes the contextual and meaning aspects of foreign language. Javorsky, Sparks, and Ganschow (1992) disagree with the whole language approach to learning foreign language for students with learning disabilities because it does not incorporate explicit instruction in the syntactic or phonetic codes. Many second language classrooms use a whole language approach in combination with overt attention to language form.

The Orton-Gillingham teaching technique, initially used within the special education population, involves "cracking" of a language code. Students who experience difficulties with phonological and syntactic codes of language may benefit from this instructional approach. The Orton-Gillingham method uses a structured, multisensory approach in which the students simultaneously see, hear, and write sounds/symbols and are directly taught rules for grammatical structures (Ganschow, Sparks, & Javorsky, 1998). Foreign language teachers carefully sequence materials, implement controlled pacing, and integrate spelling, reading, and writing as part of the Orton-Gillingham method.

Learning styles

Visual Learners

Learning styles are simply different approaches or ways of learning. Visual learners learn through seeing. These learners need to see the teacher's body language and facial expressions to fully understand the content of a lesson. They tend to prefer sitting at the front of the classroom to avoid visual obstructions. They may think in pictures and learn best from visual displays including diagrams, illustrated text books, overhead transparencies, videos, flipcharts, and hand-outs. During a lecture or classroom discussion, visual learners often prefer to take detailed notes in order to fully absorb the information.

Auditory Learners

Auditory learners learn through listening. They learn best through verbal lectures, discussions, talking things through, and listening to what others have to say. Auditory learners interpret the underlying meanings of speech through listening to tone of voice, pitch, speed, and other nuances. Written information may have little meaning until it is heard. These learners often benefit from reading text aloud and using a tape recorder.

Tactile/Kinesthetic Learners

Tactile/kinesthetic learners learn through moving, doing, and touching. Tactile/kinesthetic persons learn best through a hands-on approach, actively exploring the physical world around them. They may find it hard to sit still for long periods of time and may become distracted by their need for activity and exploration.

Multiple Intelligences

Multiple Intelligence was conceived by Howard Gardner (1993). Multiple Intelligences are seven different ways to demonstrate intellectual ability. The seven different types of Multiple Intelligence are Visual/Spatial Intelligence, Verbal/Linguistic Intelligence, Logical/Mathematical Intelligence, Bodily/Kinesthetic Intelligence, Musical/Rhythmic Intelligence, Interpersonal Intelligence, Intrapersonal Intelligence.

Visual/Spatial Intelligence is the ability to perceive the visual. These learners tend to think in pictures and need to create vivid mental images to retain information. They enjoy looking at maps, charts, pictures, videos, and movies. Their skills include reading, writing, understanding charts and graphs, creating visual metaphors and analogies, puzzle building, manipulating images, constructing, sketching, having a good sense of direction, and interpreting visual images. Students with Visual/Spatial Intelligence may do very well with reading and writing foreign languages and with understanding visual representations.

Verbal/Linguistic Intelligence is the ability to use words and language. These learners have highly developed auditory skills and are generally elegant speakers. They think in words rather than pictures. Their skills include explaining, speaking, writing, listening, storytelling, teaching, using humor, understanding the syntax and meaning of words, and analyzing language usage. These students will most likely do very well when learning a foreign language because of their unique characteristics and skill sets.

Logical/Mathematical Intelligence is the ability to use reason, logic, and numbers. These learners think conceptually in logical and numerical patterns, making connections between pieces of information. Their skills include problem solving, working with abstract concepts to figure out the relationship of each to the other, classifying and categorizing information, performing complex mathematical calculations, and working with geometric shapes. Students with Logical/Mathematical Intelligence may experience some difficulty with certain aspects of learning a foreign language. They may benefit from a clearly defined and organized structure of the materials.

Bodily/Kinesthetic Intelligence is the ability to control body movements and handle objects skillfully. These learners express themselves through movement. They have a good sense of balance and eye-hand co-ordination. Through interacting with the space around them, they are able to remember and process information.

Their skills include the use of body language, physical coordination, sports, hands-on experimentation, miming, and the expression of emotions through the body. These students may benefit from role playing in the foreign language in order to better comprehend concepts and vocabulary.

Musical/Rhythmic Intelligence is the ability to produce and appreciate music. These musically inclined learners think in sounds, rhythms, and patterns. Their skills include singing, playing musical instruments, recognizing tonal patterns, remembering melodies, and understanding the structure and rhythm of music. Students with Musical/Rhythmic Intelligence will be able to differentiate and mimic sounds and words, a skill which will greatly benefit their learning of a foreign language. These students will also learn rapidly if foreign language is put to music or rhythmic beats.

Interpersonal Intelligence is the ability to relate to and understand others. These learners try to see things from other people's point of view in order to understand how they think and feel. They often have an uncanny ability to sense feelings, intentions, and motivations. Generally they try to maintain peace in group settings and encourage cooperation. They use both verbal and non-verbal language to open communication channels with others. Their skills include listening, seeing things from the perspectives of others, understanding other people's moods and feelings, counseling, cooperating with groups, using empathy, communicating both verbally and nonverbally, and establishing positive relations with other people. These students are an asset to the classroom environment when completing group projects or community learning groups.

Intrapersonal Intelligence is the ability to self-reflect and be aware of one's inner state of being. These learners try to understand their inner feelings, dreams, relationships with others, and their own strengths and weaknesses. Their skills include reflecting and analyzing themselves, evaluating their thinking patterns, recognizing strengths and weaknesses, and understanding their role in relationship to others. Students with Intrapersonal Intelligence may be able to better understand when they are experiencing difficulty with learning new concepts and are then able to ask for assistance and support.

Case Example of a Foreign Language Program at the Middle School Level

A suburban school in Chicago begins its foreign language program in the fifth grade. Students and their parents can choose from Latin, German, Spanish, and French. These foreign language courses are taught through the twelfth grade in this school district so that the students can experience eight years of continuity in their foreign language acquisition. All students not diagnosed with a disability must take a foreign language of their choice as part of their courseload requirement starting in the fifth grade. Students diagnosed with a disability have the option of taking a study hall in lieu of a foreign language. If these students enroll in the study hall in the fifth grade, they will not have the option to enroll in a foreign language until the ninth grade. Typically students diagnosed with a disability will have a trial run in a foreign language in the fifth grade and will often transfer to a study hall by the second semester. Typically, teaching strategies and accommodations that are provided to these students in all other courses are not provided to them in foreign language, and the students are expected to succeed on their own without any assistance. According to the school district, these IEP-mandated accommodations were not required in foreign language at the fifth-grade level because foreign language is not a requirement for grade promotion. If these students were provided with some of the simple accommodations and modifications as defined in their IEP, they probably would be successful in their foreign language acquisition—just as they are in many other subjects. This is an example consistent with what many special education students endure when they attempt the study of a foreign language.

Conclusion

Today as a nation we are still working to find the pedagogical and instructional means to fully support students who receive special education services. Although we do not have all the instructional answers or, in many cases, even fully understand the basic questions related to learning issues of special education students, we have begun to realize that students with disabilities are not a "them" distinct from an "us." All students have a range of abilities and needs, and we need to provide a continuum of instructional practices to effectively meet and engage each student at his or her current level. If we truly embrace the notion that all students can learn, we will continue to expect students to succeed when they are presented with targeted instruction that meets them at their instructional level. Language is a unique human endowment, and special education students can benefit from instruction in a foreign language.

References

Arries, J. (1999). Learning disabilities and foreign languages: A curriculum approach to the design of inclusive courses. *Modern Language Journal, 83*(4), 98–110.

Drinklage, K. (1971). Inability to learn a foreign language. In G. Blaine & C. McArthur (Eds.). *Emotional problems of the student* (pp. 185–206). New York: Appleton-Century Crafts.

Freed, B. (1987). Exemptions from the foreign language requirement: A review of recent literature, problems, and policy. *ADFL Bulletin, 18*, 13–17.

Ganschow, L., Philips, L., & Schneider, E. (2001). Closing the gap: Accommodating students with language learning disabilities in college. *Topics in Language Disorders, 21*, 17–37.

Ganschow, L., Sparks, R. L., & Javorsky, J. (1998). Foreign language learning difficulties: An historical perspective. *Journal of Learning Disabilities, 31*, 248–58.

Gardner, H. (1993). *Multiple intelligences: The theory in practice.* New York: Basic Books.

Javorsky, J., Sparks, R. L., & Ganschow, L. (1992). Perceptions of college students with and without specific learning disabilities about foreign language courses. *Learning Disabilities Research & Practice, 7*, 31–44.

Jones, N. L., Apling, R. N., Mangan, B. F., & Smole, D. P. (2004). *Individuals with Disabilities Education Act (IDEA): Background and issues.* Hauppauge, New York: Nova Science.

Pimsleur, P. (1968). Language aptitude testing. In A. Davies (Ed.), *Language testing symposium: A linguistic approach* (pp. 98–106). London: Oxford University Press.

Pimsleur, P., Sundland, D., & McIntyre, R. (1964). Underachievement in foreign language learning. *International Review of Applied Linguistics, 2*, 113–150.

Smith, T. E., & Patton, J. R. (1998). *Section 504 and public schools: A practical guide for determining eligibility, developing accommodation plans, and documenting compliance, with forms.* Austin, Texas: Pro-Ed.

Sparks, R. (2001). Foreign language learning problems of students classified as learning disabled and non-learning disabled: Is there a difference? *Topics in Language Disorders, 21*, 38–54.

Stern, H. (1983). *Fundamental concepts of language teaching.* Oxford, England: Oxford University Press.

8

Toward an Ecological Vision of *Languages for All*: The Place of Heritage Languages

Guadalupe Valdés

Traditionally, the foreign language teaching profession in the United States has been concerned with teaching foreign or non-English languages to monolingual speakers of English. Although some school districts provide foreign language classes in elementary school (grades K-5), for many American students, the academic study of foreign languages begins during the middle-school years. At some schools, students can choose to study only a commonly-taught modern language such as Spanish, French, or German. At other schools, the selection of languages includes less commonly taught languages (for example, Japanese or Russian) and classical languages (Latin, for instance). At most schools, students can continue to study the selected language through the 8th grade.

The majority of students who study foreign languages, however, begin the study of Spanish, German, French, Russian, and, more recently, Japanese or Chinese in the 9th grade. Although foreign language study is not required for high school graduation, it is an entrance requirement for some colleges and universities. In California, for example, the campuses of the University of California require three years of foreign language study, and the campuses of the California State University system require only two years of a foreign language.

At the secondary level, foreign language study is seen as a college-preparatory experience of interest primarily to mainstream, middle-class, English-speaking monolinguals. Students who enroll in foreign language courses are typically academically competent and—even if not particularly interested in becoming proficient in the language studied—interested in obtaining good grades. At most high schools, courses offered in the commonly taught languages (for example, Spanish), include four full-year courses (typically, Spanish 1, Spanish 2, Spanish 3, Spanish 4). Additionally, one or two courses are offered to prepare students for Advanced Placement (AP) examinations in either literature or language. A select group of often monolingual, English-speaking students who begin the study of a foreign language in middle school or who are highly motivated enroll in AP courses and obtain college credit for foreign language study.

Foreign language study can also continue or begin at the college and university level. Students who have not studied a foreign language in middle school and high school can enroll in first-year and subsequent language courses at the college level.

Typically these students do so either for personal enrichment or to meet general education requirements. Many colleges and universities, even those that do not have a foreign language entrance requirement, have a one- or two-year foreign language requirement for graduation. At most colleges and universities, language departments administer placement examinations in order to guide students to appropriate courses. The fall 2000 survey of foreign language enrollments in institutions of higher education (Wells, 2004) reveals that among the 2,519 institutions responding, Spanish is the language with the highest enrollments, followed by French, German, Italian, American Sign Language, Japanese, Chinese, Latin, and Russian.

In general, foreign language students in the United States have primarily been fluent speakers of English who have elected to pursue foreign languages as academic subjects. While it is clear that a significant number of these students have probably been speakers of languages other than English, until about twenty years ago it had not been common for these students to enroll in the study of languages that they already spoke. Italian background students who were fluent in Italian, for example, might study Spanish or French. Spanish background students might be encouraged to study Portuguese, and Polish background students, to study Russian. In terms of "foreign" language study, students were limited to the menu of commonly taught languages offered in schools. The maintenance or development of languages already spoken by youngsters outside of school—when considered at all— was seen as the responsibility of the home and the community. As a result, traditional foreign language programs have been designed for beginners who have no background in the language to be studied. Such students have been expected to move from a state of zero proficiency to more advanced stages of learning or acquisition. Unfortunately, given national attitudes toward non-English languages and long-standing traditions of monolingualism, most American students have not aspired to develop high level professional proficiencies in the non-English languages (Haugen, 1972; Lambert, 1986; Tucker, 1984, 1991; Valdés, 1988, 2003). Many have abandoned the study of language once they have fulfilled limited language requirements for other programs of study.

Beyond the Traditional Study of Foreign Languages in the United States

At different times and for different reasons a number of individuals have publicly criticized the foreign language-teaching profession. In 1986, for example, Lambert (1986, 1987) argued for the establishment of a national agenda on foreign language instruction that could meet the "increasing challenge of internalization" (Lambert, 1986, p. 7) and that would engage in central planning and coordinating of existing scattered efforts in language teaching. From Lambert's (1986) perspective, the problem was systemic:

> It is various aspects of the system as a whole that present the problem: too limited time given to language acquisition; too many students dragging their feet in learning a skill whose utility to them is, at best, unclear; the low average level of foreign language competency of too many teachers; the compartmentalization of instruction by semesters and between primary, secondary, and tertiary schools; the lack of a way to measure well just how much competency a student really has acquired. Thus, while we welcome the growing foreign language course enrollments and requirements as recognition of the importance of foreign language competence, putting more and more students through, and pouring more and more resources into, the current foreign language teaching system will not solve the national problem. (p. 10)

For Lambert, what was needed was a national effort that focused on the importance of language, that carried out needed research on effective language pedagogies, that developed a needed common metric, and that broadly took on the examination of the specific non-English language demands facing business and national defense.

Many years later, we are once again concerned about this country's ability to develop the non-English language competencies needed for national defense. The events of September 11th made evident what Brecht and Rivers (2002) have referred to as a "language crisis" surrounding national security. What is new and different is that in the last several years, there has been an increasing interest by the intelligence and military communities (Müller, 2002) in expanding the nation's linguistic resources by both teaching non-English languages and by maintaining the heritage or home languages of the 47 million individuals who reported speaking both English and a non-English language in the latest census (U.S. Census Bureau, 2003). For many individuals concerned about language resources, the development of strategic languages can only be brought about by expanding the mission of departments of foreign languages to include the maintenance and expansion of the varieties of non-English languages currently spoken by immigrants, refugees, and their children.

The mention of heritage languages is of special importance to the language teaching profession because *deep values* within our society (Ricento, 1998) have traditionally rejected the idea that the maintenance of either immigrant or indigenous languages is intrinsically, socially, or economically valuable. In spite of the presence of persons who continue to speak non-English languages in this country, our position as a society has been to ignore available non-English language resources and to assume that the loss of ethnic languages is part of the price to be paid for becoming American. Bilingualism, as Haugen (1972) argued, has been seen, not as a characteristic of an educated citizenry, but as a characteristic of the poor and disadvantaged. Many argue that the United States does not produce large numbers of individuals who are fluent and competent in foreign languages because negative attitudes toward bilingualism are deeply embedded in what Schiffman (1996) has termed "American linguistic culture." According to Schiffman, English has been established as the dominant language in the United States by a "masked language policy" in place from the beginning of the colonial period. Schiffman (p. 234) argues that covert policies toward language have maintained that English is the language of liberty, freedom, justice, and American ideals; that non-English languages are the languages of tyranny, oppression, injustice, and un-Americanness; that children cannot learn American ideals through non-English languages; and that bilingualism is bad for children and should be discouraged in schools.

The purpose of this paper is to explore an ecological vision of *languages for all* in the United States that moves beyond the current academic goals of language teaching and learning and that views the expansion of heritage language resources as involving a close connection between families, communities, and the interests and concerns of language teaching professionals who hope to contribute to the development of a language competent society (Tucker, 1984). I first review current definitions of heritage language learners and present a brief overview of work carried out to date in the teaching of heritage languages. I then argue for an ecological vision of languages and suggest ways in which the language teaching profession can involve itself in the maintenance and development of such languages.

Heritage Students: The Problem of Definition

As pointed out above, traditionally, students of immigrant background who had developed some proficiencies in the languages commonly taught in schools did not enroll in beginning or even intermediate "foreign language" classes. Often the assumption was that these students did not need additional instruction in a language they already spoke. Often, too, there was a perception that immigrant students—even those who were fluent in English—still needed to focus on developing their English.

Given traditional views about the purposes and goals of foreign language teaching, teachers therefore did not encounter large numbers of heritage students of "foreign" or world languages in their classes until the mid-seventies. During the seventies, largely because of open enrollment policies in colleges and universities, a significant number of Latino Spanish-speaking students began to enroll in Spanish classes originally designed for beginning students of the language. To differentiate these non-traditional language students from traditional foreign language students, members of the profession referred to them using a variety of terms. When special courses were designed to meet the different needs of students who understood and spoke the target language, they were often given titles such as Spanish for bilingual students, Spanish for native–speakers (SNS), and Spanish for home-background speakers (SHBS).

Currently, the foreign language teaching profession in the United States now uses the term *heritage students* to refer to students of a target language who have been raised in homes where that non-English target language is spoken, who may speak or merely understand the target language, and who are to some degree bilingual in English and the heritage (target) language. For foreign language teaching professionals, the term refers to a group of young people who are different in important ways from English-speaking monolingual students who have traditionally undertaken the study of foreign languages in American schools and colleges. This difference has to do with *actually developed functional proficiencies* in the heritage language.

It is important to point out that within the foreign language-teaching profession the use of the term *heritage speaker* is relatively new. Its use was generalized for the first time in the *Standards for Foreign Language Learning* (American Council on the Teaching of Foreign Languages [ACTFL], 1996). Up until that time, Spanish instructors were the only members of the foreign language teaching profession who had worked with large numbers of students who already understood and spoke the language that they taught. A dissatisfaction with the terms used by the Spanish-teaching profession (for example, *quasi-native speaker*, *bilingual speaker*) led to increased use of other terms such as *home background speakers* (as used in Australia) and *heritage language speakers* (as used in Canada).

The term *heritage language student* is not unproblematic. For individuals interested in the strengthening of endangered indigenous languages or in the maintenance of immigrant languages that are and are not normally taught in school, the term *heritage language* refers to a language with which individuals have a personal historical connection (Fishman, 2001). It is the historical and personal connection to the language that is salient and not the actual proficiency of individual students. Navajo and Armenian, for example, would be considered heritage languages for American students of Navajo or Armenian ancestry even if such students were themselves English-speaking monolinguals. In terms of strengthening and preserving Navajo or Armenian in this country, such heritage students would be seen as having an important personal connection with the language and an investment in maintaining the language for future generations. Their motivation for studying Navajo or Armenian would thus contrast significantly with that of typical students of foreign languages. In terms of proficiency, however, they would be similar to beginning students of non-English languages.

The expression *heritage student*, then, rather than being a precise scientific term, is best thought of as an umbrella phrase which, as is illustrated in Figure 1, includes students who have a high personal connection with a particular group but who may or may not be proficient in the group's language. It is evident, however, that from a pedagogical perspective, it is proficient heritage students that present the most significant challenges to the language teaching profession. This is especially

+Personal Connection	+Proficient
	−Proficient

FIGURE 1 Heritage Students.

the case because heritage students vary widely in the types of proficiencies they develop in different types of communities.[1]

Heritage Language Teaching: Where Are We and Where Have We Been?

Over the past thirty years, a great deal of work has been carried out on the teaching of heritage languages, especially on the teaching of Spanish, in regular foreign language classrooms. Because of space limitations, I offer here only a broad overview of this work and refer the reader to Colombi and Roca (2003), Valdés (1995), and Valdés, Fishman, Chávez, and Pérez (in press) for more complete discussion of major trends and tendencies.

Work on the teaching of heritage languages began in the mid-seventies, at which time a number of individuals working in Spanish sought to define the field by examining the difference between foreign language and native language teaching. During the 1970s and the 1980s much attention was given to the characteristics of the Spanish language of heritage students, to concerns and questions surrounding the teaching of the standard language, and to classroom practices that appeared to be successful. By the late 1980s, however, it became clear that the problems surrounding the teaching of Spanish to bilingual speakers had not been solved. Few materials were available for the secondary level, and younger college faculty, trained primarily in Peninsular and Latin American literature, found themselves facing the same problems that others had faced a decade before. The profession had changed as well. The emphasis in foreign language teaching had shifted away from grammar-based instruction to a proficiency orientation, and there was much confusion about the right kinds of instruction and assessment. By the late 1980s and early 1990s, articles began to appear that examined old issues in new ways or that posed new questions: for example, the use of the oral proficiency interview with bilingual students (Valdés, 1989); the question of dialect and standard (Hidalgo, 1987, 1993; Politzer, 1993); the role of foreign language teachers in teaching bilingual students (Merino et al., 1993); the relationship between theory and practice (Merino, Trueba, &

---

[1] For a discussion of this point, the reader is referred to Valdés (1992) and Valdés (2001).

Samaniego, 1993); and the role of the foreign language teaching profession in maintaining minority languages (Valdés, 1992).

Beginning in the 1990s and continuing today, professional activities focusing on the teaching of heritage languages have increased enormously. The American Association of Teachers of Spanish and Portuguese (AATSP) initiated its Professional Development Series Handbooks for Teachers K-16 with *Volume I: Spanish for Native Speakers* (2000). The National Foreign Language Center (NFLC) in cooperation with AATSP developed a language-based resource, *Recursos para la Enseñanza y el Aprendizaje de las Culturas Hispanas* (REACH) <http://www.nflc.org/REACH/>, for teachers of Spanish to heritage speakers. NFLC also developed *LangNet*, a searchable database that includes Spanish and contains numerous resources for the teaching of heritage languages. In collaboration with AATSP, the NFLC also conducted a survey of Spanish language programs for native speakers (Ingold, Rivers, Tesser, & Ashby, 2002). The Center for Applied Linguistics and the NFLC launched the Alliance for the Advancement of Heritage Languages <http://www.cal.org/heritage/>. The Alliance sponsored two national conferences in 1999 and 2002 on the teaching of heritage languages; these conferences drew the participation of many language teaching professionals outside of Spanish. The first conference fostered the publication of the volume *Heritage Languages in America* (Peyton, Ranard, & McGinnis, 2001), in which much attention was given to the teaching of uncommonly taught languages, as well as the publication of a special issue of the *Bilingual Research Journal* focusing on heritage languages (Wiley & Valdés, 2000). The second conference led to the publication of a report on research priorities on the teaching of heritage languages entitled *Directions in Research: Intergenerational Transmission of Heritage Languages* (Campbell & Christian, 2003).

Collections of articles and articles in edited books and journals focusing on the teaching of Spanish as a heritage language continue to appear. For example, *Mi lengua* (Roca & Colombi, 2003) includes a range of articles on such topics as student characteristics (Carriera, 2003), revitalization versus eradication of students' varieties of Spanish (Bernal-Enriquez & Hernandez Chavez, 2003), language attitudes (Beckstead & Toribio, 2003), and theoretical principles guiding the teaching of Spanish to heritage speakers (Lynch, 2003; Valdés, in press; Valdés et al., in press).

In comparison to other heritage languages (for example, Arabic and Farsi) and even languages that are taught more commonly (such as Chinese and Japanese), the teaching of Spanish to heritage speakers is well established within secondary and postsecondary programs. However, as a recent survey and institutional study of Spanish heritage programs in California determined (Valdés et al., in press), Spanish heritage language programs have been established to respond to institutional challenges in serving an increasing population of Spanish-speaking students. No evidence was found to suggest that high schools or colleges and universities offering such programs see themselves as engaged in the process of maintaining or developing languages for professional purposes. Heritage programs (sequences of language courses or single courses) are designed to be part of existing Spanish language and literature programs. They focus on achieving traditional academic goals in the study of foreign languages and literatures.

Sadly for those who might have hoped that heritage language study might result in the development of lifelong professional strengths, the study of Spanish heritage language secondary and postsecondary programs in California suggests that an expectation that formal language programs as currently configured can and will contribute to Spanish language maintenance and development is misguided. Educational institutions do not see their role as providing support for such efforts. Rather, they see themselves as engaged in the teaching of a core curriculum centering upon the study of grammar and literature. At the high school level, the most that teachers can aspire to is having students do well on Advanced Placement examinations designed to offer college credit to traditional students of foreign languages who enter college and university departments of foreign language. In the California high schools studied, heritage students are first and foremost high school students whose success is measured, not by their ability to use Spanish extensively for a variety of purposes or by the progress they make in expanding their (colloquial and academic) range in two languages, but by their ability to sit quietly in class, to complete assignments, to do well on tests and quizzes on aspects of grammar taught to foreign language learners, and, possibly, to speak a variety of Spanish identified by their teachers as the standard. At the college/university level, faculty see themselves as either providing courses through which students fulfill a general education requirement in language or as preparing students who will major in Spanish and possibly carry out graduate work in Spanish or Latin American literature. At both the high school and college/university levels, there is a serious disconnect between what counts as success in the educational context and what those concerned about maintaining and developing heritage languages hypothesize is essential for the continued professional use of those languages in a real-world context.

While much has been written about Spanish heritage programs, there is a great deal that we do not know about the role of schools in language maintenance and language shift, about ways of measuring progress in the re-acquisition or revitalization of heritage languages, and about the most important differences between L1 and L2 learners. The scholars (e.g., Macias, Wong Fillmore, Wiley, Hornberger, LoBianco) who contributed to the research agenda created at the second national heritage conference, stated in Campbell and Christian (2003) that we need to understand the external pressures that heritage speakers are subjected to in this country, the ways in which language ideologies interact with particular pedagogical goals, and the ways in which measurement procedures can engage both community and academic norms. In establishing research directions for the study of intergenerational transmission of heritage languages, Campbell and Christian point out that numerous questions must be attended to by the research community if the formal educational system is to succeed in its efforts to maintain heritage languages.

Other Efforts to Teach Heritage and Community Languages

In many countries around the world, indigenous and immigrant languages have been taught in formal classroom settings under different conditions: (a) they have been taught by members of indigenous or immigrant communities themselves either after school or on the weekend; (b) they have been taught during the school day or after school by personnel directly contracted by the school district for that purpose; and (c) they have been taught as regular school subjects.[2]

Instruction in community languages offered by linguistic indigenous or immigrant communities themselves has had as its purpose *maintaining* or *reviving* the mother-tongue skills of students who have already acquired the wider societal language. In general, only groups who have strong feelings about maintaining the ethnic-language abilities of their children offer classes or programs to students of varying degrees of bilinguality. Additionally, such schools offer instruction in culture including religious/traditional customs, ceremonies, and texts. Examples of such groups and programs include Chinese, Korean, Armenian, Japanese, and Greek Saturday schools and after-school programs in the United States.[3] Language instruction in such programs frequently assumes that students have oral skills developed by using the language with family members and concentrates on developing reading and writing abilities in the language in question.

Instruction carried out by school personnel, either regular or specially contracted teachers, in after-school programs has been offered as a first step in responding to communities' concern about the status and long-term viability of one or several ethnic or heritage languages. In Canada, for example, a number of provincial governments set up such programs. At some schools, courses were open to students who spoke or understood the ethnic or heritage language as well as to students who had no background whatsoever in the ethnic language. Research on the outcomes and the specific methodologies and pedagogies used in these efforts beyond those studies conducted by Cummins (1984) and Danesi (1986) would be particularly useful for foreign language educators in the United States who hope to bring together heritage and non-heritage learners. As Danesi (1986, p. 3) points out, most research carried out on the teaching and learning of ancestral languages in Canadian schools has focused on the acquisition of English and has been guided by

---

[2] Valdés (1995) offers examples of these various initiatives.
[3] For a listing and description of such programs, the reader is referred to Fishman & Markham (1979) and Fishman (1985).

the following questions: (a) what effects do heritage language programs have on the learning of the dominant language or languages, and (b) how do heritage language programs affect overall academic performance and cognitive development? While interesting, this research does not contribute to our knowledge about the maintenance and development of heritage languages.

Situating heritage languages within the academic establishment has also entailed efforts that do not involve classroom instruction. In some cases, communities have been successful in positioning their languages as core or examination subjects within the curriculum. For example, the Korean community in the United States played an important role in establishing a Korean SAT II examination. This examination allows students to present their knowledge of a language that is uncommonly taught in the U.S. as evidence of academic achievement. Similarly, the Navajo community in New Mexico was successful in having the Navajo language accepted as one of the languages with which students could meet the University of New Mexico's language requirement. The careful study of both of these efforts would shed much light on the language background of students who do well on such examinations and on the kinds of proficiencies that can be measured successfully.

Promoting and Developing Language Resources: Toward an Ecological Perspective

To date the teaching of non-English languages in K-16 settings in this country has been characterized by efforts that reflect our nation's history as well as widespread ideologies that value the study of particular languages over others. For the better part of the 20th century, we neatly divided world languages into the commonly and uncommonly taught languages depending on their presence in the American curriculum, and toward the end of the century we were surprised at the waning interest in some of these core languages (for example, German). To our credit, over time we have expanded our menu of language choices at the secondary level to include uncommonly taught languages thought to be important during a particular period. During the Cold War era, for example, we included Russian among the languages available in high schools, and more recently we have added both Japanese and Chinese. The inclusion of these two latter languages probably reflects the position of Japan in the world of business during the 1980s and 1990s as well as the currently increasing interest in China by monolingual Euro-American students and by students of Chinese ancestry.

The question for the foreign language teaching profession at this point is to what degree can and should the language menu be expanded. Should it include what Gambhir (2001) has referred to as the *truly uncommonly taught languages* because there are communities of heritage speakers in this country who wish to maintain their heritage languages? Or should it expand only to those languages currently identified as *critical languages* by the National Flagship Language Initiative:[4] Arabic, Chinese, Hindi, Korean, Persian, Russian, and Turkish? Or should we leave the K-12 language menu alone and depend on institutions of higher education and government agencies to "address the urgent and growing need for significantly higher levels of language competency among a broader cross-section of professionals, particularly for those who will join Federal agencies"?[5] Finally, should we care at all about indigenous languages that are currently endangered, or should we only care about maintaining or developing those languages that are still broadly spoken?

The questions are many and the answers complex. I suggest, however, that responding to them will require that we move outside existing professional compartments and the traditional academic goals of language study. What is needed is an ecological vision of languages in the United States within which we understand the value of non-English languages in our society and the challenges involved in attempting to re-teach the languages that have undergone language shift.[6] An ecological perspective would invite us to examine not only the numbers of speakers of each language spoken in this country by both indigenous and immigrant groups, but also, as Haugen (1972) proposed, the domains of use of each language, the level of bilingualism present in communities, the internal varieties of each language, their written tradition, the attitudes of speakers toward their language, and, in Fishman's (1991) terms, their position on the Graded Intergenerational Disruption Scale (GIDS).[7] An ecological perspective would also inform vision statements guiding the activities of professional language organizations such as ACTFL. The vision statements and initiatives of such organizations would include a visualization of a world and a society that moves us outside of our traditional sphere as teachers of a limited number of non-English languages to students who do not have a background in those languages and would help us to imagine ourselves as working in a context in which language does not belong to teachers and to schools primarily or exclusively, but instead is part of a patrimony that we all nurture. Schools will not be able to teach all languages to all students, but a vision of *languages for all* must encompass advocacy for languages that we do not teach, for languages that only small indigenous communities speak, and for languages of recent immigrant groups that carry with them the values and experiences of a people.

---

[4] A description of this initiative can be found at <http://www.casl.umd.edu/nfli/>.

[5] The reader is referred to <http://www.casl.umd.edu/nfli/mission.shtml>.

[6] Language shift is defined as the change in the patterns of habitual language use by a community of speakers that involves the decreased use or abandonment of the original language of the group and the increased use of the societal or prestige language of the surrounding broader community.

[7] The Graded Intergenerational Disruption Scale (GIDS) (Fishman, 1991) describes eight stages of language disruption that can be used to determine level of abandonment of community language. In communities at Stage 8, for example, the original language is spoken only by socially isolated elders. According to Fishman, efforts to revitalize languages that have reached Stage 8 are very difficult because intergenerational transmission of those languages is no longer possible.

Times of Possibility

For heritage languages in the United States, these are times of possibility. There has been an increasing interest in the teaching of indigenous and immigrant ancestral or heritage languages not only from language-teaching professionals but also from other educators committed to the maintenance of non-English languages in this country. For the first time, individuals who teach both commonly- and less commonly-taught languages at both the secondary and postsecondary levels have come into contact with individuals who through immersion programs, dual immersion programs, and community-based language schools are working to develop the next generation's proficiencies in both indigenous and immigrant languages. For the first time also, professionals engaged in the teaching of such languages as Spanish and French have found themselves in conversations with teachers of Bengali, Zulu, and Khmer (Gambhir, 2001). More importantly, perhaps, the solicitation for the Chinese K-16 Pipeline Project by the National Foreign Language Initiative in 2005 suggests that a long program in Chinese whose aim is "to produce students with professional proficiency (level 3 and beyond) in critical languages, where the individual is capable of, for example, speaking with sufficient accuracy and vocabulary to participate effectively in most formal and informal conversations on practical, social, and professional topics" (National Security Education Program [NSEP], 2005, p. 4) will include heritage students of Chinese. The solicitation directly requires the "identification of pre-existing populations in these K-12 environments that are committed to the study of Chinese" (NSEP, 2005, p. 6).

Some individuals dare to be optimistic about the development of a coherent language-in-education policy that can support efforts to revitalize and maintain non-English languages (whether or not these languages are momentarily strategic) using the resources of existing educational institutions. In spite of Fishman's (1991) cautionary statements concerning the limitations of educational institutions in reversing language shift, many individuals—including newly-funded national defense grantees—continue to see educational institutions as a very large part of the solution.

I propose that, guided by an ecological vision of languages in the United States, the major language-teaching professional organizations build on the very fine work of ACTFL's Year of Languages initiative by identifying key steps in promoting not just the formal study of a finite menu of languages in schools, but also the maintenance and development of community languages that are spoken today by members of immigrant and indigenous communities. These steps might include:

1. Advocating publicly for *all* languages.

   At the local level, efforts by families to maintain the bilingualism of their children would be applauded by language-teaching professionals. The importance of such efforts for personal and professional purposes would be emphasized. At the state level, efforts made by communities to maintain their languages would be publicized extensively, and youngsters who have developed strong English skills and maintained their heritage languages would be identified. This public relations effort would also be reflected at the national level where the strategic importance of non-English languages would be highlighted frequently.

2. Supporting community organizations that are engaged in formal language-teaching endeavors.

    Such support might include language celebration activities carried out in school settings as well as the provision of access to school facilities for community language teaching after school hours or on Saturdays. The point of such support would be to send a clear message about the value of maintaining heritage languages for all Americans.

3. Providing assistance to language communities in obtaining training and preparation for members engaged in the teaching of heritage languages.

    Assistance might involve identifying appropriate formal study for such individuals, familiarizing them with the American education establishment, and identifying the best ways of publishing or duplicating materials in the heritage language.

4. Lobbying for the establishment of special teaching credentials in the teaching of heritage languages within school settings.

    According to Potowoski (2003), not a single state currently offers certification or a special endorsement for the teaching of heritage languages. A unified effort by language teaching professionals at the local, state, and national levels might move the profession forward in this direction and ensure the preparation of future teachers of critical heritage languages.

5. Establishing language programs in traditionally taught languages (for example, French, German) that are designed for students who have maintained a heritage language and are adding a third language.

    An ecological vision of language would imagine not only that students would maintain home and community languages, but also that they would avail themselves of opportunities to acquire other languages taught formally in schools. Language programs created with the view that entering students are already sophisticated speakers of two languages might be able to accelerate such students in their acquisition of a third language.

6. Establishing research and training programs within colleges and universities that can prepare a generation of young scholars and teachers who specialize in the study of language ecology and focus on heritage languages.

One such a program in language ecology is currently being planned by the University of California, Berkeley.[8] The establishment of such programs would help to legitimate an area of study and scholarship that has often been marginal to mainstream concerns.

The creation of a language-competent America may have to begin, not with national policies and national agendas, but with local activities that bring together grass roots supporters of community languages *and* language teaching professionals. I maintain that such professionals are unique among Americans because they understand the value of languages, the challenges involved in acquiring them, and the investment that needs to be made by all of our citizens if we are to become truly language competent. Perhaps it is time for us as a profession to question those deeply held values about language and loyalty that have consistently moved us toward the eradication of immigrant languages and to the very expensive re-teaching of these same languages for national defense.

References

American Council on the Teaching of Foreign Languages. (1996). *Standards for foreign language learning: Preparing for the 21st century*. Yonkers, NY: National Standards in Education Project.

Beckstead, K., & Toribio, A. J. (2003). Minority perspectives on language: Mexican and Mexican-American adolescents' attitudes toward Spanish and English. In A. Roca & M. C. Colombi (Eds.), *Mi lengua: Spanish as a heritage language in the United States* (pp. 154–169). Washington, DC: Georgetown University Press.

Bernal-Enríquez, Y., & Hernandez Chavez, E. (2003). La enseñanza del español en Nuevo México: ¿Revitalización o erradicación de la variedad chicana? In A. Roca & M. C. Colombi (Eds.), *Mi lengua: Spanish as a heritage language in the United States* (pp. 96–1119). Washington, DC: Georgetown University Press.

Brecht, R., & Rivers, W. P. (2002). The language crisis in the United States: Language, national security and the federal role. In S. Baker (Ed.), *Language policy: Lessons from global models* (pp. 76–90). Monterey, CA: Monterey Institute for International Studies.

Campbell, R. N., & Christian, D. (2003). Directions in research: Intergenerational transmission of heritage languages. *Heritage Language Journal, 1*(1), 1–44.

Carreira, M. M. (2003). Profiles of SNS students in the twenty-first century: Pedagogical implications of the changing demographics and social status of U.S. Hispanics. In A. Roca & C. Colombi (Eds.), *Mi lengua: Spanish as a heritage language in the United States; Research and practice* (pp. 51–77). Washington, DC: Georgetown University Press.

---

[8] Information about the program is available at <http://blc.berkeley.edu/language_ecology_proposal.html>.

Colombi, C., & Roca, A. (2003). Insights from research and practice in Spanish as a heritage language. In A. Roca & M. C. Colombi (Eds.), *Mi lengua: Spanish as a heritage language in the United State* (pp. 1–21). Washington DC: Georgetown University Press.

Cummins, J. (Ed.). (1984). *Heritage languages in Canada: Research perspectives.* Ottawa: Ontario Institute for Studies in Education.

Danesi, M. (1986). *Teaching a heritage language to dialect-speaking students.* Ontario: Ontario Institute for Studies in Education.

Fishman, J. A. (1985). Mother-tongue claiming in the United States since 1960: Trends and correlates. In J. A. Fishman, M. H. Gertner, E. G. Lowy, & W. G. Milan (Eds.), *The rise and fall of the ethnic revivial: Perspectives on language and ethnicity* (pp. 107–194). Berlin: Mouton.

Fishman, J. A. (1991). *Reversing language shift.* Clevedon, UK: Multilingual Matters.

Fishman, J. A. (2001). 300-plus years of heritage language education in the United States. In J. K. Peyton, D. A. Ranard, & S. Mcginnis (Eds.), *Heritage languages in America: Preserving a national resource* (pp. 81–97). Washington, DC: Center for Applied Linguistics/Delta Systems.

Fishman, J. A., & Markman, B. R. (1979). *The ethnic mother tongue school in America: Assumptions, findings, and directory* (Final report to the National Institute of Education). Ferkauf Graduate School, Yeshiva University.

Gambhir, S. (2001). Truly less commonly taught languages and heritage language learners in the United States. In J. K. Peyton, D. A. Ranard, & S. McGinnis (Eds.), *Heritage languages in America* (pp. 207–228). Washington, DC: Center for Applied Linguistics/ Delta Systems.

Haugen, E. (1972). The ecology of language. In A. S. Dil (Ed.), *The ecology of language* (pp. 325–339). Stanford, CA: Stanford University Press.

Haugen, E. (1972). The stigmata of bilingualism. In A. S. Dil (Ed.), *The ecology of language* (pp. 307–324). Stanford: Stanford University Press.

Hidalgo, M. (1987). On the question of "Standard" vs. "Dialect": Implications for teaching Hispanic college students. *Hispanic Journal of the Behavioral Sciences, 9*(4), 375–395.

Hidalgo, M. (1993). The teaching of Spanish to bilingual Spanish speakers: A problem of inequality. In B. Merino, H. T. Truega, & F. A. Samaniego (Eds.), *Language and culture in learning: Teaching Spanish to native speakers of Spanish* (Vol. 82–93). London: Falmer Press.

Ingold, C., Rivers, W., Tesser, C. C., & Ashby, E. (2002). Report on the NFLC/AATSP survey of Spanish language programs for native speakers. *Hispania, 85*(2), 324–329.

Lambert, R. D. (1986). *Points of leverage: An agenda for a national foundation for international studies.* New York: Social Science Research Council.

Lambert, R. D. (1987, March). The improvement of foreign language competency in the United States. *The Annals, 490,* 8–19.

Lynch, A. (2003). Toward a theory of heritage language acquisition. In A. Roca & C. Colombi (Eds.), *Mi lengua: Spanish as a heritage language in the United States: Research and practice* (pp. 25–50). Washington, DC: Georgetown University Press.

Merino, B. J. (with Samaniego, F., Trueba, H., Castañeda, E. V., & Chaudry). (1993). Language minority native Spanish speakers at the secondary level and the role of the foreign language teacher. *Peabody Journal of Education, 69*(1), 152–171.

Merino, B. J., Trueba, H. T., & Samaniego, F. A. (Eds.). (1993). *Language and culture in learning: Teaching Spanish to native speakers of Spanish*. London: Falmer Press.

Muller, K. E. (2002). Addressing counterterrorism: US literacy in languages and international affairs. *Language Problems and Language Planning, 26*(1), 1–21.

National Security Education Program. (2005). *National Flagship Language Initiative: Chinese K-16 Pipeline Project: Solicitation and application guidelines, 2005*. Retrived from <http://www.casl.umd.edu/nfli/>.

Peyton, J. K., Ranard, D. A., & McGinnis, S. (Eds.). (2001). *Heritage languages in America*. Washington, DC: Center for Applied Linguistics/Delta Systems.

Politzer, R. L. (1993). A researcher's reflections on bridging dialect and second language learning: Discussion of problems and solutions. In B. J. Merino, H. T. Trueba, & F. A. Samaniego (Eds.), *Language and culture in learning: Teaching Spanish to native speakers of Spanish* (pp. 45–57). London: Falmer Press.

Potowski, K. (2003). Chicago's heritage language teacher corps: A model for improving Spanish teacher development. *Hispania, 86*(2), 302–311.

Ricento, T. (1998). National language policy in the United States. In T. Ricento & B. Burnaby (Eds.), *Language and politics in the United States and Canada* (pp. 85–115). Mahwah, NJ: Lawrence Erlbaum.

Roca, A., & Colombi, M. C. (Eds.). (2003). *Mi lengua: Spanish as a heritage language in the United States*. Washington, DC: Georgetown University Press.

Schiffman, H. F. (1996). *Linguistic culture and language policy*. London: Routledge.

Tucker, G. R. (1984). Toward the development of a language-competent American society. *International Journal of the Sociology of Language, 45*, 153–160.

Tucker, G. R. (1991). Developing a language-competent American society: The role of language planning. In A. G. Reynolds (Ed.), *Bilingualism, multiculturalism, and second language learning* (pp. 65–79). Mahwah, NJ.: Lawrence Erlbaum.

United States Census Bureau. (2003, October). *Census 2000 brief: Language use and English-language ability* (No. C2KBR-19). Washington DC: Author.

Valdés, G. (1988). Foreign language teaching and the proposed foundation for international studies. *Profession, 88*(4), 3–9.

Valdés, G. (1992). The role of the foreign language teaching profession in maintaining non-English languages in the United States. In H. Byrnes (Ed.), *Languages for a multicultural world in transition: 1993 Northeast Conference reports* (pp. 29–71). Skokie, IL: National Textbook.

Valdés, G. (1995). The teaching of minority languages as 'foreign' languages: Pedagogical and theoretical challenges. *Modern Language Journal, 79*(3), 299–328.

Valdés, G. (2001). Heritage languages students: Profiles and possibilities. In J. K. Peyton, D. A. Ranard, & S. Mcginnis (Eds.), *Heritage languages in America: Preserving a national resource* (pp. 37–77). Washington, DC: Center for Applied Linguistics/Delta Systems.

Valdés, G. (in press). Bilingualism, heritage language learners and SLA research: Opportunities lost or seized. *Modern Language Journal, 89*(3).

Valdés, G., Fishman, J. A., Chávez, R., & Pérez, W. (in press). *The development of minority language resources: Lessons from the case of California*. Clevedon, UK: Multilingual Matters.

Valdés, G., Gonzalez, S., Garcia, D. L., & Marquez, P. (2003). Language ideology: The case of Spanish in departments of foreign language. *Anthropology and Education Quarterly*, *34*(1), 3–26.

Wells, E. (2004). Foreign language enrollments in United States institutions of higher education, Fall, 2002. *ADFL Bulletin*, *35*(2), 1–20.

Wiley, T. G., & Valdés, G. (2000). Special issue on heritage languages. *Bilingual Research Journal*, *24*(4).

9

Technology and Foreign Language Instruction: Where We Have Been, Where We Are Now, Where We Are Headed

Jean W. LeLoup
Robert Ponterio

Technology today has an impact on almost every part of our lives, and it has changed many aspects of the way world language teachers function in our profession. This chapter will discuss the role of technology in world language instruction past, present, and future. We will explore (a) a definition of technology, (b) the national mandate for technology implementation across the curriculum, (c) the use of technology heretofore in world language classrooms with some caveats about its implementation, and (d) possibilities for its use in the next ten years. A rationale for using technology in language instruction and learning will be offered that discusses some theoretical underpinnings and briefly touches on the research base for its implementation in the world language curriculum. Finally, the chapter will address the use of technology for assessment and evaluation of student learning.

What Is Technology?

A simple dictionary entry defines technology as follows:

- **noun** (pl. **technologies**) **1** the application of scientific knowledge for practical purposes (Compact Oxford English Dictionary).

From this very general definition, two words stand out: *practical purposes*. The emphasis during the past two decades on communicative competence has underscored the need to develop language learners who eventually can *use* the language in *practical* real-life situations. Technology can be seen as a useful tool providing precisely those learning scenarios that simulate real language use and, consequently, leading to meaningful learning. The shift to greater emphasis on actual language *use* has done much to counter the general public criticism that one can study a language for years in high school but not be able "to say a thing." Language learners now want to be able to employ the language successfully in practical situations that they may be likely to encounter in real life. They are not content with memorizing dialogs (delivered, by the way, technologically via tape recorders) or repeating drills with no follow-through to connect these activities to practical language use.

The following statements, taken from the New Jersey Core Curriculum Content Standards,[1] expand on this initial dictionary definition and encompass much of what teachers perceive as the definition of technology:

- Technology may be defined as the process by which human beings fashion tools and machines to *change, manipulate*, and control their environment.
- Technology is the technical means people use to *improve* their surroundings.
- Technology is the knowledge of using tools and machines to do tasks *efficiently*.
- Technology is people using knowledge, tools, and systems to make their lives *easier* and *better*. (Brzezowski, 1998 [italics added])

Technological advances in the past twenty years have increased exponentially, making mastery of these new tools follow a steep learning curve—perhaps even a vertical line. Technology has certainly *changed* our teaching and our lives; whether or not it has concomitantly *improved* or made our instruction *easier, better, and more efficient* is open to debate. Nevertheless, many teachers make a concerted effort to keep up with the innovations that will enhance their students' learning, though sometimes ruing the day "technology took over." But technology is certainly not new to the language teacher or classroom: we have been using many technologies for years in the forms of tape recorders, overhead and opaque projectors, the language lab, the VCR and videos, slide carousels, film strip projectors, laminators, photocopiers, the 16mm movie projector, even short wave radio, newspapers and magazines, and the old blackboard. These are all modes of technology that teachers have used regularly to *manipulate* and *change* the learning environment, to make teaching more *efficient, easier*, and *better*, and to *improve* learning. Nevertheless, language instruction today subsumes a plethora of newer technologies such as computers, CDs, DVDs, LCD projection, flatbed scanners, digital cameras, distance learning, and the World Wide Web (WWW) along with a host of other Internet tools. Most world language teachers would argue that these technologies are absolutely necessary now to deliver their curricula and create an optimal learning environment for their students.

Technology Across the Curriculum

The impact of technology is manifest in every educational venue. The question no longer is whether technology should be integrated into the curriculum across the board but rather how best to do so. Use of technology for instructional delivery and

---

[1] For more information on the *New Jersey World Languages Curriculum Framework*, see the following site: <http://www.state.nj.us/njded/frameworks/worldlanguages/>.

effective learning is seen as beneficial in all subject areas, not just within the world language domain. The International Society for Technology in Education (ISTE) is a leading proponent of improving teaching and learning in all subject areas by advancing the effective use of technology in K–12 education and teacher education. Within ISTE, the National Educational Technology Standards (NETS) project has laid out a set of Technology Foundation Standards for students (*NETS for Students, 1998*) in pre-kindergarten through 12th grade as well as for teachers (*NETS for Teachers,* 2000). This multiyear project describes the conditions needed to support the use of technology for learning, teaching, and institutional management across the curriculum (*National Educational Technology Standards,* 2000). Nearly every state has directly adopted or adapted their state technology plans for teacher certification and/or licensure with the NETS standards (*NETS and the States, 2004*).

In concert with the NETS project, the Standards for Foreign Language Learning includes technology as one of the principal elements in the "curricular weave" of language learning and instruction. The intent is for language learners to be able to take advantage of new technological advances that could enhance their language learning experience (*National Standards Project,* 1999). Clearly, the perception is that technology, at the very least, improves instruction and may even promote language acquisition. The concern that technology might replace the classroom teacher is not the issue. Rather, the question is how language teaching will be different because of the use of technology (Brecht, 2001). Evidence of the burgeoning interest in and inclusion of technology-driven materials is ubiquitous: the number of computer applications and communications technologies and the sheer volume of offerings on the Internet has grown at an amazing rate over the past 15 years; and many world language educators, heeding instinct, common sense, and anecdotal information, have embraced these new tools as useful instructional tools. Indeed, most all new foreign language instructional materials are accompanied by multimedia software requiring the latest technological advances; these ancillaries are often the deciding factor in materials adoption (Cubillos, 1998).

But do these "bells and whistles" really move the learner along the continuum toward successful language acquisition? There is a small but increasingly vocal cadre of second language acquisition (SLA) researchers who question whether the use of new technologies in language instruction truly furthers second language acquisition (Chapelle, 1997; Cubillos, 1998; Ervin, 1993; Garrett, 1991). Researchers lament the lack of sufficient empirical evidence to support this general belief (Burston, 1996; Salaberry, 1996) and have attempted to collect such evidence through literature reviews and calls for principled and theoretically based studies (Chapelle, 1997; Liu, Moore, Graham, & Lee, 2002; Warschauer, 1997; Zhao, 1996). Clearly, the starting point must be to work from an acceptable theoretical framework of SLA.

Theoretical Underpinnings for Technology Use

Although there are several competing theories of SLA, much of the research supports an interactionist position, underscoring the concomitant effects of the external linguistic environment and internal individual learner variables on language acquisition (Ellis, 1994; Larsen-Freeman & Long, 1991). The tenets of comprehensible input, intake, output, negotiation of meaning, and attention to both form and meaning are posited to have an impact on a learner's interlanguage progression. In addition, sociocultural perspectives on language learning, as influenced by the work of Vygotsky (Lantolf & Appel, 1994; Warschauer, 1997), provide a complementary position that considers language learners in direct relation to their social and cultural surroundings and condition. This theoretical background—reflecting both interactionist and sociocultural perspectives on second language acquisition—gives rise to some generally accepted premises regarding second language acquisition (Zhao, 1996):

1. Language learners must have meaningful second language (L2) input. In other words, they must be exposed to L2 input that is comprehensible to them and delivered in context. (Ellis, 1985, 1994; McLaughlin, 1987)

2. Language learners need to interact with the target language. They need to engage in meaningful activities that have them manipulate the L2 and negotiate meaning. (Doughty and Pica, 1986; Long, 1985)

3. Learning the culture of the target language is an integral part of learning the L2. (Lambert, 1968; Seelye, H., 1984; Seliger, 1988)

4. Motivation, although not completely understood in light of SLA, is nevertheless an important factor in L2 learning. (Lambert, 1968)

5. Language learners need exposure to authentic materials in order to be able to function in a target language environment. (Ellis, 1985)

How and where does technology fit into the above tenets of SLA? More specifically, how can we implement technologies in a principled manner to effect positive L2 learning outcomes?

Caveats for Technology Implementation in the World Language Curriculum

First, we need to agree that it *does* need to be implemented into the world language curriculum. The *Standards for Foreign Language Learning* (NSFLEP,1999) includes technology as an important component of language learning and instruction. This is an essential first step. Heretofore, as Garrett (1998) notes, the use of technology for language learning has essentially focused on the enhancement and improvement of individual courses. She advocates broadening the focus at this point to overall curriculum development, using collaborative projects and research designed to produce generalizable results.

Second, technology should fulfill a need, not create one (Ervin, 1993). Again, technology for technology's sake is a disastrous approach. We first ought to assess our language learning and instructional needs. Then we can see what technologies help meet those needs. Administrations will quickly begin to look askance at requests for technology funding if they perceive a lack of use of the equipment purchased.

Third, while technology can be a timesaver in some senses, in many others it simply is not, perhaps even taking time away from more beneficial tasks. Much of the new technology takes time to master. While world language teachers can use a tape player or VCR with relatively little anxiety, such is not necessarily the case when one sets about teaching with new communications technologies. People begin to address technology implementation in their classrooms with all levels of acumen. Faculty development and training is an absolute necessity when considering an investment in new technologies. Not only do people need to see that they will eventually be able to master these technologies, they also must see that this mastery will be well worth their time in terms of instructional productivity and language learning outcomes.

Fourth, the pedagogical soundness of technologically delivered materials must be the first consideration. Technology itself is not a methodology. It is a tool. Therefore, it relies on the effectiveness of the materials it delivers to justify its use. Some essential questions need to be asked: What will the use of technology add to the curriculum, the lesson, the activity in terms of specific pedagogical goals? Is it a facilitator, a hindrance, or just a superfluous exercise? We need to identify what the learning activities should be and then decide whether or not delivery via technology is the optimal situation (Wang, 2005). For many years, much instructional software was akin to an electronic workbook, replacing drill and practice exercises on paper with mechanical ones on the computer that did not take real advantage of the adaptive potential of the new medium to provide significant helpful or useful feedback to language learners. Little, if anything, was added by transferring these mechanical exercises from paper medium to a computerized one. Even today, one must judiciously examine all so-called multimedia ancillary materials that accompany a possible new text. Many still provide little more than "fun and games" activities that amount basically to a waste of students' and teachers' time.

Finally, we need to look at the research base in order to inform our classroom practice. Operating solely on anecdotal evidence is not a sound way to proceed when making pedagogical decisions that affect our students. It is imperative to base as much instructional planning as possible on empirical data gathered under stringent research methods. The end goal is to "connect theoretical knowledge about second language acquisition and performance with research methods in a manner that can advance practice" (Chapelle, Compton, Kon, & Sauro, 2004, p. 190).

Any use of technology in the classroom today must also take into consideration several unfortunate realities of the Internet. Children may be bombarded with inappropriate messages or images through e-mail, the Web, or instant messaging, but they and their parents have a right to expect that school activities will not be a source of such unacceptable materials. To this end, close supervision of students and teacher oversight of technology-based communication are essential to maintain the trust that we need for our schools to function. Spam, virus, and content filters will continue to improve, making this supervision easier, but they will never replace the classroom teacher's vigilance and care taken to structure assignments to prevent the intrusion of such abusive content, for instance, by screening all messages in an e-mail exchange with another school.

Teachers already face problems of students trying to use translation software to do their composition homework for their language courses. Though the quality of such translations is currently abysmal, we expect such software to continue improving. Without even considering the fairness of students obtaining grades based on a machine's work, it is clear that the student who uses this software is getting no learning benefit at all from the activity. Low-tech solutions may be the best bet to address this high-tech problem. Original writing of early drafts of at least essential parts of an assignment under the teacher's supervision may go a long way towards showing the student that he can do the assignment without the aid of machine translation.

Numerous Web sites now provide online "help" that does a student's homework, writes papers, and the like. In addition, more and more students seem inclined to copy text from Web sites and then add it to their paper as if it were their own. There are tools and services available to help the teacher detect such plagiarism. Here too, though, a greater focus on the steps in the writing process with more supervision at each step rather than placing too much emphasis on the final product can help. Being aware of the dangers is essential for anticipating problems and structuring activities to avoid them.

Bottom Line: The Benefits

One of the most acknowledged advantages to using technology in the world language classroom is the access it affords to *real target language input and authentic materials*. The Internet has opened so many doors to us as world language teachers. We can read current target language newspapers on-line daily. We can listen to and record for later use target language news broadcasts and even see them through the technologies of streaming audio and video. We can engage in synchronous and asynchronous conversations with native speakers of the target language in written, audio, and video formats on a regular basis . . . and so can our students. The ancillary materials currently available on CD-ROM, DVD, and the particular Internet sites that coordinate with world language textbooks are rife with authentic materials, native speaker input, and a cultural richness that were absent for so long from traditional texts and workbook versions. These materials contain digitized audio and video segments that expose the language learner to real-life situations, contextual language instruction, and embedded cultural information that clearly enhance the language learning experience. Digital media formats provide for lower costs, more flexibility, better integration with lessons, and hence the potential for improved pedagogical uses (over the old audio and video cassette formats) and greater availability for students. Access to authentic materials and native speaker input is a powerful argument in favor of the implementation of technology in the world language curriculum. Indeed, it is underscored by this statement from the New Jersey World Languages Curriculum Framework:

> The latest instructional technologies, particularly the most interactive technologies such as computer-assisted language learning and advanced telecommunications, enhance the possibilities of providing world languages for all students, while bringing languages and cultures into the classroom in an immediate and authentic way. Technology transforms the world languages classroom by recreating the multidimensional nature of language as it exists within the visual, social, and cultural world.
>
> (NJ World Languages Curriculum Framework, 1999, Ch. 3, p. 9)

The South Carolina Foreign Languages Curriculum Standards document also touts technology as a major resource for foreign language teachers and lists a number of benefits to students and teachers when it is used effectively:

> The use of new technologies creates experiences that are compelling for language learners. Multimedia is a way of managing and presenting the kinds of resources increasingly needed for effective language teaching, as new insights into language acquisition are developed and curricular goals are expanded. The benefits of using technology include:
>
> - access to authentic language and culture,
> - active student learning through interactive technology,
> - student self-pacing and sequencing,
> - cooperative learning environment,
> - access to the community outside the walls of the school,
> - access to various instructors and to less commonly taught languages through interactive distance learning, and
> - access to up-to-the-minute materials.
>
> (SC Foreign Language Curriculum Standards, Ch. 6, p. 4)

All of these benefits are worthy of mention, but we should underscore a few in particular.

First, the accessibility of languages to *all* learners in school districts with distance learning technology is crucial to maintaining world language study in the U.S.

It is important to view distance-learning technology as a way to share resources and provide language learning opportunities that otherwise would not exist. While some may look to distance learning as a way to save money, in fact the technological setup and time invested are quite costly and, in the end, distance learning will probably not eliminate jobs. Rather, we can use this technology to promote the sharing of resources, link foreign language colleagues (Cubillos, 1998), and offer world language courses that otherwise would fold or simply would not be offered due to low enrollments or scarcity of teachers (AP language courses, Less Commonly Taught Languages, and the like). In other circumstances, decreased school budgets and concomitant elimination of teaching positions have threatened the very existence of world language programs in some districts. Distance learning could save those programs in some circumstances by pooling resources and combining expertise and community needs in different districts (Pitkoff & Roosen, 1994).

Second, the benefit of *access to the community outside the school walls* directly relates to several of the national Standards goal areas: Cultures, Connections, Comparisons, and Communities. Through technology, language learners can explore products and practices of the target language culture and investigate the perspectives related thereto. They can then make reasonable and educated comparisons between such products and practices from the target language culture and their own. By using their language skills, learners gain access to materials and information available only through target language media (newspapers, radio, TV), much of it readily available on the Internet. Only in this way can one truly tap the perspectives held by members of the target language culture, a "must" for the dedicated language student. Additionally, exploration of these resources can continue long after the termination of formal language study, possibly leading to involvement in a target language community and hopefully leading to lifelong learning.

Sample Technologies of Today

Already mentioned above are several of the technologies that world language teachers can implement to enhance their instruction. Discussing all of them in depth is well beyond the scope of this chapter, but we will treat a few as a representative sample of the technological possibilities that exist presently. Computer technology is clearly the dominant resource, with the World-Wide Web playing a major role. Web sites exist in the millions, and certainly quite a lot are not worth the trouble of perusal. However, many quality sites exist and can serve as useful adjuncts to well-constructed foreign language lessons.[2] The trick, of course, is to locate these good

---

[2] For reviews of WWW sites of benefit to world language teachers, please see LeLoup & Ponterio, "On the Net," in *Language Learning & Technology* <http://llt.msu.edu/>. This regular column explores a different Web site in each volume.

sites with minimum time expenditure and maximum results. One way to go about this is to use a powerful search engine and to develop good search strategies: selecting useful keywords to narrow the options, searching in the target language rather than English, and using target language search engines (such as <http://fr.yahoo.com/> or <http://es.yahoo.com/>). Another way to avoid spending hours searching is to utilize collections of Web pages already generated by world language teachers. Many folks have already invested much time doing this, so there is no need to duplicate efforts.[3]

Use of electronic mail (e-mail) is pervasive in our lives today. Many world language teachers have used e-mail in their classrooms for a variety of activities. *Virtual Connections* (Warschauer, 1996) contains 125 examples of projects that world language teachers have carried out in their classrooms with various electronic communications technologies (including e-mail). E-mail provides an easy way for language students to practice their target language skills, whether it be with other language learners (through a discussion format, perhaps), their teacher (through dialog journaling, for example), or even native speakers (possibly through a penpal or keypal arrangement or project) (Knight, 1994; LeLoup, 1996).

Electronic discussion lists and Usenet groups permeate the Internet. A list is an e-mail discussion group on a topic of common interest to the subscribers. Literally thousands of lists exist on the Internet and, in actuality, hundreds are dedicated, or related in some way, to world language learning and instruction (Bedell, 1993). E-mail lists can be valuable resources for world language teachers. Through participation in the discussions on these lists, teachers can become involved in a professional dialogue about any aspect of teaching or language they wish. Exchanges abound, ranging from theoretical discussions to practical suggestions for enhancing classroom activities to comments on textbook series to advice about travel companies for student trips. This collegial exchange is a way for world language teachers to participate in ongoing professional development and networking (LeLoup & Ponterio, 2004).

An alternative to joining e-mail lists is participation in USENET newsgroups, if your service provider offers that option. Postings are read via a news reader, which keeps track of what messages have or have not been read in a particular thread or discussion topic. You can log on, select a thread, find the new messages, and read them. You can also initiate threads and post responses, much as you would post something on a bulletin board—another name frequently used for these groups. Participation in newsgroups is a popular way for many people to access information about a desired topic because it does not fill the user's mailbox; the only information stored on the user's computer is a log of which messages have been read.

---

[3] One site that offers many of these world language collections is the FLTEACH WWW Resources for Language Teachers page <http://www.cortland.edu/flteach/flteach-res.html>.

Ironically, this advantage also becomes a drawback at times. Ease of participation allows readers to come and go from topics in an irregular fashion, and a collegial or supportive atmosphere often does not result. Web-based discussions abound as well. Here all communication remains within a Web page rather than passing through e-mail or a newsgroup, thus allowing easier set-up and greater privacy.

Authoring programs exist to enable teachers to develop materials particular to their own texts and curricular goals. These programs typically are organized into templates that include a variety of answer/response formats such as multiple choice, true/false, matching, cloze, scrambled words, or sentences. Many of the programs provide for inclusion of multimedia such as digitized video and audio. Teacher authors can then tailor-make activities that coordinate with the text or topics they are covering in their class. Examples of these authoring programs are Libra (Southwest Texas University; Macintosh videodisc), WinCalis (Computer Assisted Language Instruction for Windows, Duke University; Windows platform; supports all world language texts), and Dasher (University of Iowa; both platforms), and the xMedia-Engine Template Series (Middlebury College, Macintosh).

Online instructional software applications such as WebCT and TopClass provide an environment for teachers in which entire classes can be conducted asynchronously. These Web-based programs can be used to conduct a complete class online or just to publish supplemental materials and resources for the class. Other Web-based programs such as Hot Potatoes and Quia are software applications that enable teachers to create interactive and personalized activities to coincide with their own particular teaching materials.

Conferencing systems are also available through the Internet via commercial packaging. Such systems as Daedalus or the FirstClass Conferencing system allow teachers to set up private discussion groups limited to a particular class. These systems are relatively easy to administer and tend to be of the client-server variety. They also typically support extended character sets so necessary for world language exchange. Another advantage of these conferencing systems is their moderation by a teacher, who can regulate and direct the discussion according to the class needs and curricular demands. While they are generally meant to be for asynchronous interaction, they may have provision for synchronous dialog exchange.

Opportunities for synchronous target language conversations also abound. Internet Relay Chat, or IRC, is one such application. IRC is a very popular program that presents a series of "channels" rather like a CB. By entering a channel, you can "talk" to all of the other people on the channel, no matter where they are in the world. Everything that you type will be seen instantly by all of the other people there, and you will see anything that they type. Channel names usually reflect the topics discussed, so entering a channel called "français" might be interesting for a French class, especially if you have made an appointment to meet some other Francophiles there at a specific time. IRC and similar programs do have a great potential for worldwide, interactive communication and also hold promise for small-scale target language conversation practice. You can even create private channels for your own students with the software available.

Messenger programs for real-time discussion and interchange are ubiquitous on the Web. Instant Messenger (from AOL-Netscape), Yahoo Messenger, ICQ, and MSN Messenger are but a few of the applications commonly available that allow synchronous exchange of messages, photos, and files with friends, family, and colleagues.

Commercial presentational software is very popular and includes such programs as Microsoft PowerPoint, Hyperstudio, and Visual Communicator. These programs have the capability of combining text, graphics, and video. Though not specifically designed for world language use, some language support is available, for example, diacritics. However, some of the world languages are not currently supported, notably right-to-left languages. These programs can be used to create rich cultural materials and presentations for and by language learners.

Looking Ahead

Trying to predict the future of technology has all the scientific accuracy of tarot cards, tea leaves, and chicken entrails, none of which is as dependable as the good old crystal ball. However, what we can do is to examine the question through a survey of some of today's improvements and advances we can now see appearing. By extrapolating how they will change the tools that are currently available, we can anticipate the potential modifications that might have specific pedagogical applications for the world language classroom.

The fundamental and oft-cited rule of thumb of advances in computer engineering is Moore's law, stipulating a doubling of processing power, or at least of the number of transistors in a given area of a circuit, every 18 months. While at first glance an increase in speed that stems from this transistor density might not seem terribly important to the typical world language teacher, we should note that it is not just a question of doing things faster. The consequent rise in processing power leads to improvements in the quality of everything we see and hear and can have a profound impact on our overall impression of computer-mediated communication. For instance, we have gone from the beep of the first PC to CD quality audio; from the bouncing dot in the game of Pong to DVD quality video; from the long wait as we search for a word in an electronic dictionary to transparent real-time spell-checking; from e-mail messages that appeared on our screens at a rate of less than a sentence per second to e-mail with embedded audio and video, not to mention real-time desktop videoconferencing. Will all this power make speech recognition and human-like artificial intelligence providing negotiated meaning in simulated discourse for beginning language learners a practical working reality in the world language classroom? Probably not tomorrow.

Along with continuing improvements in audio and video quality thanks to better compression of higher quality original materials, we can expect to see several additional changes thanks to a few other basic improvements in computing infrastructure. Networks, including the Internet, will continue to get faster, allowing us to move larger and larger amounts of information around more quickly. This means that we will be able to access images, audio, and video from remote locations far more quickly. Wireless networking is also likely to have an impact on the way we work. Whereas fast networks make it easier to interact with remote locations (for example, a remote digital language lab), wireless makes it easier to carry our tools around with us (for example, a teacher moving from one classroom to another while carrying all materials in a laptop that takes no time to set up). Another expected change in hardware is the continuing increase in the size and speed along with a decrease in price of memory available for both long-term storage such as hard drives, memory sticks, and optical (for example, CD and DVD formats) and internal RAM memory. Larger memory storage devices suggest the ability to store more and larger files; for the language teacher this means authentic audio and video. In addition to these technical changes, we shall certainly see software evolving in two opposing directions, as is often the case. Features are frequently added to software, making tools more powerful and capable of performing more functions, though simultaneously rendering them more complex and difficult to learn to use. But on the other hand, software designers also try to simplify their product interfaces to make them easier for typical users. This evolution generally leads to popular features that eventually do become easier to use. How might we reasonably expect such changes to impact the world language teacher? Many of them may make our lives easier, or, in other cases, perhaps more complicated, but they will not necessarily all have a direct effect on language teaching. We will examine some of the changes that we believe could have direct pedagogical importance.

Internet access to real-time audio and video programming, for instance radio and television from other countries, is already being used in many language classes. Students can see and hear authentic language use by native speakers. The quality of video and audio streams has been steadily improving, and today many, but not all, sources of these materials work well enough to be acceptable for use in the classroom. As such services continue to improve, we can be sure that many more sources will appear and more of them will be of satisfactory, even superior, quality. Eventually excellent audio and video will be the accepted norm from broadcast sources as well as from school sites where teachers are able to make specific selected audio and video available to their own students. All this works today but is often too complex for the average teacher to manage alone and still does not always work as dependably as needed for pedagogical use.

In addition to the centrally distributed audio and video discussed above, two-way interactive audio and video are also now coming into their own. Most instant messaging systems, described in a previous section, now allow for audio and often video chats, and the quality is sometimes acceptable for personal communication but not necessarily for classroom use as exposure to authentic language. Too often configuration and bandwidth problems tend to degrade this interactive audio and video, but when it works, it is quite impressive. Here too as improvements continue to be made, functional transparency and high quality will become the accepted norm. At that point, classes and individual students from around the world will be able to meet virtually and use their language skills with real native speakers. Kids from many countries are already doing this to some extent on their own with audio features of online role-play games where they talk to each other while playing.

One of the problems that teachers encounter when using audio and video in instant messaging systems is that both participants in the discussion need to be online at the same time. These messengers do allow the users to leave text messages for their contacts who happen to be off line, and a few also allow users to leave voice messages, though generally of limited length. This feature might be viewed as a sort of Internet-based voice mail system. Some e-mail programs also allow the easy attachment of voice messages or even video clips to e-mail. Expansion of such services will make it easier to exchange higher quality audio and also video messages with conversation partners who may not be online at the same moment. Such features are still in their infancy but could facilitate audio and video exchanges with classes and students in different time zones. Even when the time difference is not a problem, classes at different locations often may not meet at the same time during the day. An asynchronous message makes the communication far less interactive, but it does make interaction possible in cases where it is not practical due to scheduling conflicts.

Managing, editing, or creating audio and video materials can be daunting for the technically untrained world language teacher. Much of the software for capture and editing of a/v content has become easier to use in recent years, but technical questions of resolution, compression (quality vs. file size), sound volume, selection of recording devices, along with many other decisions that must be made routinely by anyone managing audio, video, and even image files, can still be a nightmare. Most teachers are far too busy to spend much time figuring out such things. Software for basic functions needs to be and certainly will become more transparent. Following the "Fair Use Guidelines for Educational Multimedia," teachers have plenty of leeway in terms of extracting video and audio clips, capturing and using such clips for classroom-related lessons, editing out inappropriate content, and selecting only material that supports learning goals. Ability to do such things as slow the speed of a recording without lowering the pitch can turn meaningless gibberish into comprehensible input. All of these things are possible today for the technically sophisticated, but as the software gets better more teachers will be able to take advantage of the tools that best meet their needs.

High network speeds, from gateways at large institutions to broadband at home, have made online image archives a reality, but waiting time for many images to appear is still often too long for comfortable browsing. As networks continue to improve, these waits will be significantly reduced. This should make exploring such archives seem more like browsing one's own hard drive. The resulting ease of use will lead to better interactive access to centralized data sources for images, audio, and video collections. By effectively eliminating download waits, such sources should become more attractive, giving us easier access to additional authentic and teacher produced materials. The Less Commonly Taught Languages (LCTL) project is already working with this basic technology and will certainly benefit from the expected network improvements.

One of the problems of distance learning is the cost of telecommunications. In one case of an Arabic class at State University of New York (SUNY) Cortland, the telecommunications costs were as high as the teacher's salary. Higher speed Internet will allow distance learning applications to use lower cost networks, making distance learning for LCTLs more affordable and also simultaneously sending multiple channels of high-quality data streams to students over the Internet, for example, images, audio, multiple video views, and comments by other students. In addition, the expansion of broadband access and higher broadband speeds will facilitate the extension of higher quality distance learning into the home. We already see this reality for one-on-one audio communication, which has replaced telephone office hours in many distance learning settings.

Language is about using real tools for real communication. We have long seen tools that help students learn to write better in the target language. Continuing improvements to word processor built-in grammar and spelling checkers have now integrated such support into the same programs that we use to write in our native language. Over the past ten years these tools for spell checking and grammar checking have gone from laughable to useful, but only when used with great care. Although these features sometimes give misleading information, missing basic errors or flagging well-formed sentences as wrong, overall they continue to be one of the best tools for helping students learn to write sentences in the target language with fewer spelling and grammar mistakes. More importantly, when used well, they can help students learn correct structures by providing immediate feedback showing better, more accurate forms. The built-in thesaurus can also suggest alternative vocabulary choices, helping students to expand their vocabulary. We expect these to continue to improve so that fewer misdiagnoses will crop up and more accurate alternative forms will be suggested to writers.

New tools are becoming available for readers as well. Reading is one of the best sources of vocabulary development and authentic language that can be digested at the reader's own speed, but limited vocabulary is a major hurdle to the novice foreign language reader. Some turn to very bad machine translations of online texts to try to get the gist, but this does not often work well and it certainly does not help one improve language skills. Better, that is, more transparent, integration of bilingual dictionary help for electronic reading materials puts glossing decisions under the reader's control. Dictionaries both online and installed on one's personal computer may be set to allow instant lookup of words in either a bilingual or monolingual dictionary simply by clicking on the unknown word. Rather than providing a translation that might be no better than a wild guess, these give complete dictionary entries allowing students to interpret the word according to the context. This practice improves the comprehensibility of the authentic text for the student, as long as there are not too many words that need to be looked up. A major advantage of these systems is that they do not require any advance preparation of the text by a teacher, such as adding glosses. By making the lookup interactive and instantaneous, the interruption of the reading process is reduced to a minimum, thus improving the overall quality and benefit of the reading experience (LeLoup & Ponterio, 2005).

The operating systems now being developed include improved tools for organizing content, not only text, but also audio, video, and images. For instance, a song in the target language can be tagged with searchable comments about the topic, the grammar structures present, the level of difficulty, links to additional online information, images, lyrics, audio, in essence, about any information that the teacher or student might find useful. All of these things are then found at the teacher's fingertips when needed, either in class or when preparing a lesson. Currently teachers need to organize such materials in folders, but not everyone has good organizational skills; and, even so, the folder model does not allow multiple organizational criteria, such as by book chapter, topic, grammar points, class level, and the like, all at the same time. Few teachers know how to make good use of databases for this purpose. Although the integration of advanced search features in the operating system is not truly a tool specific to foreign language, the enhanced ability to search for audio and video materials by predefined criteria is of particular use to the language teacher who often needs to locate authentic language samples meeting specific criteria for a particular lesson.

The USB memory stick is also a device that does not really have a specific foreign language application, but, as the memory stick becomes easier to use and grows in memory size and speed, it is becoming possible to carry all of the materials one might ever need in one's pocket. This is a boon to any teacher who travels from classroom to classroom or prepares materials at home for use in school. The memories of these devices, at least in their upper range, are now becoming large enough to carry audio and video as well as other files. In cases where Internet access to student audio recordings is not possible, this can now be a satisfactory option for accessing these recordings outside of the lab. Of course, they can also be used much like a writable or rewritable DVD disk to bring digital a/v materials, captured from a variety of outside sources, into the classroom (for instance, current mp3 players). But they are easier to use than rewritable data DVDs, appearing to the teacher and functioning just like an external hard drive.

Ten years ago, using a portable computer for a presentation in a school or at a conference was often a nightmare. It was always likely that something would not work, and teachers could often be seen scurrying around trying to find a technical guru to solve the inevitable problems. Today the integration of different devices tends to be more and more standard, so we can usually count on everything working after we connect a few fairly simple standard cables. Yet every new feature seems to yield another potential incompatibility. In the future, we may expect such connections to be wireless, eliminating the need to make cable connections, though some security will certainly be required to ensure against outside intrusions and to be sure that the presentation in room 12 does not appear on the screen in room 13. As these devices do a better job talking to each other, the teacher has less to do to ensure that correct settings allow the systems to function. A good example of such simplification can be seen in mp3 players that can send audio to your car's radio.

Many new and improved devices develop potential applications or become more accessible as they become easier to use. Digital cameras and camcorders have been gaining ground in the classroom as the software for using them becomes simpler. In the language class this means more time doing language and less time manipulating the technology, connecting cameras, downloading files, scanning images. Many teachers are making good use of the PDA, smart boards, classroom management systems, electronic grade books. Here too such devices are useful for all teachers, not specifically the world language teacher. On the other hand, some tools might not at first appear to have a foreign language benefit, but turn out to present a crucial advantage. The integration of Java software in Web pages has much promise for large businesses that may be able to save money on computer maintenance, but the potential to make foreign-language-specific software available to students over the Internet without installing a program on the computer that the student is using is an interesting way to make this nongeneral use software accessible where it would not otherwise be installed.

Most people think first of voice recognition as a key to the future of world language technology. Voice recognition has certainly come a long way and is used successfully in some world language applications, but it still has a long way to go to achieve seamless human-like interaction, anticipation of learner errors, and pedagogically sound feedback. Many native speakers of a language find it difficult to interact with a language learner, and we are a long way from teaching a computer to do something that is a problem for so many native speakers. Teachers often hear the hype about such products but need to do careful testing to verify their usability with real learners in the actual classroom or home setting.

The language lab has undergone significant transformations in recent years, going from audio cassette tapes to Internet-connected computer stations. The traditional language lab functions—primarily listening and recording simultaneously on two audio tracks, distributing audio to multiple student audio stations, and allowing teacher monitoring of student work—have also been expensive because the devices used were not standard on the electronics market; analog networks required complex switching; and management of a huge number of possible functions, many of which were not utilized by many individual teachers, required big investments. Digital and virtual language labs have the potential to replace many of these traditional language lab functions and indeed provide new functions as well, with software-only solutions that can make use of general purpose computers with standard audio cards, inexpensive headsets and microphones, standard Internet connections, and basic Web servers. A digital lab simply means that the audio and video are stored and moved around in digital format instead of the analog form of cassette tapes. Many current labs use proprietary devices to combine analog and digital signals. Moving to digital only can represent a significant savings, but it does exclude some possible uses of materials that are not in digital format. Making the move is a big step and a very personal decision for the teacher, especially in settings where there is already a significant collection of analog materials on tape, but as digital formats come to replace all analog media, it becomes easier to work around the exceptions.

The virtual language lab makes use of material in digital format outside the language lab by representing devices for listening or viewing materials on the computer screen. Software might be located in a lab, be installed on a student's computer at home, or even be contained in a Java applet on a Web page so that any computer where the student happens to be sitting will instantly become a language lab station. The high-speed Internet access that we discussed earlier makes it possible to extend the virtual language lab beyond the walls of the classroom, giving access to materials and functions wherever the student and teacher happen to be. Many virtual language labs today offer remote access to digital audio and video files for student use, but we expect to see the generalized extension of many traditional language lab functions (for instance listening to a teacher track while recording a student track) to remote generic computers as well.

Predicting the future is a tricky and dangerous business. In fact, we may safely predict that the predictions we have suggested here will be inaccurate, but they represent a fairly conservative anticipation of the likely evolution of useful technology in the coming years.

Technology and Assessment

Technology has a number of specific applications and implications for assessment in the world language classroom. Our profession has long reflected on what represents good assessment, and we certainly want technology to help us assess well, not lead us towards easier but less effective or pedagogically unsound assessment. From computer-adaptive testing to alternative assessment to performance-based assessment, and including tools to help teachers design testing materials, technology can be seen playing a role.

One of the most obvious technical applications for assessment can be seen in tests that are taken and automatically graded at the computer terminal. Such tests are limited in their ability to evaluate real language production, which is gaining in importance as we see in the evolution of the written component of the SAT exam. Computer adaptive testing is based on the notion that a student's language ability can be described according to a set of levels, for example, the ACTFL proficiency scale. The test, like an Oral Proficiency Interview (OPI), uses criterion-referenced performance indicators through test items that have been evaluated for this purpose to verify whether a student is performing at a certain level of proficiency. If so, the student is checked for performance at the next level, and so on, until the test determines the student's level. Such tests have been effectively used as placement tools.

A potential problem of technology-mediated assessments has long been the affective block that makes using the technology difficult for some students. These test takers may have trouble performing or simply function less well using a computer than taking a paper and pencil test. Materials may be designed to reduce, perhaps even to eliminate, this effect, but the possibility that the medium could negatively impact a student's performance is a serious issue that must be considered. On another front, the clever or technically astute test taker may find a way to use the technology itself to cheat in a testing situation. Some computerized test settings need to be specifically designed to prevent such cheating, leading institutions to set aside a dedicated secure testing lab, but then the equipment may no longer be able to perform the general purpose functions that make computers so valuable in the first place. Such a solution could be very expensive indeed.

Alternative assessments may involve the production of written communication with authentic technical tools that are commonly used for real communication. These may involve such things as word processors, publishing tools, presentations, and video recordings. In these cases the teacher must monitor the time spent learning to use the tools versus the attention given to the language production. In terms of assessment, it is also essential to be sure we are assessing the language use, not the bells and whistles of the tools employed. The advantage in using such programs should be their role as real communicative tools as used by native speakers in a culturally authentic situation. The goal is then to come as close as possible to real communication, not to focus more on form than on content, which may be a danger when such tools take over a project.

There is certainly an overlap between alternative assessment and performance-based assessments. In many cases the function of technology specific to performance-based assessments is to capture and store a student's performance for closer evaluation by the instructor at a later time. Audio and video cassettes have long played this role. The advantage of digital technology is easier storage and more flexible availability of the performance to the evaluator. Faster access to student samples, the ability to instantly jump around to specific locations in the student's performance, and the possibility of much more easily comparing the performances of several students represent clear advantages offered by the technology during the evaluation of such tasks.

For all kinds of assessment methods and formats, technology can help the teacher prepare materials. We can now much more easily integrate authentic language through audio and video listening comprehension segments. Images can be presented in a variety of media formats to help provide the context necessary for the presentation or simulation of more realistic communicative acts. Even the simple act of using a word processor to write tests tends to help us reduce typographical errors, make modifications for multiple versions of tests, and mix and match test segments and items from past exams. Even software that helps teachers design rubrics can lead to more attention to the effectiveness of the test instrument, better evaluation of the student's language, and more effective communication with the student and parents about what needs to be learned, what skills need to be acquired, and how these will be evaluated.

Publisher resources are an integral part of textbook adoption, and more and more of these resources are technology based. For assessment, this means that the teacher has easier access to a variety of materials provided by the publisher and designed to support teaching and evaluation of the material in specific chapters of the text. These materials cover the same broad range that we have already mentioned for teacher-designed materials.

Organizations intended to support teachers are also using technology to help teachers design lessons and assessments. An excellent example is the Center for Advanced Research on Language Acquisition (CARLA) that supports teachers through a number of online services, for instance, the Content-Based Language Teaching through Technology (CoBaLTT) Web site <http://www.carla.umn.edu/cobaltt/>, where technology is used to provide access to a variety of resources, including resources to aid the teacher in designing and creating good assessments. CARLA is also the home of the LCTL project Web site that serves many functions including access to royalty-free images, audio, and video for teachers' use. These resources can be used not only as aids in building lessons but also as the basis of assessment materials. LCTLs are languages where publishers do not have sufficient financial incentive to produce materials for teachers, so teachers have a great interest in sharing materials with each other to create their own common stock of media. Such initiatives are excellent examples of the use of technology at the grassroots level helping teachers help each other.

The computer's role in assessment has come a long way from Scantron® forms for multiple choice tests. No matter what the assessment philosophy or medium, technology can play a role in aiding the teacher in an area that is not always the favorite part of the classroom teacher's job.

Conclusion

Mirroring its increasing role in all aspects of our daily lives, the impact of technology in the world language classroom has become an essential consideration for the language teacher. We must keep in mind that our purpose is to teach people to use the language. Where technology can help us do a better job, it certainly behooves us to consider using it. Yet we should beware of using technology for its own sake; it must never detract from our primary goal of language learning. Where technology helps us communicate as we do in practical real-life situations, it will have a positive effect. Certainly, its most powerful function in the world language classroom is to improve access to high-quality, up-to-date, authentic language. In those cases where a native would use a technology for communication, it only makes sense that language learners should themselves practice communicating via that technology, manipulating real language as would a native. Today's teacher uses technology to communicate in the real world as a matter of course, so it is only natural for these tools to find their uses in the classroom. Still, we should remember that very often the best communication technology is two chairs in which two people can sit face-to-face.

References

Bedell, S. (1993). Review of electronic lists for language learning. *Athelstan, 5*, 13–15.

Brecht, R. D. (2001). Testing the future of language education in the United States: Five "easy" questions. In R. Z. Lavine (Ed.), *Beyond the boundaries: Changing contexts in language learning* (pp. 1–20). Northeast Conference Reports. Columbus, OH: McGraw-Hill.

Brzezowski, E. H. (1998). *New Jersey core curriculum content standards: Integration of technology in the classroom.* Last revised 4/23/98. Retrieved May 17, 2005, from <http://www.fes-nj.com/Technology/Core-Tech/core_tech.html>

Burston, J. (1996). CALL at the crossroads: Myths, realities, promises and challenges. *Annual Review of Applied Linguistics, 19*(2), 27–36.

Chapelle, C. (1997). CALL in the year 2000: Still in search of research paradigms? *Language Learning & Technology, 1*(1), 19–43.

Chapelle, C., Compton, L., Kon, E., & Sauro, S. (2004). Theory, research, and practice in CALL: Making the links. In L. Lomicka & J. Cooke-Plagwitz (Eds.), *Teaching with technology* (pp. 189–208). Boston: Heinle.

Compact Oxford English Dictionary. Retrieved on May 17, 2005, from <http://www.askoxford.com/concise_oed/technology?view=uk>

Cubillos, J. H. (1998). Technology: A step forward in the teaching of foreign languages. In J. Harper, M. Lively, & M. Williams (Eds.), *The coming of age of the profession: Issues and emerging ideas for the teaching of foreign languages* (pp. 37–52). Boston: Heinle.

Doughty, C., & Pica, T. (1986). "Information gap" tasks: Do they facilitate second language acquisition? *TESOL Quarterly, 20*, 305–325.

Ellis, R. (1985). *Understanding second language acquisition.* Oxford, UK: Oxford University Press.

Ellis, R. (1994). *The study of second language acquisition.* Oxford, UK: Oxford University Press.

Ervin, G. L. (1993). Can technology fulfill its promise? *IALL Journal, 26*(2), 7–16.

Garrett, N. (1991).Technology in the service of language learning: Trends and issues. *Modern Language Journal, 75*(1), 74–101.

Garrett, N. (1998). *Are we on the right path to reach our long-term objectives?* Paper delivered at CALICO 98, San Diego, CA.

Knight, S. (1994). Making authentic cultural and linguistic connections. *Hispania, 77*(2), 288–94.

Lambert, W., Gardner, C., Olton, R., & Tunstall, K. (1968). A study of the roles of attitudes and motivation in second-language learning. In J. Fishman (Ed.), *Readings in the sociology of language* (pp. 473–491). The Hague: Mouton.

Lantolf, J. P., & Appel, G. (Eds.). (1994). *Vygotskian approaches to second language acquisition.* Norwood, NJ: Ablex.

Larsen-Freeman, D., & Long, M. H. (1991). *An introduction to second language acquisition research.* London: Longman.

LeLoup, J. W. (1996). But I only have e-mail—What can I do? *Learning Languages, 2*(2), 10–15.

LeLoup, J. W., & Ponterio, R. (2004). FLTEACH: On-line professional development for preservice and inservice foreign language teachers. In L. Lomicka & J. Cooke-Plagwitz (Eds.), *Teaching with technology* (pp. 26–44). Boston: Heinle.

LeLoup, J. W., & Ponterio, R. (2005). On The Net: Vocabulary support for independent online reading. *Language Learning & Technology, 9*(2), 3–7. Available at <http://llt.msu.edu/vol9num2/net/>

Liu, M., Moore, Z., Graham, L., & Lee, S. (2002). A look at the research on computer-based technology use in second language learning: A review of the literature from 1990–2000. *Journal of Research on Technology in Education, 34*(3), 250–273.

Long, M. (1985). Input and second language acquisition theory. In S. Gass & C. Madden (Eds.), *Input in second language acquisition.* Rowley, MA: Newbury House.

McLaughlin, B. (1987). *Theories of second language learning.* London: Edward Arnold.

National Educational Technology Standards for students (1998). Eugene, OR: International Society for Technology in Education (ISTE).

National Educational Technology Standards for teachers. (2000). Eugene, OR: International Society for Technology in Education (ISTE).

National Educational Technology Standards (NETS) and the states. (2004). Retrieved May 17, 2005, from <http://cnets.iste.org/docs/States_using_NETS.pdf>

National Standards in Foreign Language Education Project. (1999). *Standards for foreign language learning in the 21st century.* Lawrence, KS: Allen.

New Jersey world languages curriculum framework. (1999). Retrieved May 29, 2005, from <http://www.state.nj.us/njded/frameworks/worldlanguages/chap3.pdf>

Pitkoff, E., & Roosen, E. (1994, September). New technology, new attitudes provide language instruction. *NASSP Bulletin,* 36–43.

Salaberry, M. R. (1996). A theoretical foundation for the development of pedagogical tasks in computer mediated communication. *Calico Journal, 14*(1), 5–34.

Seelye, H. (1984). *Teaching culture: Strategies for intercultural communication* (2nd ed.). Lincolnwood, IL: National Textbook Company.

Seliger, H. (1988). Psycholinguistic issues in second language acquisition. In L. Beebe (Ed.), *Issues in second language acquisition: Multiple perspectives*. New York: Newbury House.

South Carolina foreign language curriculum standards. (1998). Retrieved on May 18, 2005, from <http://www.myscschools.com/offices/cso/foreign_language/documents/standards/studies/chapter6.pdf>

Wang, L. (2005, May). Technology integration in foreign language teaching demonstrates the shift from a behavioral to a constructivist learning approach. *THE Journal Online*. Retrieved on May 26, 2005, from <http://www.thejournal.com/magazine/vault/A5357C.cfm>

Warschauer, M. (1996). *Virtual connections*. Honolulu: University of Hawaii Press.

Warschauer, M. (1997). Computer-mediated collaborative learning: Theory and practice. *Modern Language Journal, 81*, 470–81.

Zhao, Y. (1996). Language learning on the World Wide Web: Toward a framework of network based CALL. *Calico Journal, 14*(1), 37–51.

10

Globalization and Its Implications for the Profession

John M. Grandin

With his declaration that the world is flat, Thomas Friedman (2005) has coined the metaphor for the age in which our students will live and work. While many of us still envision a round world with American skill and know-how as the main driving force, the Internet, rapid and convenient travel, and the global spread of the free market system have caused things to change radically. As Friedman points out, the already smaller world has now become tiny, the playing fields have been leveled, and the long-standing American competitive advantage is disappearing. Given head-on competition with diligent and highly educated peers from rapidly emerging economies in countries such as in India and China, young people today will need to meet global standards of education, work harder and smarter than their predecessors, and be involved internationally.

Fields such as business, technology, science, law, and medicine can no longer be limited to a single national context in today's level or "flat" world. Companies large and small are now exposed to intense competition on a worldwide basis and must be engaged in the global marketplace if they wish to keep pace. Research enterprises and scientific communities can likewise no longer consider the implications of their work solely on a local basis. Just as it is unthinkable that Ford or Microsoft would design products solely for the U.S. market, legal decisions, scientific and medical studies, as well as public policy decisions, must be undertaken with global considerations.

Mercedes-Benz is a good example of an organization redefined by this wave of change, which we now generally call *globalization*. Always the ultimate symbol for products *Made in Germany*, the Mercedes is now built in numerous global locations, and its parent corporation is even responsible for non-German products. Daimler-Chrysler AG makes cars, trucks, and other products in North America, South America, Europe, Africa, and Asia and sells them under many different names, such as Chrysler, Freightliner and Mitsubishi. The historic Mercedes-Benz, therefore, is no longer a German company in the traditional sense, but rather a part of a global enterprise, located throughout the world, owned by stockholders across the world, designing, manufacturing, selling, and competing in the world marketplace.

Of special interest to language educators is the fact that the shrinking, leveling, and "flattening" of the world has changed the kinds of qualifications needed and expected of today's young professionals. In the 70s and 80s, a machine tool manufacturer in New England might have seen Michigan as its primary export market and four or five other firms in the United States as its competitors, thereby not giving any thought to distant lands, to language or cultural considerations. That same company today, however, will only survive in a global context, face-to-face with competitors from many different nations. Whether working for a giant like Daimler-Chrysler or the small local manufacturer of machines or parts for companies such as DaimlerChrysler, employees of such companies must know the competition worldwide, be able to seek out markets for goods throughout the world, and coordinate work with peers, partners, and customers who speak different languages and view the world through many different cultural lenses.

The implications of globalization for American education are, therefore, enormous, especially so for those of us in the profession of teaching language and culture. As shown in a study by the Rand Corporation (College Placement Council, 1994), cross-cultural communication skills are in high demand in the global workplace even though these skills continue to be largely ignored by American higher education. While engineering students in the European Union, for example, are expected to learn English and at least one other European or Asian language, U.S. educators, especially in the professional fields most affected, are only beginning to talk about the issue and have done little to change curricula or even inform their students of the needs and requisites for the global workplace. The danger looms, therefore, that young American professionals will not meet the basic qualifications for leadership-track positions in global firms and that companies will look increasingly to experts from abroad to fill their key personnel needs. In his *New York Times* review of Friedman's book, *The World is Flat*, *Newsweek's* Fareed Zakaria (2005) points to the irony that America is least prepared for globalization, even though it created the forces driving it. "While hierarchies are being eroded and playing fields leveled. . . ., are we conducting ourselves in a way that will succeed in this new atmosphere? Or will it turn out that, having globalized the world, the United States had forgotten to globalize itself?" (p. 11)

In this chapter, it will be argued that the "flattening" of the world has powerful implications for language teaching in America, both in terms of challenges and opportunities, and that our success or failure over the next decade will depend upon our responses to this new era. Though some would argue, for example, that English is already predominant as the new *lingua franca*, thereby obviating the need for other languages, strong arguments to the contrary exist, calling for a vigorous response from the language profession. In the following pages, we will first explore the phenomenon of Global English and its implications for the language teaching profession. What is Global English, how far will it spread, and what are its limits? Secondly, we will examine the implications of globalization for the language curriculum and departmental structure. To what extent is the profession acknowledging the sweeping changes of globalization and adapting accordingly? What opportunities does this new era bring and what challenges does it present? Is it necessary to change? If so, in what ways? What models exist which might point us in new directions and which might ultimately help us to carve out a stronger position for language learning in the overall educational curriculum? How far have we come in that effort and where do we see ourselves in the coming years?

Who Needs to Study a Language When the Whole World Speaks English?[1]

This may not seem like a serious question to multilingual language educators. At the very least, it is annoying to those of us who travel and work abroad periodically and who know that communication with partners in other cultures is incomplete if we do not have access to their language. It strikes us as very naïve and reminds us that the battle to make language learning relevant to Americans is never ending.

Like it or not, however, we cannot retreat from the fact that English is indeed the global language of our era. Always a strong contender as a means of international communication, anyone traveling throughout the world today knows that its use has increased with a vengeance in the last two decades, even in the last few years. The bad news for the language teaching profession is that the people who control the educational purse strings, the people who fund teachers and programs, who decide the future of our tenure-track lines, who determine that Johnny and Suzy have to learn to read, write, and do math, but not necessarily speak another language, also know this.

The power of English as a global language has a long history. It really goes back to British colonialism in the 18th and 19th centuries, which took English to so many parts of the globe and includes the founding and growth of this country with English as the primary language. To appreciate the long historical trend of English as a global language, one need only note these words written by John Adams in 1780 as part of his proposal for an American Academy:

> English is destined to be in the next and succeeding centuries more generally the language of the world than Latin was in the last or French is in the present age. The reason of this is obvious, because the increasing population in America, and their universal connection and correspondence with all nations will, aided by the influence of England in the world, whether great or small, force their language into general use, in spite of all the obstacles that may be thrown in their way, if any such there should be.
>
> (as cited in Crystal, 1997, p. 66)

---

[1] This section of the chapter is based upon addresses given to the Rhode Island Foreign Language Association (RIFLA) and the Massachusetts Foreign Language Association (MAFLA).

A second big factor was the industrial revolution of the 19th Century, which likewise had its origins in England and bolstered the prestige and importance of English as it was exported to other parts of the world. The current surge of English is more an American phenomenon than British and is attributable to American economic and military dominance and to the power and attractiveness of the free market system.

To understand the rapidly growing role of English in recent decades, we need to consider at least three very influential developments. First of all, regardless of the turmoil in the Muslim world, we live today in an era of American dominance. With the fall of the Wall in Berlin and the concomitant end of the Cold War, we were left as the only superpower and our style of free-market capitalism was accepted much more broadly and adopted by the world marketplace. Eastern Europe, Latin America, Asia, Southeast Asia, and other parts of the world are doing their best to follow our model and to become competitive players in the global market. They want to play our game, and that often means speaking our language.

Second, we have accelerated the shrinking of the world with incredible systems of transportation, computer networking, and telecommunications. A Bostonian can be in Frankfurt in just over six hours, and it is a non-stop flight from Chicago to Shanghai. Short of that, one can easily be in contact with partners around the world on a daily basis by way of the computers on our desks or the fax machine in the outer office. The facts are there, and the numbers are astonishing:

- Hundreds of thousands of passengers cross the Atlantic each day.

- Daily worldwide currency exchange has grown from $590 billion per day in 1989 to $1.9 trillion in 2004.[2]

- The number of calls made from the U.S. to other countries increased from 200 million in 1980 to 5.9 billion in 2002.[3]

- About 31 billion e-mails were sent daily in 2003, and this figure is expected to triple by 2006.[4]

Third, along with the expansion of our market system and our technology, our language has been accepted as the common or default language to be used when people of different nations need to speak with one another and do not have the ability to communicate in their mutual languages. English is the language of international conferences; the language of most international organizations; the language of scientific and medical journals; the first second-language in a rapidly growing number of nations; the official language of most global companies; the growing

---

[2] See: <http://www.bis.org/publ/rpfx04.pdf>.
[3] Federal Communications Commission News (May 6, 2004). May be found at: <http://www.fcc.gov/Bureaus/Common_Carrier/Reports/FCC-State_Link/IAD/trend504.pdf>.
[4] See: <http://www.sims.berkeley.edu/research/projects/how-much-info-2003/execsum.htm>.

language of instruction at universities in many non-English speaking countries such as Sweden, Holland, and Finland; the language likely to be used in multinational business meetings; the most common language in the modern music scene, the motion picture industry, the tourist industry, the international news industry (CNN and MSNBC, for example), and the fast-food industry; the international marketing language; the language of international sports; the lingua franca of the Internet; and, yes, even a key language for international terrorism.

If this is so, why do we as Americans need to speak anything but English? There is no sign that English will decline as the primary language for global communication. Indeed, many speculate that the use of English will only intensify in the coming years. Some believe that English will become the language of the European Union, with its expansion to Eastern Europe and current membership of 25 nations. Some theorize that smaller countries like Holland or Slovakia will eventually give up their native tongues in favor of English as a matter of practicality, in short, that English will become so predominant that language after language will slip away in favor of an emerging global English. Thus, the question persists: Who needs to study a language when the whole world speaks English? Though language professionals might snicker and shake their heads about this kind of attitude, the question will not go away, and Americans remain simply too pragmatic to accept vague theoretical responses or rationales for language study, such as broadening the horizons of our students or learning to understand our own language better.

There is long-term hope if we take an historical perspective. Though it would not be politic to suggest in any way that American civilization could decline, there is powerful evidence that external or global languages do drift in and out of fashion on a large scale without forcing native tongues into extinction. Latin, of course, played an enormous role in Medieval Europe as an academic and official language. In the 18th century, French was so "in" that Prussian King Frederick the Great claimed he only spoke German with his horse grooms. German was so prevalent in the former Austro-Hungarian Empire that literary figures, like Kafka in Prague, chose German as their medium for artistic expression. Consider also the dominance of Russian in the many nations and republics behind the Iron Curtain, which has all but disappeared in many regions in as little as one generation. The East Germans are no longer interested in speaking Russian (if they ever were); the Czechs learn German for business purposes, as even the man on the street is very likely to get by in English.

Such an historical perspective is certainly interesting, and it encourages speculation about the future of English. As the voice of American culture, English tends to be either loved or hated—or both—by much of the rest of the world and is thereby subject to accusations of linguistic and cultural hegemony and to potential backlash and rejection. Nevertheless, language teachers probably should not go to their school boards with the argument that English, based on examples of the past and the precariousness of the world political situation, might be significantly diminished in 50 years in favor of Chinese or Spanish. On a shorter term basis, it is important to know how widespread or pervasive English really is. Who speaks English and who does not and how does that affect us in our lives and careers? We also need to ask what the nature of Global English is, how far one can get with Global English, and what the disadvantages are for those who are limited to it. We also need to ask what native speakers of English are missing if they do not learn other languages.

How Widespread is Global English?

As suggested already, the use of Global English is growing and growing fast. Europeans hoping to progress in their professional careers, for example, know that they are expected to be proficient in English and one other foreign language. Most companies do their international work in English, and chances are continually greater that students outside of the UK and the USA will do at least part of their postsecondary studies in English.

But, there are limits to this apparent global spread of English which many Americans do not understand—and it is critical that we define and clarify these limits for our non-language colleagues, our school administrators, and school boards. First of all, it is ridiculous to think that Europeans are going to scrap their native tongues in favor of English. Dutch will always be the first language of the Dutch and Swedish will always be the first language of the Swedes. Despite the European Union and other forces, nationalism remains a powerful force and native tongues remain the prime cultural marker and cornerstone of personal and national identity. Secondly, English is a popular and necessary second language for many peoples around the world, but it is precisely that—a second language, a language of convenience for international meetings, and not the language of daily thoughts, not the language used in the family setting, not the language spoken with colleagues in their own national environment, and not the language used when subtleties are involved. If we really want to understand the Dutch, the Swedes, the Japanese, the Chinese, if we really want to speak to their minds and hearts, we must approach them through their native tongues. Thirdly, as we shall see in more detail below, the English used globally is predominantly not the English spoken by native speakers, but rather a simplified and often topic-specific language of convenience.

Who Speaks Global English?

At certain levels, English is widespread and spoken extremely well, but this ability is not as prevalent as many would like to think. If an American plans to tour or do business travel abroad, confining oneself to hotels and restaurants catering to the global community, in other words, to linguistically and culturally safe zones, then English will clearly suffice. Or if one interacts only with the management levels of global companies or with academics in professional meetings, English will be adequate. But English by no means permeates organizations abroad, even when they are global in structure and nature and have English as an official language. Parallel to tourism where one is linguistically safe on Main Street, the business world is safe for English when associating with the right groups. Strong English skills are common to the domain of upper management but rapidly fall off at other structural levels. Middle management, sales forces, and service people, as well as engineers, tend to focus on the immediate and local issues through the medium of their own tongue and find themselves pressed when forced to work in English. Moving to the technician level or to the shop floor reduces even more dramatically the chances of speaking in English.

This author was recently part of an American group visiting a company in Spain, the Spanish subsidiary of a French-owned firm which had established English as its official language. Their presentation to us as a group of Americans was in English, but despite official policy our group was surprised at the clear inadequacy of their English language skills. The Spaniards acknowledged that inadequacy and confessed that German was actually more important to them at their facility because their customers were German. (They make seats for Volkswagen.) English played a large role in global strategy sessions, but these generally were limited to the company's top players. One can have similar experiences with global firms such as DaimlerChrysler, whose official language is also English. Based upon this author's visits to several branches of the company in Germany, there is little indication that this impacts the daily routine of the majority of employees. Board decisions are certainly sent around the world in English, but if one wants to access the research and development teams, the test engineers, the production facilities, and the like, German is highly desirable. Even the annual corporation meetings are held in German.

In an article in the *Journal of Language for International Business* (Dehmel and Grandin, 1997), which was the result of a survey of engineers who worked for the TRW Corporation in locations in Germany, France, Spain, and England, language needs were also found to be complex. Though English is the company's official language, it was found that English was not necessarily used in cross-national communication, in part because of inadequacy, but also in part because of national pride. People felt strongly that there should be an effort to learn each other's languages and that English should not be the only language of communication. In actual practice, TRW employees communicate across cultures in a variety of languages, generally choosing the language of least resistance, or, in some cases, the language of the person presumed to have the highest status among the players at a particular meeting.

The Nature of Global English

It is important to note that there is a Global English used internationally by non-native speakers of English as a common language, for example, when an Italian, a Japanese, a Dane, and a Brazilian get together to negotiate an agreement or when a group of any single nationality must meet with monolingual Americans. In most cases, the English that they speak in such meetings is not the English spoken by a native speaker, but rather a simplified international variant that is very different in significant aspects and deserves, for that reason, a special name. *Global English* is an easily understood designation, but it could be Inter-English, World Standard Spoken English (WSSE, as designated by the linguist David Crystal, 1997, p. 150), or some other similar name.

Global English should more accurately be designated as a default language than as a language of choice. It is the language most likely to be known by international groups communicating with one another on common topics. When the various parties are coming to a meeting in Malaysia, for example, one might envision one group en route speaking Indian English amongst themselves, the Germans speaking German, the Japanese speaking Japanese, the group from South Africa speaking Afrikaans, and the Finns speaking Finnish. But, when they meet, they all give up the languages defining their national and cultural identities and communicate with each other in their own forms of Global English.

Global English tends to be a stripped-down English, grammatically uncomplex, avoidant of subtleties and nuances, limited in vocabulary, and culturally neutral. It is not a personal language, it is not a native language, it is not the language of nonnative speakers' innermost thoughts, feelings, beliefs, or aspirations. Global English is a utilitarian language, and, as such, a less than impressive English from the point of view of the native speaker. The crudest examples are known today as Seaspeak, Emergencyspeak, AirTraffic English, and Computerspeak. But even the English used in academic settings is often wanting in terms of style, vocabulary, or grammatical perfection. As one executive of a large German-based global company told this author on the basis of his many years of experience, "The language of international business today is bad English."

One of the great ironies of Global English is that it is not spoken well by native speakers. For Americans to succeed at communication in Global English, they must learn to simplify their language and avoid imagery and metaphors and other expressions rooted in culturally specific terms. Monolinguals, a term describing most Americans, tend to be unaware of the linguistic barriers or the subtleties separating them as native speakers of their language from those who have learned or are learning their language as a second language or as a language for a specific purpose. In Global English, one would say, for example, that he or she bought something at a good price, whereas an American might well say that he or she bought something "dirt cheap" or "for a song" or that he or she "stole it right out from under" someone. In turning down an offer, Americans often say that they are "all set" or that they will "pass" or that they are "good." This can be confusing to the global traveler who has learned to simply say, "No, thank you." While the nonnative speaker of English would say that he or she did not succeed at a particular venture, the American is likely to be more colorful with phrases such as "I struck out," "I screwed up," "I never even got to first base." A phrase as simple as "I don't know" offers a whole range of possibilities for Americans which would flop in the global business setting: "Beats the hell out of me;" "I don't have a clue;" "I don't have the slightest."

What Are the Disadvantages for Those Limited to English?

Global English is a risky and limited form of communication. Aside from its purely linguistic limitations and the resulting potential for misunderstanding, it bars us from cultural nuances and isolates us from the inner language of our conversational partners. It keeps us at the surface level and never lets us into the other person's world. As Wallraff (2000, November) observed in the *Atlantic Monthly*, "the globalization of English does not mean that . . . we'll soon be able to exchange ideas with anyone who has anything to say. We can't count on having much more around the world than a very basic ability to communicate."

Jay Oliva, the past President of New York University, spoke on this topic at the Northeast Conference on the Teaching of Foreign Languages in New York in 2001. His argument was that English is a "language of convenience" available to the global community, but not the "language of the soul." If you want to truly understand your partners abroad, then you must reach them through their languages, the languages of their thoughts, and of their innermost selves. Without this, discussion remains at the superficial level.

At the Kentucky Foreign Language Conference in April, 2001, similar thoughts were echoed by American businessman Edward Cohen. He argued that business is 90% social, that things happen through personal contacts and through personal relationships. Here again, the only real way to interact with persons from other cultures is through their own view of the world, and that means their language.

This author recently visited the subsidiary of an American company in Germany, which makes valves for Volkswagen engines. Though their official corporate language is English and some of the managers are Americans, they were quick to point out that German is the language they need to speak when they meet with Volkswagen engineers, in other words, that they would be at a distinct disadvantage and would most likely lose this very important customer if they could not negotiate in German. Indeed, negotiations might well commence in English, but it is not at all uncommon for the engineers on the Volkswagen side to retreat to a discussion amongst themselves in German, potentially excluding the other side from important considerations.

Americans are often warned in the current political climate that we need to be reaching out to the hearts and minds of the Muslim populations so that they understand who we Americans are and what we want. Yet we have few experts who can translate appropriate messages into clearly communicative Pashto and Dari, which are the most commonly spoken of the 45 languages in Afghanistan. Indeed, the federal government has been advertising in search of people with expertise in these languages and even recruiting native speakers among Washington cab drivers.

Can we really understand the Muslim extremist if we can only access his or her thoughts through the Global English which he despises? If we value our relationship with Iran, maybe we should encourage more Americans to learn Farsi and to study the Iranian culture. If we really want the Uzbeckis and the Turks and the Afghans to be on our side, maybe we should invest in the study of the languages which provide them with their national identities.

We must get the message across that there is a world standard for global communication. Though English may be the symbol of that standard for others, *the heart of that standard is not English, but rather bilingualism and cross-cultural communication.* Though we might think of it as an advantage, the spread of Global English has become a national handicap for us, for it has given us a false sense of security and actually clouded our understanding of the world beyond our borders. Being born speakers of the global *lingua franca* enables us to be lazy, to confine ourselves to a monolingual perspective, and it limits us to superficial conversation with our partners. It allows us to "let the other guy make the extra effort" to communicate in our language. It denies us access to the innermost world or the personal world of our partners from other cultures. It translates into ignorance and loss of power. As Wallraff (2000) points out in her article: "Outside certain professional fields, if English-speaking Americans hope to exchange ideas with people in a nuanced way, we may be well advised to do as people elsewhere are doing: becoming bilingual."

In the current world political climate, language professionals have an opportunity to make some impressive arguments, among them that the superficial conversation afforded by Global English is not sufficient for complex issues. When our political leaders confer with their counterparts from Saudi Arabia, Pakistan or Uzbekistan, they no doubt are counting on the Uzbeks or translators who might even be supplied by the other side to understand everything they say. And one hopes they are being as straightforward as possible with very few nuances or subtleties in their words. I would hope that our military and State Department leaders have speakers of the pertinent languages on staff, cognizant of and experienced with the cultural subtleties of those societies. Or, are they relying on the other side's translators? Americans do not have a good track record in these things. Can we really afford to remain as linguistically and culturally limited as we are?

This author's experience has been more in the realm of global business than in global politics, and here there has been a detectable awakening among Americans.

Global business people value and seek bilingualism increasingly as an appropriate credential for the global workplace. We can offer proof of that through our International Engineering Program at the University of Rhode Island where global companies eagerly recruit our graduating bilingual engineers. It has also been our experience that the private sector is an ally for language faculty today. We have had direct contact with numerous corporate leaders who clearly subscribe to the notion of bilingualism as a fundamental qualification for work in this age of globalization and who are willing to speak up. They have helped us in Rhode Island and have made it clear that international education is in the direct interest of corporate America. Given this experience and the evidence provided in the report to be released by the prestigious Committee on Economic Development <http://www.ced.org>, it is clear that language faculty have the potential of collaborating with powerful allies from a broader spectrum of society to overcome the national lethargy with regard to language study. In short, there is now a greater potential for convincing the American public that our monolingualism is a handicap that we can no longer afford to ignore. Or, as Mexican President Vicente Fox stated at the 2nd International Congress on the Spanish Language in Valladolid on October 16, 2001: ". . . el monolingüismo ya no es la condición natural del hombre." (". . . monolingualism is no longer a natural condition of man.")

New Challenges and New Opportunities

If we accept Thomas Friedman's view that the global marketplace has become a level playing field, with no guaranteed competitive advantage for Americans, and if we accept the argument that bilingualism is a fundamental qualification for global citizenry and professional success, then the implications for American educators are enormous. Though there are many isolated language teaching success stories across the country, there is no national foreign language policy and there is no consistent K-12 or K-16 articulated pattern of language learning such as one finds in other parts of the world. While American grade school pupils may have a positive language experience in the early grades, it is not uncommon for the middle or high school language courses to be unrelated to the earlier experience or even to each other. Students at the high school level often repeat what they have done at earlier levels, only to do the same at the postsecondary level and to then drop out with finality at the intermediate or even the beginning level. In short, our national neglect of foreign language study has left us vulnerable in an age when cross-cultural and cross-linguistic communication has become a necessity.

Challenges Within Schools

Unfortunately it is not difficult to paint an even gloomier picture of language learning in the United States. Budgetary pressures are squeezing out language courses with weaker enrollments to the extent that many school systems are moving toward

Spanish as the sole language of instruction. The so-called less-frequently-taught languages such as Chinese, Arabic, or Japanese are struggling in many areas of the country, as are German and French. There is a trend to offer language learning and support programs for heritage speakers, and yet these too are under pressure by political forces demanding the elimination of bilingual programs and the granting of official status to English as the sole national language.

The place of language learning at the college and university level is also far from secure, in part due to political and budgetary pressures, but also because of 19th century traditions which shaped the mission of language study at the post-secondary level. Language requirements have tended to be eliminated over the last three decades, and those that remain serve mainly to enforce strong enrollments at the elementary and intermediate levels. While we have regular reports from the Modern Language Association (MLA) on postsecondary language enrollments, we do not have information on the numbers of students enrolled in languages in courses at the upper levels. If we were to learn how many American students graduate at the bachelor's level with a working proficiency in a second language, which is the norm for students in other countries across the globe, the results would be very bleak. Little progress has been made, and we are still sending future leaders into the world who will look back at their language learning experience and declare it a waste of time: "I took three years of [insert a language] in high school and two semesters in college and I can't even order a meal in a restaurant or buy a loaf of bread!"

Though college and university language departments are now engaged in debates about their mission, often by necessity, traditions remain strong. How often we are reminded by colleagues that we are deeply rooted in the humanities and that our main mission is literary scholarship; indeed our greatest accomplishments rest in the preparation of students who will attend graduate school and follow in our own literary footsteps. Colleagues bound to this monolithic tradition tend to ignore the fact that the numbers of students eager to pursue the purely literary track have diminished and that our cash-strapped institutions can no longer support programs with tiny upper-level courses and small numbers of majors. The result is often a bitter battle with deans who have no other options but to withdraw resources, leading to lost faculty positions, cancelled majors, and an ever smaller place in the curriculum for language programs.

Challenges in the Economic Sector

It is ironic that language programs should struggle or even lose ground in a time of intense globalization, when it appears obvious that young people need to be educated for working and living together with peers from other cultural and linguistic backgrounds. We in the profession need to step back, therefore, and see ourselves in a larger context and assess the role that we should be playing in a time of such drastic change. We need to accept the fact that there are multiple reasons for language learning, not the least of which is to ensure the economic well-being of the nation. Though, for some of us, markets may smack of forces degrading to the traditional humanities, these fears mask the potential of new partnerships and new allies with whom we can jointly reshape the American attitude toward languages other than English and toward language learning. Ironically, our new allies from the workplace and marketplace could well help to strengthen the overall place of the humanities in the American educational curriculum.

It is indeed becoming easier and easier to argue that second language skills are directly relevant to the national economic well-being. It is, for example, a sign of the times that the prestigious Washington-based public policy group, the Committee for Economic Development <http://www.ced.org> is releasing a 2005 study on this very issue, with an unequivocal recommendation that the nation develop a clear language learning policy and that our expectations for language learning be substantially raised. The call is heard increasingly from the business community, as corporations find themselves managing multiple locations, working with cross-national research and development teams, and marketing to locations across every continent. As was published in the Rand Corporation study (College Placement Council, 1994) over 10 years ago, corporate leaders are calling for professionals in all areas of expertise to be skilled in cross-cultural communication. In a recent survey of executive recruiters, Korn/Ferry International found clear agreement that bilingualism was strongly tied to success in today's business environment and that this skill would be even more important in the future ("Multilingual Execs," 2005). In short, the language teaching community must acknowledge and embrace the fact that the business community and the global economy are calling upon educators at all levels to work together to prepare students with real-life second language abilities and international experience.

Challenges From the Political Arena

Parallel to the economic arguments for language learning, the current political environment has also focused attention on our monolingualism as a national liability and vulnerability from a defense and homeland security point of view. The federal government could not find sufficient numbers of speakers of Pashto, Urdu, Farsi, or Arabic in the wake of 9/11. Hearings of the National Commission on Terrorism Attacks Against the United States identified the shortage of language specialists as "an ongoing problem" and found that thousands of hours of audiotapes and pages of written material are not being reviewed or translated in a timely manner (National Commission on Terrorism, 2000). These and other concerns led to a National Language Conference of leaders from the U.S. Department of State with members of the educational and private sectors in 2004; this group released a federal white paper strongly endorsing heightened national attention to language learning in the interest of both national defense and economic well-being (National Language Conference, 2005).

Responding to the Challenges: Globalized Language Programs

Language faculty need to realize that the age of globalization, with all of its ambiguities, challenges, and anxieties, is demanding greater intercultural knowledge and sophistication of all school and university graduates and therefore is opening the doors of opportunity to language programs. Responding to this demand is not simple, however, since the opportunities are often associated with student and curricular audiences outside of the traditional humanities framework, for example, in engineering, business, law, and other professional programs. It can be understandably intimidating or threatening to think of tailoring language programs for the scientist or the engineer, and language faculty want least of all to see themselves reduced to a service function for other disciplines.

A specific need for language skills, whether pragmatic or not, will bring students to the classroom, and those who have worked to accommodate new audiences have been able to reinvigorate their departments, save their faculty lines, and, indeed, carve out a much larger place for themselves in the overall undergraduate curriculum. As will be seen through the following case studies where faculty have attempted to build a language department for the age of globalization, the result is not only a larger number of majors with greater personal and intellectual diversity, but also a program of outreach for the humanities, where bridges are being built between the humanities and the scientific, technical, and business disciplines. Language faculty are thereby beginning to see themselves not as service entities, but as the focal point in the undergraduate curriculum where all other disciplines can converge and blend with one another in a manner appropriate to an age of interdisciplinarity.

The University of Michigan, Department of Germanic Languages and Literatures

One such language program is The University of Michigan's Department of Germanic Languages and Literatures[5] where faculty have substantially increased the number and variety of internship and study abroad opportunities offered to students and have broadened the curriculum to include a wide variety of interdisciplinary courses. As a result, undergraduate enrollments have increased dramatically. In the past six years, the number of German majors has risen from 60 to 149, almost all of whom are double majors, and an additional 95 students are currently pursuing the recently introduced German minor.

Beginning in the early 1990s, the department developed an extensive Business German sequence: Contemporary German Society and Business Culture (4th semester), Business German (3rd year), German Civilization and Culture for International

---

[5]Information on this program was provided by Drs. Hartmut Rastalsky and Janet VanValkenburg.

Relations (3rd year), Advanced Business German (4th year), Marketing and Management (4th year). The department has since introduced a 4th semester course in Scientific German and two 3rd year courses in Engineering German and is developing a minor in Engineering German. The range of courses in German literature, film, music, history, and politics has also been substantially expanded. The transition to this broader array of upper-level courses has been facilitated by the replacement of the traditional 4th semester language course by special topics sections such as Introduction to German Film, Mozart's *Magic Flute*, Legal German, German Crime Stories, Classics of German Literature, as well as those mentioned above.

During their studies at Michigan, roughly 90% of the German majors spend an extended time in a German-speaking country. Recognizing the importance of linking undergraduate students with the professional world, the department has cooperated with the International Cooperative Education (ICE) program, International Association for the Exchange of Students for Technical Experience (IAESTE), AIESEC, and the Robert Bosch Foundation to find summer internships for students in Germany. Most importantly, the department has entered a partnership with CDS International and now accommodates its Midwest office. CDS arranges individualized internships for students and recent graduates. To encourage students to pursue internships abroad, the department offers financial assistance and has developed a one-credit pre-internship course as well as a three-credit course through which students can earn credits for the successful completion of an internship.

Study abroad options include summer courses at the Goethe Institut, for which the department has streamlined the process of awarding transfer credits; a summer program in Graz; a popular new one-semester program in Tübingen; and a one-year program in Freiburg. As with internships, departmental or university financial assistance is available for participants in all these programs. To ease the cultural and academic transition, the department offers a one-credit course that serves as an extended orientation.

With this varied range of curricular and practical initiatives, the Department of Germanic Languages and Literatures strives to reach out to students of all academic backgrounds and interests. Students gain practical knowledge and experience as well as intercultural skills that not only make them more marketable, but also personally enrich their lives in the context of the opportunities and challenges of today's globally interconnected world.

University of Rhode Island, International Engineering Program

A second example of creative outreach by a language program to other disciplinary partners may be seen in the International Engineering Program (IEP) at the University of Rhode Island, which is directed by the author of this chapter.[6] The IEP is a

---

[6] For further information on this program, see: <www.uri.edu/iep>.

five-year undergraduate curriculum through which students simultaneously complete the Bachelor of Science in any of the engineering disciplines and the Bachelor of Arts degree with a major in French, German, Spanish, or Chinese. Key components of the IEP are specialized language courses for engineering students, a semester of study at a partner university abroad, and a six-month professional internship with a company in the target culture. The IEP also has developed its own residential complex on campus, enabling students to live in either of two IEP Houses, thereby interlinking their academic program with their residential life on campus.

The IEP was initiated by the German faculty along with the dean of the College of Engineering. Both parties understood the need for engineers with strong cross-cultural skills, the educational value of melding the humanities with the technical fields, and the potential for the institution as a whole by innovating in a time of broad social change. The IEP reinvigorated the German language program, which now has over 100 majors, and has, in the meantime, likewise provided a substantial boost to the numbers of majors in French and Spanish. The IEP has proven to be a powerful force for the College of Engineering, as it has helped to recruit an ever stronger and more talented student body and has created an award-winning educational model, recognized and praised by many groups across the educational spectrum. Twenty percent of URI's engineering undergraduates, one-third of whom are women, are earning a second degree in a foreign language through the International Engineering Program.

The Rhode Island program has become a national resource center for the collaboration of engineering and language groups and now organizes an annual conference on the subject, the Annual Colloquium on International Engineering Education. The language faculty, once a threatened breed at the University of Rhode Island, now find themselves in the center of national and international cross-disciplinary educational activities. They are often called upon by colleagues across the country for their expertise in designing and offering language courses appropriate to students in the science and technology areas. Locally, they are seen as the leaders of a cutting-edge program which has attracted outstanding students to campus and taken major steps in adapting the university curriculum to the needs of the global age.

San Diego State University, International Business Program

Yet another example of language and professional school collaboration is the International Business Program (IB) at San Diego State University (SDSU).[7] International Business is an interdisciplinary major that culminates in a Bachelor of Arts degree offered jointly by the College of Arts and Letters and College of Business Administration. This program integrates course work in regional and cultural

---

[7] Information on this program was provided by its director, Professor Steven Loughrin-Sacco.

studies, business administration, and language, with students completing an emphasis in one of seven regional/cultural studies: Africa, Asia, Central Europe, Latin America, Middle East, North America, or Western Europe. For the degree, 3 1/2 years of language study on campus are required, plus a semester-long study-abroad or internship component, which may be expanded to include completion of dual or even triple degree programs with partner universities abroad.

The International Business Program is supported by the Center for International Business Education and Research (CIBER) at SDSU. This Center is funded by a grant from the U.S. Department of Education and is administered by SDSU's Colleges of Arts and Letters and Business Administration in order to promote international business education and research in the region. SDSU is one of 27 universities nationwide to be designated as a "national center of excellence" in international business.

Studies required for the IB major follow the same pattern as the preparation for the regular language or business majors. Courses are required in regional/cultural studies, business, and language. Regional/cultural studies may include courses in traditions, literature, theatre, ancient and modern civilization, history of area business and trade, international relations, philosophy, religion, economics, labor, and political systems. Studies in business include finance, production and operations management, marketing, international business strategy and integration, and global marketing strategy. In language, course work includes grammar, composition, conversation, translation, civilization, plus special commercial Chinese, French, German, Japanese, Russian, and Spanish courses. The IB is an excellent example of interdisciplinary work with language study as a significant part of the core. The university Web site <www.sdsu.edu> makes it clear that the institution takes pride in this program, which now boasts over 725 majors.

Georgia Institute of Technology

The language faculty at Georgia Institute of Technology have also realized significant language program growth through interdisciplinary collaboration.[8] On the one hand, the language colleagues have benefited from the foresight of an administration cognizant of the implications of globalization and most notably from a university-wide plan to internationalize the curriculum and prepare each and every student for the global workplace. On the other hand, the language faculty have understood the opportunities of internationalization, have adapted their programs to the overall needs of the institution, and have succeeded in locating language learning at the center of the international core. The result has been an almost 80% increase in the enrollment of their eight-language School of Modern Languages over the past four

---

[8] Information on this program was provided by the language chairman, Professor Phillip McKnight.

years. Georgia Tech faculty offer the Bachelor of Science in International Affairs and Modern Languages (IAML) with concentrations in French, German, Japanese, Spanish, and Chinese. The IAML degree is now the most sought after by incoming freshman enrolling in the Ivan Allen College of Liberal Arts. To this successful model, the College has added a parallel program in Global Economics and Modern Languages. The language faculty have also developed intensive summer programs in China, France, Germany, Japan, Spain, and Mexico, which are known collectively as the Language for Business and Technology Programs. In support of these programs, Georgia Tech has exchange partnerships with several universities around the world and offers extensive professional internship opportunities as well.

Georgia Tech has its own campus in Metz, France (GT Lorraine), and is expanding the original masters programs in electrical and mechanical engineering to include considerable undergraduate offerings. Georgia Tech will set up a similar campus in Singapore and agreements have been signed with three universities in China, most notably with Shanghai Jiao Tong University and with Peking University, for whom Georgia Tech will help build an Engineering School, including a new summer program with Shanghai Jiao Tong University.

> The School of Modern Languages prepares future participants in the global workforce through applied studies in foreign languages that are designed to develop advanced communication skills, creative thinking, and professional competency in the language. The School is building bridges between the languages it teaches and the engineering and technology units at Georgia Tech by integrating into its programs the kind of professional and social language students expect to use after entering the workforce. At the same time, the School offers an opportunity to develop a broad understanding of culture and literature, and of daily life in other countries and cultures.
>
> (Phillip McKnight, Chair, School of Modern Languages, Georgia Tech)

It is important to note that outreach and cross-disciplinary efforts involving language programs have not been limited to larger, state institutions where the potential of collaboration with professional schools such as engineering or business might seem more obvious. Many excellent programs have evolved at smaller, private liberal arts institutions as well, likewise with a focus on collaboration with other disciplines, likewise as a response to preparing young people for lives and careers in a complex global society. Indeed, many fine institutions are staking their identity on their ability to offer higher level language training and high-quality international experiences as part of their undergraduate studies.

St. Olaf College, Foreign Language Across the Curriculum

St. Olaf College, for example, has attracted national attention to their Foreign Language Across the Curriculum (FLAC) program, which links the language learning process with other disciplines and the major interests of students throughout the institution. St. Olaf faculty have redesigned selected courses in areas such as economics, history, religion, and political science to allow students to do some of their coursework in those subject areas in Chinese, French, German, Norwegian, Russian, or Spanish, thereby enabling them to gain deeper knowledge of their major fields, while continuing to build their language skills. FLAC succeeds in melding language learning with the students' primary interests and also serves to bring faculty together from multiple disciplines, as they co-design and even co-teach such courses in collaboration with their language colleagues.

FLAC and language learning at St. Olaf have worked hand-in-hand with the institutional leadership, which has identified international education as one of its major directions in its formal mission statement, as have many institutions in recent years:

> St. Olaf College, through International and Off-Campus Studies, creates and provides programs that serve the mission of the College at sites in the United States and abroad. These programs are characterized by the integration of academic and experiential education. The experiential component of these programs amplifies and extends the liberal learning that occurs on campus and enhances students' global perspective by helping them encounter and understand changes confronting our world in a context of global community and world citizenship.

Consonant with the overall institutional goals and in collaboration with language faculty, St. Olaf sends over 800 students per year to its programs in Europe, Asia, the Middle East, Africa, and North, South, and Central America. Some programs extend the scope of particular majors, language concentrations, or area studies; all add a cross-cultural dimension to a liberal arts education. Study abroad, of course, provides motivation for students to study other languages in depth in preparation for their departure, and the study abroad experience, in turn, prepares students for doing advanced language work back at the home campus. St. Olaf faculty have thus been very creative in encouraging interest in language learning for the student body as a whole and in defining a central place for themselves in the institutional mission and daily life. As a result, language courses are a relevant and dynamic part of the curriculum.

Dickinson College

Dickinson College is a second small liberal arts institution which has tied its identity closely to language and international study. Dickinson's strategic plan[9] strives to create "an educational program of the highest quality and challenge that turns the campus from a single site into the hub of a truly global network. The Dickinson global education model should be characterized by sustained, in-depth study; an

---

[9] See <www.Dickinson.edu>.

imaginative variety of opportunities that reach across disciplines; and close integration of study elsewhere with the program on the home campus."

It is of more than symbolic value that Dickinson's Office of Global Education (OGE) is a well-staffed, state-of-the-art facility located in the center of campus, which also houses the academic departments of East Asian studies, international studies, and international business and management. Dickinson sponsors more than 40 programs abroad on six continents in 24 countries, with options including academic year programs, semester programs, summer programs, Globally Integrated courses that include a January international field experience, and specialized programs which combine domestic study with international study. Over 60 of its faculty have served as directors of programs abroad.

Dickinson has underscored its commitment to preparing students for the global workplace by means of two of its newer programs. The International Business and Management Program provides a solid grounding in business and economics while exploring international cultural, political, and business environments. Each student selects a single international region—Latin America, the Far East, or a European country—for additional course work, which can be supplemented by study programs and/or internships abroad. The International Studies major focuses on the politics, history, culture, and economics of a particular global region, be it the Far East, Latin America, Europe, Africa, or Australia. Students can customize this major in consultation with an adviser and often pursue the program in combination with a language major and study abroad.

And, according to Dickinson Provost Neil Weissman, the college is having considerable success in meeting its goals. Of this year's Dickinson graduating seniors, 15% had majored in modern foreign languages and 29% in international fields (foreign language, International Studies, International Business & Management, area studies) that require advanced work in foreign language. The college's IIE Open Doors Report "study abroad participation rate" was 94.4%. Some 54% of the graduating senior class had studied abroad, 80% of these in Dickinson's own programs run in partnership with foreign universities. Of Dickinson students studying abroad each year between one quarter and one third are enrolled abroad for a full year.

Other Programs

It is perhaps unfair to focus this discussion on a few institutions when there are many other progressive programs and projects underway with language faculty at the core. Kalamazoo College, Earlham College, Iowa State University, Eastern Michigan University, the University of South Carolina, the Thunderbird School of International Management, Brigham Young University, and others are actively developing and refining programs with significant foreign language involvement, which may be characterized as appropriate responses to the new world described so aptly by Thomas Friedman. Lest we become too optimistic, however, it is unfortunately clear that these examples represent new and bold initiatives, but by far not the national norm. We are thus left with an open future for American language learning. Will we seize the opportunities presented in this age of globalization, or will we cling to the traditions which have become so limiting?

Conclusion

The examples described above provide us with inspiration and suggest some core characteristics of successful language programs for the era in which we live. This essay will conclude with a summation of these traits or concepts and some basic generalizations about the necessary ingredients for vital language programs in the coming years. Though no two institutions have the exact same set of dynamics, it may still be argued that certain qualities are necessary in defining those programs in our students' best interests:

- **Outreach**: Language faculty at any institution need to ask what role they may play in collaboration with non-language colleagues and departments in their given and specific location and in the context of their overall institutional mission and then how to initiate action. It might be a language/business program or interaction with a college of engineering or agriculture. It may mean joint programs with colleagues in economics, political science, communications, or hotel and restaurant management. Though each partnership will differ, success will depend on reaching out and finding like-minded colleagues and establishing creative programs with language learning as a significant component. In the current historical moment, one may safely assume that there are colleagues, departments, and disciplines open to innovation and to programmatic developments from which all can benefit. These are only available, however, to those willing to take proactive steps.

- **Interdisciplinarity**: Educational theorists are in agreement that the existing silo or vertical nature of American educational curricula must be overcome, in other words, that specialization in one area without consideration of other fields is no longer appropriate in a complex global age. Just as the mechanical engineer can no longer ignore the dimensions of electrical or manufacturing engineering, he or she can also no longer ignore the social and political dimensions of working as part of a diverse, multifaceted, complex, global organization. The call for interdisciplinary education is heard uniformly today, and this fact alone extends special opportunities and challenges to language faculty. It is in and with the study of language that all fields—whether business, engineering, the social sciences, or the study of culture—can merge, and the current wave of globalization provides powerful motivation for that to happen.

- **Flexibility**: There are those who create change, there are those who watch change, and there are those who resist change. If language faculty wish to take advantage of the new opportunities to weave language learning into the core of the educational curriculum, then they must join the ranks of those creating change. They must be able to see opportunity, and they must be able to respond to opportunity quickly and creatively. Evidence of this may be seen in the programs discussed above and at other schools where faculty have been open to change, flexible, and eager to act.

- **Entrepreneurialism**: Though such a term might appear to some as an affront to the humanities, we should not shrink from entrepreneurialism on behalf of the humanities. If we assume that a humanistic education and a bilingual and multi-cultural perspective will enrich the lives and careers of all persons, especially in this age of globalization, then we should aggressively work to make this possible. Even though we were trained to work in libraries and in the classroom, it has become possible, appropriate, and necessary for language faculty to assert their place in the curriculum and in the academic community in the form of new and creative programs. Among the many possibilities, this can mean new curricula; it can mean joint programs, collaborative teaching, and distance learning; it can mean study abroad, internships abroad; it can mean the merging of the classroom with residential life.

- **Partnerships**: Language faculty must learn to transcend the outdated traditions and confines of the departmental unit and to form new organizational structures, not only together with colleagues from numerous disciplines across the institutional whole, but also with partners from the private and public sectors. The examples cited above show that language faculty can partner with engineering professors and administrators, with business faculty, with colleagues in the social sciences, with senior-level provosts, vice presidents, and presidents. They also show the potential of collaboration with global companies and with public sector groups eager to adapt education to contemporary needs. The challenge is to find like-minded, hard-working colleagues and to reach out to the corporate sector in order to understand their needs and to create joint educational experiences from which everyone—especially the student—can derive benefit.

- **Cross-Cultural-Communication**: Language faculty can benefit by embedding themselves more deeply into the issues of cross-cultural training. While we have always taught culture, language programs have leaned most heavily on the concepts of high culture and less so on the issues of day-to-day communication in venues such as the workplace. In an age, however, when young people can expect to spend part of their professional lives abroad or, at the very least, in close communication with peers from other cultural perspectives, it is imperative that more attention be paid to the issues of cross-cultural communication. If we wish to expand study abroad programs, international internship experiences, and joint programs with professional schools, then this must become an area of serious teaching and research for faculty in language programs.

* **International Education**: It is ironic and unfortunate that language educators and international educators do not necessarily work together, attend the same conferences, or see themselves as part of an intricately interwoven common agenda. It is time for language faculty to collaborate closely with those who wish to "internationalize the curriculum" or "globalize" higher education. Granted, many opportunities for students abroad can be undertaken without language, but it is the role of the language faculty to work with their institutions as a whole in preparing students for in-depth cultural experiences in countries where English is not the native language. The programs described above are successful, in large part, because they have closely linked the language classroom with preparation for study and experiential learning abroad.

References

College Placement Council. (1994). *Developing the global work force—Insights for colleges and corporations.* A CPC Foundation/Rand Corporation Report. Bethlehem, PA: College Placement Council.

Crystal, D. (1997). *English as a global language.* Cambridge, UK: Cambridge University Press.

Dehmel, E. W., & Grandin, J. M. (1997). Educating engineers for the global workplace: A study of cross-cultural issues. *Journal of Language for International Business, 8*(2), 1–15.

Friedman, T. (2005). *The world is flat: A brief history of the 21st century.* New York: Farrar, Straus & Giroux.

Multilingual Execs in Demand. (March, 2005). *Hispanic Business,* 15.

National Commission on Terrorism Against the United States. (2000). Staff Statement No. 12.

National Language Conference. (2005). *A call to action for national foreign language capabilities* [white paper]. Washington, DC: Office of the Undersecretary of Defense (Personnel and Readiness).

Wallraff, B. (2000, November) "What Global Language?" *Atlantic Monthly,* 52–66.

Zakaria, F. (2005, May 1). The wealth of yet more nations [Review of the book *The world is flat: A brief history of the 21st Century*]. *The New York Times Book Review, 11.*

11

Advancing Less Commonly Taught Language Instruction in America: The Time Is Now

Antonia Y. Schleicher
Michael E. Everson

Introduction

While it is no secret that modern language enrollments in American education are dominated by French, German, and Spanish, national leaders in education, business, and government continually point to the need for competency in a variety of African languages, Arabic, Chinese, Hindi, Indonesian, Japanese, and Russian, just to name a few. While Spanish is clearly a critical language in both domestic and international terms, a host of contemporary political crises, diplomatic challenges, threats to national security, and economic opportunities are taking place in areas of the world populated by those who speak languages that are often referred to as less commonly taught languages (LCTLs). Yet, the fact of the matter is that the teaching of even the more widely publicized LCTLs such as Japanese and Chinese, representing 6% of foreign language enrollments in higher education, is a very small enterprise in American education when compared to the number of learners studying the more commonly taught languages of Spanish, French, and German, which in higher education represents 74.4% (Welles, 2004) and in high school almost 92% (Draper & Hicks, 2002) of all foreign language enrollments. So whether you know them as LCTLs, "strategic languages," "critical languages," "truly foreign languages," or just "other," they have traditionally occupied a marginal place in our educational system. Yet, there are signs that LCTLs will become a more prominent fixture on the American foreign language education landscape as our nation moves more deeply into the 21st century.

To support this assertion, this chapter will give a brief history of LCTLs within the American educational context after World War II. It will then discuss where the LCTLs are now in terms of initiatives and programs designed to nurture their growth in a time when both national security needs and educational priorities demand for them a more dominant place in our society. Our last section will focus on where we would like to be in 2015 with LCTL initiatives, a place that is attainable only by finding ways to bring vastly different elements in education and government together to work in greater cooperation.

Supporting and Organizing the LCTLs

The learning and teaching of LCTLs in the United States have benefited from several global developments, of which the launching of Sputnik 1 on October 4, 1957, by the Soviet Union was a major one. As a result of this watershed event, the United States Congress immediately passed the National Defense Education Act (NDEA) in 1958 to respond to the threat of the Soviet Union's superiority in technology. The NDEA was instituted primarily to stimulate the advancement of education in science, mathematics, and modern foreign languages. Many LCTL programs and area study centers in the United States were formally established in the late 1950s as an integral and crucial component of the NDEA (Dougherty, 1993; Ruther, 1994; Swenson, 1999). For example, Lambert (1973) reports that in 1958, before the introduction of the NDEA, there were only a few students studying LCTLs such as African languages, Asian languages, Slavic and East European languages, and Middle Eastern languages. The enrollments in these LCTLs rose by a dramatic 440% about five years after the legislation of the NDEA.

Having recognized the lack of practical language training, United States legislators approved the revised NDEA (Higher Education Act) under the Title VI programs. This program provides grants to institutions of higher education or consortia of institutions of higher education to establish, strengthen, and operate comprehensive and undergraduate language and area/international studies centers that will be national resources for the following:

- Teaching of any modern foreign language;
- Instruction in fields needed to provide full understanding of areas, regions, or countries in which the language is commonly used;
- Research and training in international studies;
- Language aspects of professional and other fields of study; and
- Instruction and research on issues in world affairs.

To some extent, the establishment of these Title VI National Resource Centers brought attention to the teaching and learning of LCTLs such as African, Central Asian, East Asian, South Asian, South East Asian, Latin American, Middle Eastern, and Slavic and East European languages.

Aside from providing federal funds for establishing National Resource Centers where these LCTLs could be learned and taught, this Title VI program also provides academic year and summer fellowships (Foreign Language and Area Studies Fellowship [FLAS]) to institutions of higher education to assist graduate students in foreign language and either area or international studies. The goals of the fellowship program include (a) assisting in the development of knowledge, resources, and trained personnel for modern foreign language and area/international studies;

(b) stimulating the attainment of foreign language acquisition and fluency; and (c) developing a pool of international experts to meet national needs.

As a result of the Peace Corps Program during the 1960s, many Peace Corps returnees who were exposed to LCTLs during their service years decided to pursue the study of these languages at the academic level. The majority of these Americans were able to do so through FLAS fellowships. Aside from the NDEA/HEA Title VI programs that provided different opportunities for learning and teaching LCTLs, the National Association of Self-Instructional Languages Programs (NASILP) became the first North American LCTL professional organization to promote the learning and teaching of LCTLs. According to d'Aquin (1999), NASILP "as we know it today, represents the evolution of an idea first presented by Peter Boyd-Bowman some thirty years ago" (p. 16). Between the late 1950s and early 1960s, many institutions of higher learning started realizing the need to broaden their foreign language curricula to include some of the less commonly taught languages of Africa and Asia. At this time, a lack of qualified instructors and the uncertainty of sufficient enrollments in any single LCTL did not justify the cost of formal programs at any particular institution. As a result, Dr. Boyd-Bowman prepared an instructional manual for college administrators who were interested in establishing self-instructional programs specifically dealing with LCTLs. His program offered a way to present basic instruction "in non-Western languages potentially so inexpensive and so simple to initiate that it could be duplicated on any campus in the U.S." (d'Aquin,1999, p. 16). This program is based on guided independent study, with available texts and tapes, supervised by native speakers of the target languages. Students are given prochievement tests at the end of each term by "Visiting Examiners" who are specialists and instructors of the languages that are tested. Using this method of instruction, between 1963 and 1965 Dr. Boyd-Bowman coordinated a program including Modern Spanish, Mandarin Chinese, Hindi-Urdu, Japanese, Persian, Portuguese, and Swahili. By December 1972, NASILP was formed at the National Conference of Self-Instruction in Critical Languages held in Buffalo, NY. Ever since, NASILP has been promoting the learning of over forty LCTLs, from Arabic to Zulu, at various member institutions that could not afford to have regular classes for these LCTLs. Other organizations such as the Foreign Service Institute (FSI) were also instrumental in developing audio-lingual text materials and cassette tapes for many LCTLs in the early to late 1960s.

The 1990s: A Seminal Decade

Entering the 1990s, advocates of LCTL endeavors sought to articulate a coherent and systematic vision to insure the sustainability of their efforts. One of their primary concerns was how the foreign language community traditionally viewed growth and development. That is, when one looks for some sort of metric with which to measure growth in foreign language, it is typical to quote statistics attesting to the numbers of students currently studying foreign language or the number of programs in which specific languages are taught. While this certainly can give us a feel of language education in the United States, Brecht and Walton (1994) felt that there was a misplaced overemphasis on language programs, especially in terms of how many resources were allotted to language programs at the expense of other areas in foreign language education where resources should be devoted. In their seminal article, the authors argued for establishing a comprehensive architecture for specific language fields that would support and enable LCTLs to deliver instruction in a more principled manner.

To form this field architecture, Brecht and Walton (1994) first argued that we must account for the total supply capacity for language in America, which they believe comes from four sectors: the federal, private, academic sectors, and domestic ethnic language preservation or enhancement sector, more commonly known now as the *heritage* sector. To marshal these diverse and often competing resources within a language field, work at a more foundational level must take place, work on what the authors termed "superstructure components" and "infrastructure components," while language programs would constitute the third element of this field architecture. The superstructure of a field helps an organization make plans and coordinate effort and consists of its expertise base, its language-learning framework, an ongoing strategic planning process, and field-based proactive organizations. These elements are there to make sure that in addition to knowing its expertise base from which they can draw resources and disseminate information among professionals, planners can derive a well-informed learning framework so as to avoid wrongheaded experimentation in the development of teaching methodologies as well as concentrate on collaborative planning to avoid wasteful reduplication of effort.

Infrastructure components include a host of initiatives to make sure that instructional programs can be implemented with a high degree of success. These include establishing relations between programs, scholars, countries where the target language is spoken, institutions, area studies programs, the U.S. ethnic community, and international organizations and networks. It also includes the need to establish a vibrant research tradition to nurture its language learning framework and to help in the production of well-designed materials.

Given this base, language programs form the third component of the field architecture, but it can be seen that programs are the natural manifestation of fields that are well grounded and reflect the health and vibrancy of their superstructure and infrastructural elements. Brecht and Walton (1994) used the analogy of a tree, whereby the superstructure of a language field is like a tree's roots and trunk, with the infrastructure of the language field being its branches, and the language programs, its fruit. They argue that traditional resource allocation that has concentrated on programs is like the gardener who only waters the fruit of the tree. In the long run, not tending to the other parts of the tree will have devastating consequences for the entire enterprise, as has been witnessed among LCTL program managers who have tried to start up programs with no superstructure or infrastructure elements in place. Even with such powerful initiatives as the Title VI National Foreign Language Resource Centers (NFLRCs), the authors warn that these initiatives are given to institutions and not to fields, pitting members of the same field against one another and thus producing the potential for the dissipation of collaborative energy and organization.

Given this framework, scholars at the National Foreign Language Center (Jorden & Lambert, 1991; Moore, Walton, & Lambert, 1992) began research on two of the more prominent LCTLs in American education, those of high school Chinese and pre-collegiate/postsecondary Japanese, to establish the expertise base involved in the teaching of these languages at these levels, as well as to investigate the challenges confronting these teachers so that an infrastructure could be developed with a strong language learning framework and accompanying strategic planning. The results of these surveys indicated a dismaying lack of standards and commonality between programs in virtually every aspect of language program management, be it teacher preparation, curriculum development, materials, assessment, classroom methodology, or educational standards. Especially problematic was teacher development. In fact, the findings from both studies indicated the importance of the teacher in the whole process, with the Chinese study stating that in ". . . the view of the principals, the students, the teachers themselves, and the site-visit teams, the success of a program depends most heavily on the skill and enthusiasm of the teacher. Another major indicator of the success of a program is the degree of the teacher's professionalization" (Moore et al., 1992, p. 118).

Given such compelling evidence that teacher professionalization was one of the cornerstones—if not *the* cornerstone—upon which LCTL programs must be built, a task force was formed to provide prospective teachers with a language learning framework that could be used to guide professionals involved in program development for LCTLs. Based on survey research, the group concluded that students who study LCTLs do so to interact with the cultures of these languages. This being said, the task force determined that if learners are to interact with the people of other cultures in a linguistically and culturally appropriate manner, a foundational principle of the learning framework must be that LCTLs have to be taught as a lifelong learning endeavor (Walker & McGinnis, 1995). To facilitate this journey, learners and teachers must continually expand their expertise in their knowledge of language learning and language teaching so that appropriate teaching methodologies are employed for the various proficiency levels. It is also important for learners and teachers to realize that they have important responsibilities for themselves and for each other in the learning process. For example, because so much of the learning of LCTLs takes place in other than traditional classroom settings, a premium is placed on students developing independent learning strategies so as to insure the development of their language skills in these environments. The task force also stressed the need for language learning to be culturally based so as to continually insure that language learning is properly imbedded within a cultural framework. Finally, the task force recommended the importance of adapting LCTL programs to local conditions.

In addition to these initiatives, LCTL advocates in the 1990s made more of an effort to delineate how LCTL teacher preparation programs might differ from teacher preparation programs for languages more commonly taught in our nation's schools, given the unique characteristics of LCTLs. The late pioneer of LCTL advocacy, A. Ronald Walton, used to be fond of saying, "Japanese isn't just hard French." What he meant by this, of course, was that LCTLs present unique challenges to learners, program developers, and materials designers due to their unique phonetic systems, grammatical structures, orthographic properties, and cultural aspects of the societies that employ these languages. Consequently, that language pedagogy can employ teacher education strategies and classroom methodologies for these languages that are akin to those used in more commonly taught language programs has long been thought to be misguided.

To demonstrate the differences that learners experience with LCTLs, there is a variety of research that speaks to their challenges. The Foreign Service Institute (FSI), for instance, using the performance history of learners in its school, has classified all the languages it teaches into four categories in terms of how long it takes American learners to reach specific levels of proficiency. Four prominent LCTLs—Chinese, Japanese, Korean, and Arabic—are the sole examples of what they term "Category IV" languages, or those that take the most instructional time. Walton (1992) has stated that the FSI experience has demonstrated that it takes 480 contact hours to reach a proficiency level of 2 for languages such as Spanish, French, and German, but 1,320 contact hours to reach this level of proficiency for a Category IV language. It should be remembered that government agencies such as the FSI and the Defense Language Institute (DLI) employ intensive language programs where students are immersed for many months over several hours a day. Given the nature of collegiate programs, Walton stated that it would take a learner approximately eight years of academic language study to reach this proficiency level in a Category IV language.

Clearly one of the more obvious reasons for this is that the Category IV languages employ orthographic systems that are challenging for American students to master, especially given the fact that their native language of English is represented in print by the Roman alphabet. Chinese, for example, uses a logographic system whereby each character represents a word or morpheme where the pronunciation is almost impossible for beginning learners to discern from the structural properties of the actual character. This inability to bring one's phonetic reading background to bear on the reading task makes learning Chinese characters a memory- and labor-intensive endeavor for learners and makes the learners reliant on romanization systems to learn large amounts of Chinese vocabulary in short periods of time. Japanese is also challenging as it employs three different orthographic systems, two of which are syllabary systems and one of which is the Chinese character system borrowed from China throughout various periods of Japanese history. Korean also uses Chinese characters along with a Korean alphabet. Lastly, Arabic employs a non-Roman alphabet that typically does not display vowel markings. When combined with the fact that students have a very incomplete command of the language when they are learning to read in these languages, these learners are further challenged because they do not have the spoken resources necessary to facilitate their reading development.

While reading in these languages has perhaps attracted the most interest from researchers, there have been recent attempts to move the discussion away from matters that might be considered more "code-based" and toward understanding how cultural aspects embedded in the language can also inhibit learner's proficiency development (Nara & Noda, 2003). Thus, we are beginning to see more comprehensive theories of how many of the LCTLs need to be viewed if we are to design effective teaching methodologies, materials, and teacher development programs. These newly emerging theories have also been discussed in terms of how well they will be able to propel LCTL learners to attain advanced levels of proficiency, a goal that has been extremely difficult to realize (Byrnes, 2005).

Perhaps the difference between LCTLs and more commonly taught languages most apparent to foreign language teachers is how LCTLs are accepted and valued differently in the schools, often making it difficult for these languages to become mainstreamed. Consequently, these programs tend to be extraordinarily vulnerable to elimination, with low enrollments, teacher turnover, and capricious administrative decision-making often bringing about the end of an otherwise successful LCTL program. As it is not uncommon for LCTL programs to be run by one person, these programs have no "defense in depth" to weather such vagaries as instructor turnover. Additionally, teachers in start-up programs have found conditions in schools that seem to symbolize and personify their more marginalized place in the school, such as being without a permanent classroom, lacking a common core of experience with other foreign language teachers in terms of professional development, having an itinerant teaching schedule between different schools and buildings, or holding classes for multiple levels of the language simultaneously in the same classroom (Schrier & Everson, 2000). In the collegiate environment, it is not uncommon for a teaching assistant or professor to be told that if they do not take a teaching overload, the students who are continuing on to a second year of a LCTL will be unable to continue their study, thus putting additional pressures on faculty and staff to overload themselves for the good of their program.

Where Are We Now, and Where Are We Going?

For even the most casual observer of current events, it is difficult not to be struck by the abundance of news dealing with countries whose inhabitants speak LCTLs. An issue of *Newsweek* magazine devoted a large segment of the magazine's content to its cover story entitled "Does the Future Belong to China" (Zakaria, 2005), prominently featuring a story of the growth and interest in Chinese language learning in America. A cover story in *The Atlantic* deals with the expansion of the Chinese military under the ominous title "How We Would Fight China" (Kaplan, 2005). These are, of course, alongside the stories about the American military presence in Iraq and Afghanistan and on the heels of stories during the winter holidays of 2004 when an earthquake spawned a tsunami that in the blink of an eye killed upwards of 180,000 people across Asia. Given the generally marginalized place that LCTLs have occupied in our educational system, yet still being associated with countries so prominent in world affairs, one might ask what the years of infrastructure building in the LCTLs have produced and what is being done to anticipate the challenges ahead of us. The short answer, of course, is that much has been accomplished, but much needs to be done.

The 1990s brought about several new federal and nonfederal initiatives that are meant to enhance the teaching and learning of the LCTLs. One of those initiatives was the establishment of National Foreign Language Resource Centers (NFLRCs) within Title VI of the Higher Education Act, which, according to Brecht and Walton (1993, p.1), "was intended to provide fresh focus on language study which over a hundred comprehensive language and area studies centers have apparently failed to do over nearly three decades." As of 1990, there were three NFLRCs, but the number has grown to fourteen after the events of September 11, 2001. The NFLRCs are to serve as resources for improving the nation's capacity for teaching and learning foreign languages through teacher training, research, materials development, and dissemination projects. By the year 2002, six of these fourteen NFLRCs were specifically funded by the Department of Education to enhance the learning and teaching of African languages, Central Asian languages, East Asian languages, Middle Eastern languages, Slavic and East European languages, and South Asian languages. These regional NFLRCs are developing different research-based materials for the LCTLs in their respective regions. Many of these regional NFLRCs are also providing summer professional development opportunities for teachers of their respective LCTLs, and several undertake various research endeavors in the learning of many LCTLs and more commonly taught languages. Other NFLRCs concentrate on the assessment of learning different languages, including the LCTLs. As a result of the work of some of these NFLRCs, especially the regional ones, some LCTLs now have up-to-date research-based materials for learners and instructors.

Title VI International Research Studies also have funds that can be competed for to develop materials in and do research on different foreign languages. Many text and technology materials for LCTLs exist today as a result of funds from this program.

In order to confront the difficult challenge of bringing LCTL learners to enhanced proficiency levels, the National Flagship Initiative (NFLI) of the National Security Education Program (NSEP) is co-sponsored by the federal government and higher education and designed to produce advanced-level speakers in a number of

LCTLs with pilot programs ongoing in Arabic, Chinese, Korean, and Russian at U.S. campuses. These programs use a combination of in-country immersion and on-campus language instruction " . . . to produce, across a broad spectrum of fields and disciplines, professionals and students with 'professional competency' (ILR level 3) in critical foreign languages" (National Security Education Program, 2004). The NSEP also hopes to continue to meet the increased demand for programs in these languages in the future, while also hoping to establish programs in Hindi, Japanese, Persian/Farsi, and Turkish.

In addition to these, a call for proposals for a new and ambitious NFLI initiative in Chinese is ongoing that targets the development of a K-16 pipeline project. The objectives of the 2005 project are to (a) establish a Chinese Flagship program that addresses the needs of students already at the advanced proficiency level and (b) work closely with one or more geographically proximate elementary/middle/high school systems to establish an articulated Chinese language program that progresses from the elementary grades into advanced Chinese at the university level. Consistent with all NFLI programs, the final outcome of the program is expected to be students with superior (3) level proficiency in Chinese. This project is exciting for a number of reasons. First, it gives all participants in this project, from curriculum designers to language researchers, a unique opportunity to evaluate longer sequences of language instruction, something that typical programs in American schools have traditionally been unable to accomplish. Secondly, it provides a unique opportunity for a variety of stakeholders to participate jointly, thus bridging some of the fault lines that have appeared in the articulation between elementary schools and high schools, high schools and higher education, as well as between the teachers, researchers, and administrators who run these programs. Lastly, it emphasizes the need for the program to be based on solid second language research evidence and thus provides a laboratory for more of this research evidence to be gathered and reported.

Aside from government initiatives to promote the LCTLs there are also organizational-level initiatives that began to thrive in the 1990s that are still ongoing at the present time. One such organization that has played a major role in the advancement of the LCTLs is the National Council of Less Commonly Taught Languages (NCOLCTL). The Council, originally based at the National Foreign Language Center (NFLC) in Washington, DC, was specifically established by Richard Brecht and A. Ronald Walton to help strengthen the position of the LCTLs, to ensure the formulation of a national strategy for establishing priorities, and to address problems common to the instruction of these languages. The Council grew out of three annual conferences beginning in 1987, with support from the U.S. Department of Education, the National Foreign Language Center, and the Ford Foundation. The Council has served as an umbrella organization for the major organizations representing the languages of Africa; East, Southeast, and South Asia; Eastern and Central Europe; and the Middle East. Early meetings of the Council established such policy priorities as the need for better organizational structures, for a stronger voice in setting a national agenda for the LCTLs, and for the regular collection of data on needs and resources in these languages. In the instructional domain, the Council identified improved teacher training, standardized curricular design, new and improved instructional materials, and the effective use of new technologies as priorities.

The Council also successfully effected changes in the organizational, policy, and instructional domains, changes which have had major implications for the LCTL profession. It provided advice and assistance on organization to the African Language Teachers Association and to the teachers of South Asian and South East Asian languages; it has supported the American Association of Teachers of Slavic and East European Languages and the American Council of Teachers of Russian in a joint national discussion on future developments in the profession; and it helped the American Association of Teachers of Arabic establish a database to serve the field of Arabic language training. The Council also brought together experienced LCTL program managers to plan pilot workshops for LCTL teacher trainers; in addition, it supported the Association of Teachers of Japanese, the American Association of Teachers of Turkish, and the National Association of Professors of Hebrew in research and development of LCTL curricular design and materials production, including exploration of the uses of technology. Without NCOLCTL many of the LCTL professional organizations would not exist today. Now an individual membership organization, NCOLCTL has definitely helped to raise the academic bar for many LCTLs through its annual national and international conferences, where teachers, learners, scholars, administrators, government officials, business personnel, and any other individuals interested in promoting the LCTLs can meet to discuss issues related to the LCTLs.

Also on the national and international level, the American Council on the Teaching of Foreign Languages (ACTFL) has been working very hard to promote the LCTLs in its activities. Since 1999, every president of ACTFL has made it a point to attend the NCOLCTL annual conference to lend support to the activities of the Council. Many LCTL professionals are now playing active roles in ACTFL, with more LCTL papers being presented at the ACTFL annual conference, while Standards for Foreign Languages have been published dealing with LCTLs. Recently, with support from ACTFL, the LCTL Special Interest Group was put in place in 2004, thus giving all involved in LCTL endeavors another place to meet and share their ideas at the annual ACTFL meeting.

A View of LCTLs in 2015

When trying to set a course for where LCTLs should be in 2015, it is important to note recent developments in the government and educational sectors of the United States that will have a huge impact upon the future of LCTL education, and, for that matter, world language education in general. In a speech given by Congressman Rush Holt at the National Language Conference organized by the Defense Department and the Center for Advanced Studies of Languages (CASL) in June, 2004, he said, "Immediately after September 11, 2001, Americans found themselves again facing a Sputnik moment. They realized that they were caught flat-footed, unprepared to confront Al Qaeda terrorists. We need a national commitment to languages on a scale of the National Defense Education Act commitment to science, including improved curriculum, teaching technology and methods, teacher development and a systemic cultural commitment" (National Language Conference, 2005, p. 2). To address these crises, significant events pertaining to LCTLs education have been put forth that can have wide-ranging impact on how LCTL education will develop. In viewing these events, it is important to realize that they represent a continuity and coherence of purpose that planners spoke of long before the tragic events of September 11th. Among the watershed meetings and proposed legislation are the initiatives described below:

- A National Foreign Language Conference was held in June of 2004, co-sponsored by the Department of Defense and the Center for Advanced Study of Language (CASL), a university-affiliated research center. Attended by leaders in all sectors of the government, academia, and industry, its white paper "A Call to Action for National Foreign Language Capabilities" (National Language Conference, 2005) details the need for a new and visionary approach to implementing a national strategy for foreign language education and awareness. Among the many rallying points put forth in the paper is the necessity for American leadership in the world through foreign language proficiency and cultural competence, a goal that can only be realized through cooperation between government, academia, and the private sector;

- The ACTFL/Year of Languages National Language Policy Summit was held at The University of North Carolina at Chapel Hill in January 2005. Participants from academe, business, and government convened on-site, joined by over 3,500 others via various electronic media. The participants addressed the issues raised in the Department of Defense's "A Call to Action for National Foreign Language Capabilities" by exploring strategies to respond to those issues. The report of this summit, "A Blueprint for Action on Language Education" (Müller, 2005), sets forth the actions to be taken and identifies the parties responsible for each proposed action;

- The *Defense Language Transformation Roadmap*, whereby language skill and regional expertise are now viewed ". . . as important as critical weapons systems" (U.S. Department of Defense, p. 3), was approved in February 2005. The *Roadmap* proposes to build and manage language assets in the defense community and to uncover and organize the capabilities of linguists that already exist. It also proposes to require a cadre of members to reach level 3 proficiency in speaking, reading, and listening;

- Senator Akaka put forth a bill in 2005 to establish a National Foreign Language Coordination Council chaired by a National Language Director charged with the development and implementation of a national language strategy. The bill very specifically addresses LCTLs and calls for the Council to take leadership in working with the various sectors of foreign language stakeholders;

- The National Security Language Act co-sponsored by Representative Rush Holt focuses on a variety of foreign language initiatives such as early foreign language learning, foreign language education for science and technology, heritage community language learning, the flagship initiative, and loan forgiveness to foreign language students;

- Senators Lieberman and Alexander sponsored in 2005 the United States-China Cultural Engagement Act which provides support for, among other things, Chinese language instruction in American elementary and secondary schools;

- Senators Dodd and Cochran introduced in 2005 The International and Foreign Language Studies Act of 2005. The purpose of this act is to increase study abroad and foreign language study opportunities for undergraduate and graduate students.

In view of all the above initiatives, the immediate question that comes to mind is how can we leverage these growing interests in the LCTLs to expand and improve the LCTL infrastructures? The first answer to this question is the need for collaboration between the academic, business, private, community and government sectors to get us to where we want to be by 2015. As stated in the 2005 White Paper, "No one sector—government, industry, or academia—has all of the needs for language and cultural competency, or all of the solutions" (National Language Conference, 2005, p. 12).

Our reaction to these proposals for how things will look for LCTL education in 2015 is quite simple—LCTL educators must become activists, as must educators of all foreign languages. By this we mean that we have seen reports before such as *A Nation at Risk* (National Commission on Excellence in Education, 1983) that stated vehemently, "if an unfriendly foreign power had attempted to impose on America the mediocre educational performance that exists today, we might well have viewed it as an act of war." This report was equally articulate and vehement in its assertion that America is woefully unprepared to meet the challenges of the future and needed to improve the learning and teaching of foreign language. Yet, here we are in 2005 with new reports essentially saying that we are still nowhere near where we need to be if we are to meet the challenges of the 21st century. As activists, it is important that we keep abreast of these developments of such concern to foreign language education and that we make sure that we participate in a process that furthers these initiatives. We think it is also important to point out that the recommendation of an appointment of a National Language Director who will provide top-down leadership has not been met without criticism by language professionals, many of whom are LCTL educators. We welcome this debate, as it is important to hear all voices as we move on with this serious endeavor. As LCTL professionals who have spent much of the time in the margins of American education and who have often lived from semester to semester with no guarantee of job security due to the problems we have mentioned in this chapter, we feel the time has come to participate in a process whereby we can be empowered as educators to work within this framework to maximize LCTL viability.

Secondly, if we are to be a force in education in 2015, we must become knowledgeable about the ramifications of *No Child Left Behind* (NCLB) for LCTL education and, again, foreign language education in general. The "Perspectives" section in the summer 2005 issue of the *Modern Language Journal* speaks directly to this matter and makes the case that if foreign language is not one of the testing priorities for NCLB, the dire consequences for schools and teachers for not meeting its standards are that the testable subjects will receive all of the school's attention and resources. If this is the case, foreign language will be further marginalized, with LCTLs programs taking on the major brunt of the closings. We find it interesting how on the one hand the government is sounding the alarm for a call to action to make our society more linguistically proficient, while on the other is putting systems into place that in reality act as obstacles for forward progress in the area of foreign language education. We recommend, therefore, that LCTL advocates stop viewing themselves as second-class citizens in the language learning community and take their place with the more established foreign languages. To do this, LCTL advocates must remind the future National Language Director, should one be appointed, of the factors marginalizing LCTLs that are being hardwired into our educational system, factors that militate against the very objectives that the federal government states it wants to achieve.

Thirdly, it is important to meet the current, more pressing needs of curriculum development and materials, the lack of which has consistently and constantly plagued LCTL educators. Our vision for 2015 is that no LCTL thought worthy enough to be taught in our society will be faced with having no materials for its teachers and learners. It is important to remember that the language learning framework mentioned previously in this chapter underscored the fact that LCTL instruction will normally take place in non-traditional settings. Therefore, the NFLRCs, as well as projects such as LangNet materials development, must continue to make available materials both in printed form and over the Internet so that both teachers and learners will not have to endure the frustration that all involved in LCTL education have had to endure or are still enduring due to a lack of instructional materials.

Fourthly, we would like to talk about topics such as the place of the LCTLs in a seamless K-16 environment, but it is difficult to project what this will be in the year 2015. Given some of the grave concerns about the place of even the more commonly taught foreign languages in our schools due to NCLB, LCTL advocates feel more concern due to their experience with the "last in, first out" policy of employment termination. Given that there is much we cannot control, at a minimum our goal for 2015 will be that every LCTL teacher will be guaranteed access to a teacher education program, as recent surveys highlight this as a continuing need for LCTLs (Johnston & Janus, 2003). In the meantime, it will be critical to watch a program like the K-16 Chinese Flagship as it unfolds to evaluate whether this model can be adapted to other LCTLs, as we are attracted by its potential to serve as a model for the kind of collaborative efforts needed by all the different sectors to help us have the infrastructure that we need for the LCTLs. LCTL advocates need to watch the K-16 Chinese Flagship program closely and, if it is successful, work with the government sectors to encourage other LCTL K-16 Pipeline Projects. Just as the goal of this pipeline project cannot be reached by one single sector, it is critical for us in the LCTLs to have the kind of collaboration called for in the Model Chinese K-16 Pipeline Project so that by 2015 we can have projects like it for Arabic, Hindi, Swahili, Persian/Farsi, Korean, Yoruba, and similar languages. Without a fully connected infrastructure that the Chinese K-16 Pipeline Project is calling for, we will continue to find ourselves in the endless cycle of sporadically building programs that will eventually disappear.

Lastly, we wish to point out the importance of establishing a coherent research agenda for the LCTLs. Conducting empirical research among learners of LCTLs has been a fairly recent endeavor (Everson, 1993), yet it should be pointed out that researchers have been able to carry out research projects that have been influential in furthering our understanding of the processes involved for American learners coping with non-alphabetic writing systems (Everson, 2002; Nara & Noda, 2003; Koda, 2005), the furtherance of language proficiency through study abroad (Davidson, 2005), and the needs and developments of language professionalization (Schrier & Everson, 2000), as well as studies into second language acquisition (Hatasa, 2003). Importantly, another federal government initiative that promises to enhance the acquisition of the LCTLs and other foreign languages is the establishment of the Center for Advanced Studies of Languages (CASL), which is one of the University Affiliated Research Studies Centers. The mission of CASL is to improve the performance of Foreign Language Professionals (FLPs) in the federal government. This is accomplished through a unique partnership between academe and government, the goal of which is to guarantee that research be innovative, of the highest quality, and informed by a deep understanding of the operational environment of language professionals in the federal government. Its work is driven by the explicit requirements of the federal workforce involved with language and by academe's best vision on how these requirements can be met.

In establishing our research, however, it is important that we again become activists in letting policymakers know that foreign language education has a research agenda that must take into consideration areas of interest specifically germane to our discipline. For example, under NCLB, Rosenbusch (2005) points out that foreign language educators are concerned that we are being told that our research agenda must be focused towards documenting how foreign language education contributes to ". . . 'scientifically based research' that provides statistical evidence that the study of a FL enhances cognitive functioning and results in improved student performance on tests of the core academic subjects of language arts/reading, mathematics, and science" (p. 257). We believe that this is akin to asking track and field coaches to justify their existence by documenting how participation in their sport develops better football and basketball players. Clearly, the physical conditioning derived from participation in track and field can help any athlete perform at a higher level since physical conditioning is a basic building block of athletics. Yet, the sport of track and field has much to recommend itself due to its specific characteristics that are not shared with other sports, hence its value and inclusion in the athletic community. Likewise, while research into how foreign languages study relates to other academic skill development is worthy, research informing policymakers about the unique contributions that research in second language acquisition, foreign language education, and applied linguistics can provide that are unique to our field is paramount. It is important to realize that every LCTL and foreign language initiative cited in this chapter in some way demands that we bring learners to advanced level, culturally appropriate language proficiency acquired in a variety of settings across learners of various ages and linguistic backgrounds. This will only be accomplished by doing more research in our primary domains of expertise, and no one is more capable of framing this research agenda than we are.

In addition, we need to inform these policymakers about the value of different research paradigms that are becoming more frequently used in foreign language research. For instance, if by "scientifically based research" we mean only studies that are based on experimental/quasi-experimental designs from a more cognitively-based theoretical paradigm, we have work to do in informing policymakers about more socio-cultural frameworks that analyze different types of data—and which are becoming more and more prominent—to investigate language within its socio-cultural environment. Therefore, by 2015 we need to have not only articulated a research philosophy and produced a document that states a plan of research for the LCTLs, but to have already moved that agenda along in this ten-year period through a series of completed projects.

Conclusion

As 2005 is the Year of Languages, LCTL advocates should be pleased that recent initiatives are highlighting the importance to expanding the capacity for LCTL education in America. Yet, we remain somewhat skeptical about the long-term effectiveness of these initiatives because we have "been there" before in a flush of fervor in 1957 that produced a mandate for the expansion of Russian language programs in the United States. With the dissolution of the Soviet Union, however, came the unilateral dismantling of much of the Russian language program infrastructure in this nation. It is therefore important that we actively monitor the progress of these recent LCTL initiatives so that by 2015 they are characterized by strength, sustainability, and follow-through, characteristics that have been sorely lacking in many of the LCTL initiatives of the past.

We also wish to state that we understand that writing a chapter on LCTLs should cover many other initiatives that are ongoing in the United States. For instance, we have not discussed the work of many language preservationists who toil energetically to study and preserve Native American languages and the heritage and history they represent to our nation. Equally important are the efforts of the many who work to maintain the teaching of LCTLs such as the Scandinavian or Celtic languages that represent the heritage of many of Americans but do not receive a great deal of recognition because they are not prominent in conversations dealing with national defense.

Perhaps, then, this speaks to the larger issue of language policy within the United States, or perhaps better termed the "non-issue," as this country has been accused of not having one. As we began this chapter, we focused on LCTLs as primary pieces of an overall language issue. Even its term "other" for languages other than Spanish, French, and German indicates to many the fact that we do not have an overall policy for the managing of our nation's linguistic resources. With that, we will include on our wish list that a language policy be in place by 2015 so that LCTLs can be recognized as a unique and vibrant characteristic of the many peoples who populate our nation. Without a policy to organize and disentangle the many elements that need to be working together towards more common goals in LCTL language education, we fear that in our conversations across education, government, and the private sectors, we will be speaking different languages.

References

Brecht, R. D., & Walton, A. R. (1993, December). *National strategic planning in the less commonly taught languages.* Occasional Papers. Washington, DC: National Foreign Language Center.

Brecht, R. D., & Walton, A. R. (1994). National strategic planning in the less commonly taught languages. In R. D. Lambert (Ed.), *Foreign language policy: An agenda for* change. *Annals of the American Academy of Political and Social Science, 532*, 190–212. Thousand Oaks, CA, Sage.

Byrnes, H. (2005, Spring). The privilege of the less commonly taught languages: Linking literacy and advanced L2 capabilities. *Journal of the National Council of Less Commonly Taught Languages, 2*, 21–44. Madison, WI: National African Language Resource Center Press.

D'Aquin, J. (1999). NASILP: Twenty-five Years of a Unique Organization. In E. H. D. Mazzocco (Ed.), *National Association of Self-Instructional Language Programs Journal, 27*, 16–21.

Davidson, D. E. (2005, April). *L2 and study abroad: Who gains, how much gain?* Paper presented at the 8th annual meeting of the National Council of Less Commonly Taught Languages, Madison, WI.

Dougherty, J. V. (1993). *A history of federal policy concerning college or university-based foreign language and area studies centers, 1941–1980 (Army Specialized Program, National Defense Education Act).* Doctoral thesis: University of Maryland-College Park.

Draper, J. B., & Hicks, J. H. (2002). *Foreign language enrollments in public secondary schools, fall 2000.* Yonkers, NY: American Council on the Teaching of Foreign Languages.

Everson, M. E. (1993). Research in the less commonly taught languages. In A. O. Hadley (Ed.), *Research in language learning* (pp. 198–228). Lincolnwood, IL: National Textbook.

Everson, M. E. (2002). Theoretical developments in reading Chinese and Japanese as foreign languages. In J. Hammadou Sullivan (Ed.), *Literacy and the second language learner* (pp. 1–16). Greenwich, CT: Information Age.

Hatasa, Y. (Ed.) (2003). *An invitation to second language acquisition research in Japanese: In honor of Seiichi Makino.* Tokyo: Kurosio.

Johnston, B., & Janus, L. (2003). *Teacher professional development for the less commonly taught languages.* Minneapolis: Center for Advanced Research on Language Acquisition.

Jorden, E. H., & Lambert, R. D. (1991). *Japanese language instruction in the United States: Resources, practice, and investment strategy.* Washington, DC: National Foreign Language Center.

Kaplan, R. D. (2005, June). How we would fight China. *The Atlantic, 295*(5), 49–64.

Koda, K. (2005). *Insights into second language reading: A cross-linguistic approach.* Cambridge, UK: Cambridge University Press.

Lambert, R. D. (1973). *Language and area studies review* (American Academy of Political and Social Science Monograph No. 17). Philadelphia: American Academy of Political and Social Science.

Moore, S. J., Walton, A. R., & Lambert, R. D. (1992). *Introducing Chinese into high schools: The Dodge initiative.* Washington, DC: National Foreign Language Center

Müller, K. E. (2005). *A blueprint for action on language education: Summary of the proceedings at the National Language Policy Summit, January 10–11, 2005.* [white paper]. Alexandria, VA: American Council on the Teaching of Foreign Languages.

Nara, H., & Noda, M. (2003). *Acts of reading: Exploring connections in pedagogy of Japanese.* Honolulu: The University of Hawaii Press.

National Commission on Excellence in Education. (1983, April). *A nation at risk: The imperative for educational reform.* Available: <http://www.ed.gov/pubs/NatAtRisk/risk.html>

National Language Conference. (2005). *A call to action for national foreign language capabilities* [white paper]. Washington, DC: Office of the Undersecretary of Defense (Personnel and Readiness). Available: <http://www.nlconference.org.docs/White_Paper.pdf>

National Security Education Program. (2004). *National Flagship Language Initiative (NFLI): Addressing national needs for language proficient professionals.* Available: <http://www.ndu.edu/nsep/NationalFlagshipLanguageInitiativeUpdateJan2004.pdf>

Rosenbusch, M. H. (2005). The No Child Left Behind Act and teaching and learning languages in the U.S. schools. *The Modern Language Journal, 89*(2), 250–263.

Ruther, N. L. (1994). *The role of federal programs in internationalizing the United States higher education system from 1958–1988.* Doctoral thesis, University of Massachusetts, Amherst.

Schrier, L. L., & Everson, M. E. (2000). From the margins to the new millennium: Preparing teachers of critical languages. In D. W. Birckbichler & R. M. Terry (Eds.), *Reflecting on the past to shape the future* (pp. 125–161). Lincolnwood, IL: National Textbook.

Swenson, S. R. (1999). *International education and the national interest: The National Defense Education Act of 1958, the International Act of 1966, and the National Security Education Act of 1991.* Doctoral thesis, University of Oregon, Eugene, Oregon.

U.S. Department of Defense (2005). *Defense language transformation roadmap.* Available: <http://www.defenselink.mil/news/Mar2005/d20050330roadmap.pdf>

Walker, G., & McGinnis, S. (1995). *Learning less commonly taught languages: An agreement on the bases for the training of teachers.* Columbus, OH: The Ohio State University Foreign Language Center.

Walton, A. R. (1992). *Expanding the vision of foreign language education: Enter the less commonly taught languages.* Washington, DC: National Foreign Language Center.

Welles, E. B. (2004). Foreign language enrollments in United States institutions of higher education, fall 2002. *Association of Departments of Foreign Languages Bulletin, 35*(2–3), 7–26. Retrieved June 25, 2005, from <http://www.mla.org/pdf/enrollments.pdf>

Zakaria, F. (2005, May 9). Does the future belong to China? *Newsweek, 145*(19), 28–47.

About the Authors

Martha G. Abbott, Director of Education, American Council on the Teaching of Foreign Languages. Marty served as co-chair of the Year of Languages Working Committee in her position as Director of Education at ACTFL. Prior to this, Marty worked in the Fairfax County Public Schools (VA) as a language teacher, foreign language coordinator, and Director of High School Instruction. Her leadership positions include Chair of the Northeast Conference in 1999 and President of ACTFL in 2003. She holds her B.A. degree in Spanish with a minor in Latin from Mary Washington College and a Master's Degree in Spanish Linguistics from Georgetown University. <mabbott@actfl.org>

Christine Brown, Assistant Superintendent, Glastonbury (CT) Public Schools. Christine Brown, former Director of Languages, has overseen the Glastonbury language program, the nation's oldest continuous grade 1 to 12 language program for the last 22 years. She is a past president of the Connecticut Council of Language Teachers, the National Network of Early Language Learning, and the American Council on the Teaching of Foreign Languages. She is a past Chair of the Northeast Conference and the Chair of the writing task force of the national foreign language standards project. She co-chaired the 2005 Year Languages working committee. <Brownc@Glastonburyus.org>

Anne Conzemius, President, QLD Learning. Anne Conzemius brings a broad range of experience to her practice. Prior to establishing QLD Learning, Anne served as Assistant State Superintendent for Wisconsin's Department of Public Instruction. From 1988 to 1990, Anne served as Director of Employee Development and Training for the State of Wisconsin. Anne worked in the public schools for eight years as a school psychologist. Her work has been published in local, state, and national educational newsletters and journals, and she is co-author of three books with Jan O'Neill. Anne holds two Master's degrees from the University of Wisconsin-Madison, one in Educational Psychology and one in Industrial Relations. <annec@qldlearning.com>

Sandra Brunner Evarrs, Assistant Clinical Professor, School Psychology Program, The University of North Carolina at Chapel Hill. Dr. Evarrs teaches courses in psychoeducational assessment, intervention, and clinical practice at The University of North Carolina at Chapel Hill. Prior to joining the faculty at UNC she earned her B.S. in Elementary Education from DePaul University and began her career as a first-grade teacher in the inner city of Chicago. At Loyola University Chicago she earned a M.Ed. and Ph.D., focusing her research on autism and related disorders. In addition to teaching, Dr. Evarrs has serviced students with varying disabilities in both urban and suburban Chicago as a school psychologist. <evarrs@email.unc.edu>

Michael E. Everson, Associate Professor of Foreign Language Education, The University of Iowa. Michael E. Everson is program coordinator for the Foreign Language and ESL Education

217

program in the College of Education, The University of Iowa. His research interests include all aspects of less commonly taught language instruction, with an emphasis on how foreign language students learn to read in Chinese and Japanese. He is currently president of the National Council of Less Commonly Taught Languages (NCOLCTL), a member of the Chinese Language Teachers Association (CLTA) Executive Board, and longtime member of the American Council on the Teaching of Foreign Languages (ACTFL). He also sits on the Editorial Board for *The Modern Language Journal*. <michael-everson@uiowa.edu>

John M. Grandin, Professor of German and Director of the International Engineering Program, University of Rhode Island. At URI, Grandin directs an interdisciplinary curriculum through which students complete simultaneous degrees (BA and BS) in German, French, or Spanish, and in an engineering discipline. Grandin has received numerous awards for his work, has published widely on such cross-disciplinary initiatives, has been the principle investigator for several funded grants, and organizes the Annual Colloquium on International Engineering Education. In earlier lives Grandin served as associate dean and acting dean of URI's College of Arts and Sciences and as chair of the Department of Languages. He also has published several articles and a book on Franz Kafka. <grandin@uri.edu>

Audrey L. Heining-Boynton, Professor of Education, The University of North Carolina at Chapel Hill. At UNC-CH she is a world language/English as a Second Language teacher educator. She has also taught K-16 Spanish and French. Heining-Boynton has co-authored *¡Atrévete!*, *¡En español!*, and *¡Anímate!* and has published in a variety of journals. Her state/national service includes board member for the Foreign Language Association of North Carolina and for the Michigan Foreign Language Association and president of the National Network for Early Language Learning. She is the recipient of the American Council on the Teaching of Foreign Languages (ACTFL) /NYSAFLT Anthony Papalia Award for Excellence in Teacher Education and served as the President of ACTFL in 2005. <ahb@email.unc.edu>

Steven E. Knotek, Assistant Professor, School Psychology Program, The University of North Carolina at Chapel Hill. Dr. Knotek is in the School Psychology Program at The University of North Carolina at Chapel Hill. His clinical work and research focuses on consultation, prevention, and early intervention to support students at-risk for academic failure in regular education settings. <sknotek@email.unc.edu>

Jean W. LeLoup, Professor of Spanish and Coordinator of Adolescence Education, SUNY Cortland. Jean W. LeLoup is Professor of Spanish at SUNY Cortland and is also the Coordinator of Adolescence Education, responsible for the language teacher-training program. She is the co-founder and co-moderator of FLTEACH, the Foreign Language Teaching Forum <http://www.cortland.edu/flteach/>, a listserv list for FL professionals, and the co-editor of "On the Net," a regular column in the electronic journal Language Learning & Technology. She has taught courses in multimedia development for international communication at the graduate and undergraduate levels and has developed many online materials for language teaching and learning. Dr. LeLoup is a recipient of the ACTFL/FDP-Houghton Mifflin Award for Excellence in Foreign Language Instruction Using Technology with IALL. <leloupj@cortland.edu>

Myriam Met, Senior Research Associate, National Foreign Language Center, University of Maryland. Myriam Met is a Senior Research Associate, National Foreign Language Center, University of Maryland, where her work focuses primarily on K-12 foreign language policy. Her previous positions include supervisor of foreign language programs K-12, English for Speakers of Other Languages, and bilingual education for major urban and suburban school districts. Mimi is co-chair of the New Visions in Foreign Language Education and currently serves on the Executive Council of the American Council on the Teaching of Foreign Languages. She has been a president of the National Association of District Supervisors of Foreign Languages and was a founding member and later president of the National Network for Early Language Learning. <mmet@nflc.org>

Kurt E. Müller. Kurt E. Müller (Ph.D., Rutgers University) has taught in a variety of institutions: Hunter College, The College of New Jersey, Rutgers University, four military language schools, including the Defense Language Institute, and an ethnic-language school. He has held research appointments at the University of Maryland and the Institute for National Strategic Studies of the National Defense University. He served on the staff of the Modern Language Association and the Association of Departments of Foreign Languages and was executive vice president of the National Council on Foreign Language and International Studies. His research interests include language policy; he has published in six languages. Müller has also undertaken several government assignments. <MullerKE@cs.com>

June K. Phillips, Dean of the College of Arts & Humanities and Professor of French, Weber State University (UT). A past-president of the American Council on the Teaching of Foreign Languages, Phillips received the Palmès Académiques and the Nelson Brooks Award of the Northeast Conference. She directed the Foreign Language Standards project and co-chaired development of the *ACTFL/NCATE Program Standards for the Preparation of Foreign Language Teachers*. She has consulted with curriculum and testing projects including the Spanish NAEP and the Annenberg/WGBH video library, has published extensively on pedagogical topics, and has edited volumes for ACTFL and Northeast. <jphillips@weber.edu>

Robert Ponterio, Professor of French, SUNY Cortland. Ponterio is the co-founder and co-moderator of FLTEACH, the Foreign Language Teaching Forum <http://www.cortland.edu/flteach/>, a LISTSERV list for FL professionals, and the co-editor of "On the Net," a regular column in the electronic journal *Language Learning & Technology*. He holds a Ph.D., University of Illinois, Urbana-Champaign. He regularly teaches graduate courses in technology in the foreign language classroom and in teaching French civilization. <PonterioR@ CORTLAND. EDU>

Antonia Folarin Schleicher, Professor of African Languages and Literature, The University of Wisconsin-Madison. Schleicher is the Executive Director of the National Council of Less Commonly Taught Languages (NCOLCTL), and the founding Director of the National African Language Resource Center (NALRC). Her area of specialization is in Linguistics and Second Language Acquisition. She has published seven books, four multimedia language CD-ROMs, several articles, and has edited several journals. All her publications are in relation to less commonly taught languages. She is the series editor for the first set of communicatively oriented textbooks for African languages. She is a member of the UW-Madison Teaching Academy. She is also on the Board of Directors of Joint National Council on Languages (JNCL). <ayschlei@wisc.edu>

Bernard Spolsky, Bar-Ilan University. Born in New Zealand in 1932, Bernard Spolsky was educated at Victoria University and the University of Montreal. After teaching at McGill University and Indiana University, he moved to the University of New Mexico where he was Professor of Linguistics, Anthropology, and Elementary Education, and Graduate Dean. In 1980, he became Professor of English at Bar-Ilan University, retiring in 2000. He has been associated with the National Foreign Language Center since 1991 and with the new Center for the Advanced Study of Language since its creation. He has written and edited a dozen books and published over 200 chapters and articles. Founding co-editor of the journal *Applied Linguistics*, he is currently editor-in-chief of *Language Policy* and of the *Journal of Asia TEFL*. <spolsb@mail.biu.ac.il> <http://www.biu.ac.il/faculty/spolsb/>

Guadalupe Valdés, Stanford University, Bonnie Katz Tenenbaum Professor of Education, Stanford School of Education. Guadalupe Valdés' has a joint appointment in the Department of Spanish and Portuguese and the School of Education. Valdés' research has focused on both elective bilingualism and on circumstantial bilingualism. She has worked extensively on the teaching of Spanish to heritage learners and on foreign language learners of Spanish. A member of ACTFL since 1972, Valdés was a member of the Task Force on National Standards for Foreign Language Education and a member of the committee that developed the National Board Certification Standards for World Languages Other than English. Valdés received the Distinguished Service to the Profession Award from the American Departments of Foreign Languages in 1996. <gvaldes@stanford.edu>